MW00782159

From the Library of

THE RICHES OF WATCHMAN NEE

COMPILED BY
THE EDITORIAL SECTION
LIVING STREAM MINISTRY

BARBOUR
PUBLISHING, INC.
Uhrichsville, Ohio

© MCMXCIX by Living Stream Ministry

ISBN 1-57748-585-8

All rights reserved. No part of this publication may be reproduced or transmitted in any form or by any means, electronic or mechanical, including photocopying, recording, or by any information storage or retrieval system, without written permission of the publisher.

All New Testament Scripture quotations are taken from the Recovery Version of the Bible, copyright© 1999 by Living Stream Ministry, Anaheim, CA. Used by permission.

Old Testament quotations are taken from either the Recovery Version or the King James Version of the Bible.

Published by Barbour Publishing, Inc., P.O. Box 719, Uhrichsville, Ohio 44683
http://www.barbourbooks.com

 Member of the
Evangelical Christian
Publishers Association

Printed in the United States of America.

THE
RICHES OF
WATCHMAN
NEE

CONTENTS

PART 10: THE BELIEVERS

PART 11: THE CHURCH

PREFACE

Watchman Nee was a unique gift to this age, raised up by the Lord and given to His church "for the perfecting of the saints unto the work of the ministry unto the building up of the Body of Christ." Although much of Brother Nee's ministry was lost, that which survived has recently been published in its entirety in a sixty-two volume work entitled *The Collected Works of Watchman Nee.* This present publication is a short extract of the riches contained in that body of work.

The book is divided into twelve sections: 1) God, 2) the eternal plan of God, 3) the incarnation of God, 4) Christ—the Son of God, 5) the death of Christ, 6) the resurrection of Christ, 7) the divine life, 8) the Spirit, 9) Christ's redemption and God's salvation, 10) the believers, 11) the church, and 12) the New Jerusalem. The things which Watchman Nee preached and spoke from the Bible are broad, deep, and far-reaching, but these twelve items are their center, their course, and their goal. These items are essential; they constitute the center of the Christian faith, the course of the Christian race, and the goal of every believer's pursuit.

We commit this book to the Lord's blessing hands, that through it our departed brother will yet minister to God's children for the accomplishing of His purpose.

EDITORIAL SECTION
LIVING STREAM MINISTRY
ANAHEIM, CALIFORNIA

FOREWORD

In creation God ordained that man should replenish the earth and have dominion over all created things (Gen. 1:28). In redemption the Lord commissioned His disciples to go into all the world to preach the gospel and disciple all the nations for His kingdom on earth (Mark 16:15; Matt. 28:19). Following Pentecost, the territory around the Mediterranean Sea was evangelized in less than half a century, and the gospel was spread to Europe within the first two centuries. However, it was confined there for over ten centuries. Following the discovery of America, the gospel was brought to the Western Hemisphere through European immigration, but it never properly spread to the Far East before the defeat of Spain.

The Nestorians brought their religion from Persia to China in the seventh century. Nestorianism was a deviation from the divine revelation. It was not the pure gospel of life. Three emperors of the Tang Dynasty in China received this religion. However, after two centuries Nestorianism was banned and vanished because of its inaccuracy and lack of life. After that, there was no trace of Christianity in China in any form until the arrival of the Franciscans in the thirteenth century and the Jesuits in the sixteenth century. They, with their Western learning, were also lifeless and full of traditional ordinances. They were not prevailing in winning the conservative Chinese, who were saturated with the ethical teachings of Confucius and misled by the superstitions of Buddhism. It was only from the beginning of the nineteenth century that the pure gospel and the Bible were brought to China.

After the defeat of Spain, which was the power of the Catholic-dominated world in the sixteenth century, many

Protestant missions under God's sovereign grace were raised up both in Europe and in America to send hundreds of missionaries to heathen countries. More missionaries were sent to China than to any other country. Robert Morrison landed in Canton, capital of the southernmost province of China, in the early years of the nineteenth century. The Congregationalists, Methodists, and Anglicans came to the southern province of Fukien. The American Presbyterians and the Southern Baptists arrived in the northern province of Shantung. The Christian and Missionary Alliance reached the international port of Shanghai. The China Inland Mission pioneered a number of inland provinces, and other missions settled in many other territories. Many of these missionaries, especially the pioneers, were men of God. They sacrificed much for the Lord's commission and suffered a great deal for the gospel. Through their pioneering work, many doors in China were opened and thousands of people who were in darkness and sin were led to the Lord and received the Lord's salvation. These missionaries brought with them three treasures: the Lord's name, which is the Lord Himself, the gospel, and the Bible. We thank the Lord for this! However, the gospel was not adequately presented to the educated Chinese class, and the truth concerning life and the church was not effectually released until the first decade of the twentieth century.

In 1900 Satan instigated the Boxer Rebellion. In this uprising many missionaries and a great number of Chinese believers were martyred. Satan's intention was to terminate the Lord's move in China. But under God's sovereignty this persecution aroused a great burden among the saints in the Western world to pray desperately for the Lord's move in China. We believe it was through the Lord's answer to those desperate prayers that some prevailing evangelists among the

Chinese believers were raised up after the Boxer Rebellion. These "native" preachers became prevailing in gospel preaching, and their preaching reached the students of China's new generation. Around the year 1920 the gospel penetrated many schools, and a good number of high school and college students were captured by the Lord throughout the country from the far north to the far south. A number of brilliant ones were called and equipped by the Lord to do His work.

The Raising Up of Watchman Nee

One of these outstanding students was Nee Shu-tsu. His English name was Henry Nee. His paternal grandfather, Nee Yu-cheng, studied in the American Congregational College in Foochow and became the first Chinese pastor in northern Fukien among the Congregationalists. Nee Shu-tsu's paternal grandmother was a student in the American Congregational Girls' College in Foochow. His father, Nee Wen-shiu, a second generation Christian, studied in the American Methodist College in Foochow. Nee Wen-shiu was well trained in classical Chinese and became an officer in the Chinese customs. Nee Shu-tsu's mother, Lin Ho-ping, also a second generation Christian, studied in the Chinese Western Girls' School in Shanghai. This school maintained a high English standard. Nee Shu-tsu, a third generation Christian, studied in the Anglican Trinity College in Foochow. This school was a two-year college which maintained a high standard both in Chinese and English. After being raised up by the Lord to carry out His commission, he adopted the new English name Watchman Nee and the new Chinese name To-sheng, which means, the sound of a watchman's rattle. As a newly regenerated

Christian called by the Lord, he considered himself a watchman, raised up to give the sound of a rattle to people in the dark night. He eventually became, by the Lord's bountiful mercy and grace, a unique gift to this age. Watchman Nee was given by the Lord to His Body for His move of recovery on the earth, not only in China but also throughout the entire world.

(Taken from *Watchman Nee—A Seer of the Divine Revelation in the Present Age,* pp. 7–9, by Witness Lee)

A Word of Explanation

The content of this book is taken from *The Collected Works of Watchman Nee,* published by Living Stream Ministry, Anaheim, California. Each excerpt is followed by an exact citation of its source. In many cases the source material has also been published as part of a stand-alone book. In these cases, the individual publication has been cited.

The excerpts taken from volumes 33, 39, and 40 of *The Collected Works of Watchman Nee* are from *The Normal Christian Life, Love Not the World,* and *What Shall This Man Do?,* respectively. The rights to these titles are held by Kingsway Publications, Lottbridge Drove, Eastbourne, East Sussex, England, BN23 6NT.

All New Testament quotations in *The Collected Works of Watchman Nee* are taken from the Recovery Version published by Living Stream Ministry. Quotations from the Old Testament are taken from either the King James Version or the Recovery Version.

CHAPTER 1

GOD

THE DIVINE TRINITY

God is triune. Although the word *triune* is not found in the Bible, this is definitely a major teaching in the Bible. The Bible testifies everywhere that the Father is God (2 Tim. 1:2, etc.). The Bible also attests that the Son is God. Hebrews 1:8 says, "Of the *Son,* 'Your throne, O *God,* is forever and ever. . . .' " This shows us clearly that the Son is God. John 1:1 says clearly that "the Word was God." The Lord Jesus Himself also said, "I and the Father are one" (John 10:30). We can see from the Holy Spirit's source and work that He is also God. Moreover, the Bible says explicitly that the Holy Spirit is God. Acts 5:3–4 says, "But Peter said, Ananias, why has Satan filled your heart to deceive the *Holy Spirit. . . ?* You have not lied to men but to *God.*" From the above verses we can see that the Father is God, the Son is God, and the Holy Spirit is also God. Then why do we say that He is the Triune God? First Timothy 2:5 says, "For there is one God." There is one God. Yet the Father, the Son, and the Spirit are all God. Since there are not *three gods,* there must be a *Triune* God. This conclusion does not contradict the biblical teaching of one God, nor does it annul the divinity of the Son and the Holy Spirit. It is the most scriptural expression. However, the doctrine of the Trinity is most mysterious, and we can only know about it without understanding it. We should remain quietly before Him and meditate on His greatness, rather than trying in vain to understand what God has not revealed to us (Deut. 29:29). (Note: It is better to say the Triune God than to say the Trinity.) *(The Collected Works of Watchman Nee,* Vol. 7, pp. 1015–1016)

In eternity past, God ordained that there be a house and that the second person of the Godhead, the Son, rule over this house. God committed all things to the Son, and the Son inherits all things. Everything is of the Son, through the Son, and unto the Son. The Father plans, the Son inherits what the Father planned, and the Spirit accomplishes what the Father planned. The Father is the planning One, the Son is the inheriting One, and the Spirit is the accomplishing One. From eternity past, the Father has loved the Son; He is the "Beloved of the Father." God has loved Him from eternity past. When the Son came to earth, the Father still declared, "My Son, the Beloved" (Matt. 3:17). The Father loves the Son and has given Him all things. Before the Lord died, He knew "that the Father had given all into His hands" (John 13:3). When He resurrected and ascended, it was so that "He might fill all things" (Eph. 4:10). *(The Collected Works of Watchman Nee,* Vol. 11, p. 734)

The Father as the Source

Abraham's original name was Abram. Later, God changed his name to Abraham (Gen. 17:5). Within both of these two names is the root *Abra,* which in the original language means "father." Abraham was a father himself, and the lesson he learned was to know God as the Father. Throughout his whole life, he learned this one lesson—knowing God as the Father.

What does it mean to know God as the Father? It means that everything is from God. The Lord Jesus said, "My Father is working until now, and I also am working" (John 5:17). He did not say, "My God is working until now," but "My Father is working until now." For God to be the Father means that God is the Creator, the unique Initiator. The Son was sent from the Father. "The Son can do nothing from Himself except what He sees the Father doing, for whatever that One does, these things the Son also does in like manner" (v. 19). This must be our experience. We must receive grace from God to realize that we cannot initiate anything. We are not worthy of initiating anything. Genesis 1 begins by saying, "In the beginning God. . . ." In the beginning it was not us, but God. God is the Father, and everything originates from Him.

The day that God shows you that He is the Father will be a blessed day. On that day you will realize that you cannot do anything and that you are helpless. You will not have to try to hold yourself back from doing this thing or that thing. Instead you will ask, "Has God initiated this?" This is the experience of Abraham. His experience shows us that he had no thought of becoming [the father of] God's people. Abraham did not initiate anything. It was God who initiated. It was God who brought him from the other side of the

Euphrates River (Gen. 12:1–5). God wanted him, and He called him out. Abraham never thought of this. Hallelujah! God wanted him and God did the work.

God is the Father. Abraham did not volunteer to go to the land flowing with milk and honey. God said it first, and then Abraham went and possessed it. He did not know anything about it beforehand. When he was called to go out, he did not know where he was going (Heb. 11:8). He left his father's land without knowing where he was going. This was Abraham. God was the Initiator of everything for him; he had nothing to do with it. If you know that God is the Father, you will not be so confident and will not say that you can do whatever you want. You will only say, "If the Lord is willing, I will do this and that. Whatever the Lord says, I will do." This does not mean that you should be indecisive. It means that you truly do not know what to do and that you only know after the Father has revealed His will.

This was not all. Abraham did not know that he was going to beget a son. He even had to receive his son from God. Abraham could not initiate anything. His son was given to him by God. This was Abraham.

Abraham knew God as the Father. This kind of knowledge is not a knowledge in doctrine. It is a knowledge in which one is brought to the point of confessing, "God, I am not the source. You are the source of everything, and You are my source. Without You, I cannot have a beginning." This was Abraham. If we do not have Abraham's realization, we cannot be God's people. The first lesson we have to learn is to realize that we can do nothing and that everything depends on God. He is the Father, and He is the Initiator of everything. *(The God of Abraham, Isaac, and Jacob,* pp. 8–9)

(14:16–20). Another name for the Holy Spirit is "the Spirit of Jesus" (Acts 16:7). He is also called "the Spirit of Christ" (Rom. 8:9). When the Lord Jesus put on the Holy Spirit, He became a "receivable" Lord. If He had not become such a Lord, we would not be able to enjoy Him. Christ has resurrected and put on the Holy Spirit. When we receive the Holy Spirit, we receive Christ; in the same way, when we receive the Son, we receive the Father. When men in the past saw the Father, they saw the Son; in the same way, when men know the Spirit today, they know the Son. The Lord Jesus has resurrected, and He is in the Holy Spirit. Therefore, we can receive Him into us to be our life. All those who have received the Lord Jesus, whether they are clear or not, have received this experience from God. *(The Collected Works of Watchman Nee,* Vol. 36, pp. 170–171)

Now we must see how the Holy Spirit conveys the work of the Lord to us. The Lord's work includes all that He has done on the cross, in His resurrection, in His ascension, in His second coming, and in everything that He bestows upon us. We cannot go into detail concerning all these items. There is too much to say about them. To speak of them, we would have to mention the work of the Holy Spirit in the entire New Testament. Tonight we can only mention it in brief. The coming of the Holy Spirit is not merely for conveying the Lord's work to us. It is also for conveying the Lord Himself to us. The purpose of the fellowship of the Holy Spirit is to convey the Lord Jesus and His work to us. If a man has not received the work of the Lord, the Holy Spirit conveys this work to him. If a man has not received the Lord Jesus, the Holy Spirit conveys the Lord Himself to man. At the time we were saved, the work of the Holy Spirit was to convey the work of the Lord to us. Later His work is to convey the Lord Himself to us. The ministry of the Holy Spirit is to manifest the Lord Jesus.

A week ago, two sisters came to me asking me how to translate the English phrase *to minister with Christ* into Chinese. This is a difficult phrase to translate. It means to serve others with Christ, like serving someone with a cup of tea or a bowl of rice. The work of the Holy Spirit is to serve the Lord Jesus to us. When we received the Lord, the Holy Spirit transferred the Lord's work to us. Hence, all the work that the Lord has accomplished, such as the gift of repentance, forgiveness, cleansing, justification, sanctification, and joy, are accomplished by the Holy Spirit in us. Matters such as regeneration or the receiving of eternal life are accomplished in us through the Holy Spirit. The work of the Holy Spirit is to convey the life of the Lord Jesus to us. It is similar to a wire conveying electricity from the power plant at Willow Tree Creek to us. Through the Holy Spirit, we receive a new life, a new heart, and a new spirit (cf. Ezek. 36:26). When we receive a new spirit and a new heart, the Lord Jesus is able to abide in us through the Holy Spirit. Hence, regeneration is the Holy Spirit preparing a new temple for the Lord.

Since we are of the flesh, the Lord Jesus cannot dwell in us. We are like the world under judgment at the time of Noah. After the water subsided, Noah released a dove from the ark (Gen. 8:8–9). But the dove found no place of rest; it could not abide anywhere. In the same way, we are full of sin. The Lord Jesus can find no place to abide in us. That being the case, God gave to us the Holy Spirit. The Lord accomplished everything objectively. Now the Holy Spirit gave us a new spirit subjectively, so that the Son of God can abide in our spirit. The Holy Spirit came first to prepare a dwelling for the Lord Jesus. Then the Lord came to live in us. *(The Gospel of God,* Vol. 1, pp. 158–159)

One verse which we are all familiar with and which is often used by pastors in the denominations for their benedictions is 2 Corinthians 13:14: "The grace of the Lord Jesus Christ and the love of God and the fellowship of the Holy Spirit be with you all."

Why does this verse speak of the love of God, the grace of the Lord Jesus Christ, and the fellowship of the Holy Spirit? Can we change it to "the grace of God," "the love of the Lord Jesus Christ," and "the fellowship of the Holy Spirit"? No, because the characteristic of God is love. God is love. God in heaven is the source of all love. He is the source of love. Then Christ came to the earth to actually accomplish God's work of love. He died on the cross; He was crucified by men for the redemption of man. This is the work of God's love for man, which is grace. Therefore, God's characteristic is love and Christ's characteristic is grace. The fellowship of the Spirit is the flowing into us of all that Christ has accomplished for us. The source is God. Following God's love is Christ's work which is His grace. God is love and Christ came to manifest this love. But if it merely stops there, it is still of no benefit to us. Christ died on Calvary. He died on the cross to accomplish the work of redemption for us. This is good. But the accomplishment of Christ can only be applied to man through the Spirit. God's love is the source, Christ's grace is the operation of God's love, and the Spirit's fellowship channels this work of Christ to man. The Spirit changes the objective things of Christ into subjective experiences of Christ. He wroughts that which is outside of man into man. This is why 2 Corinthians 13:14 says, "The grace of the Lord

Jesus Christ and the love of God and the fellowship of the Holy Spirit be with you all."

An illustration of this can be found in the hospital where a doctor gives a prescription, a pharmacist dispenses the medicine, and the nurse ultimately delivers the medicine to the patient. If you only know the kind of medicine you need without having anyone deliver it to you, the medicine cannot get into your body. You need to have all three before the medicine can take effect. Hence, 2 Corinthians 13:14 speaks of the love of God, the grace of Christ, and the fellowship of the Spirit. *(The Collected Works of Watchman Nee,* Vol. 43, pp. 562–563)

HIS ATTRIBUTES

Love

The Bible never fails to point out the love of God. In our Bible study this time, we will cover the truth of the gospel only in a sketchy way. We will mention a lot of things, but will not consider them in detail. Tonight I cannot cover every aspect concerning the love of God found in the Bible. I can mention this matter only briefly. We must consider three aspects of the love of God. First, God is love. Second, God loves man. And third, the expression of God's love is in the death of Christ.

God Is Love

Let us come to the first point: God is love. This is recorded in 1 John 4:16. Here it does not say that God loves. Nor does it say that God may love, or that God can love, or that God has loved or will love. Rather, it says that God is love. What does it mean to say that God is love? It means that God Himself, His nature and His being, is love. If we can say that God has a substance, then God's substance is love.

The greatest revelation of the Bible is that God is love. This revelation is what man needs the most. Man has many conjectures and theories about God. We ponder all the time about what kind of God our God is, what kind of heart our God has, what intentions God has toward man, what God Himself is like. You can ask anyone about his idea of God, and he will give you his concept. He will think that God is this kind of God or that kind of God. All the idols in the world and all the images made by man are products of man's imagination. Man thinks that God is a fierce God or a severe God. He pictures God this way and that way. Man is always trying to reason and to explore what God is like. In order to correct the different conjectures man has concerning God, He manifests Himself in the light of the gospel and shows man that He is not an unapproachable or unfathomable God.

What is God then? God is love. This statement will not be clear to you unless I give an illustration. Suppose that there is a patient person. He has patience no matter what he encounters and no matter how difficult or bad the conditions are. For such a person, we cannot say that he has acted patiently. The adverb *patiently* cannot be used to describe him. Nor can we say that he is patient, using an adjective. We must say that he is patience itself. Perhaps we would not refer to him by his name. Instead, behind his back we would say that Patience has come or that Patience has spoken. When we say that God is love, we mean that love is the nature of God. He is love from inside to outside. Therefore, we would not say that God is loving, using an adjective, or that God loves, using a verb. Rather, we would say that God is love, applying the noun to Him.

In our friend Patience we cannot find rashness. The man is patience itself; he is not simply patient. He is just a lump of patience. Would you think that with such a person there could be rashness? Could he lose his temper? Could he exchange sharp words with others? It is impossible for him to do such things because there is no element in his nature to do such things. There is no such thing as temper in his nature. There is no such thing as rashness in his nature. He is simply patience.

The same is true with God, who is love. God as love is the greatest revelation in the Bible. For every Christian, the greatest thing to know in the Bible is that God is love. It is impossible for God to hate. If God hates, He will not only have a conflict with whomever He hates, but will also have a conflict with Himself. If God hated any one of us here today, He would not have a problem with that one alone; He would have a problem with Himself. God must develop a problem with Himself before He can hate or do anything in a way that is not in love. God is love. Although these three words are most simple, they give us the greatest revelation. The nature of God, the life-essence of God, is just love. He cannot do anything otherwise. He loves, and at the same time, He is love.

If you are a sinner today, you may wonder what you must do before God will love you. Many people do not know God's mind toward them. They do not know what God is thinking or what intentions God has. Many think that they should do something or that they should suffer or should be very conscientious before they can please God. However, only those who are in darkness and do not know God will think this way. If there were no gospel today, you would be able to think this way. But now that the gospel is here, you cannot think this way anymore, for the gospel tells us that God is love.

We human beings are nothing but hatred. For us to love is extremely difficult. Likewise, it is equally difficult for God to hate. You may think that it is difficult to love and that you do not know how to love others. But it is impossible for God to hate. You have no way to love, and God has no way to hate. God is love, and for Him to hate is for Him to act contrary to His nature, which is impossible for Him to do.

God So Loved the World

This is not all. God Himself is love, but when this love is applied to us, we find that "God so loved the world" (John 3:16). "God is love" speaks of His nature, and "God so loved the world" speaks of His action. God Himself is love; hence, that which issues out from Him must be love. Where there is love, there must also be the object of that love. After showing us that He is love, God immediately shows us that He loves the world. God has not only loved us, but has also sent forth His love. God could not help but send forth His love. He could not help but love the world. Hallelujah!

The greatest problem the world has is that it thinks that God always harbors evil intentions for man. Man thinks that God makes severe demands, and that He is strict and mean. Since man has doubts about the love of God, he also doubts that God loves the world. But as long as God is love, He loves the world. If love is His nature, He can conduct Himself toward man in no other way except in love. It would make Him uncomfortable if He did not love. Hallelujah! This is a fact! God is love. He cannot help but love. God is love, and what spontaneously follows is that God loves the world.

We can blame ourselves for our sins, for being suscepti-
ble to Satan's temptation, for being entangled by sin. But we
cannot doubt God Himself. You can blame yourself for com-
mitting a sin, for having failed, for succumbing to temptation. But if you doubt God's heart toward you, you are not
acting like a Christian, for to doubt God's heart toward you
is to contradict the revelation in the gospel.

I cannot say that you will never fail again. Nor can I say
that you will never sin again. Perhaps you will fail and you
will sin again. But please remember that for you to fail or sin
is one thing, but God's heart towards you is another. You
must never doubt God's feeling toward you simply because
you have failed or sinned. Although you may sin and fail,
God does not change His attitude toward you, for God is
love and He loves the world. This is an unchangeable fact in
the Bible.

On our side, we change and turn. But on the side of the
love of God, there is no change or turn. Many times your love
can change or become cold. But this does not mean that
God's love is affected. If God is love, no matter how you test
Him, what comes forth from Him is always love. If there is a
piece of wood here, no matter how you hit it, you will always
get the sound of wood. If you hit it with a book, it will give
you the sound of wood. If you hit it with your palm, it will
still give you the sound of wood. If you hit it with another
piece of wood, it will again give you the sound of wood. If
God is love, no matter how you "hit" Him—if you reject
Him, deny Him, or cast Him aside—He is still love. One
thing is sure: God cannot deny Himself; He cannot contradict Himself. Since we are just hatred itself, it is altogether
natural for us to hate. Since God is love, it is altogether natural for God to love. God cannot change His own nature.

Since God's nature cannot be changed, His attitude toward you cannot be changed. So we see that God loves the world.

God's Expression of Love

Does the whole matter stop with God loving the world? "God is love" speaks of God's nature; it speaks of God Himself. "God so loved the world" speaks of God's action. But God's love toward us has an expression. What is this expression of His love? Romans 5:8 says, "But God commends His own love to us in that while we were yet sinners, Christ died for us." God's love has an expression. If I love a person and merely tell him that I love him, that love has not yet been consummated. Unless love is expressed, it is not consummated. There is no love in the world that is without an expression. If there is love, it must be expressed. If a love is not expressed, such a love cannot be considered love. Love is most practical. It is not vain and is not merely a verbal matter. Love is expressed through actions. If you put a ball on a surface that is not level, you can be sure that something will happen; it will end up rolling down. The same is true with love. You can be sure that it will have an expression.

Since God loves the world, He has to be concerned about man's need. Hence, He must do something for man. We are sinners. We have no other choice but to go to hell, and no other place to be except in the place of perdition. But God loves us, and He will not be satisfied until He has saved us. When God says, "I love you," His love will step up to bear all our burdens and remove all our problems. Since God loves us, He must provide a solution to the problem of sin; He must provide the salvation that we sinners need. For this reason, the Bible has shown us this one great fact: the love of God is manifested in the death of Christ. Since we are sinners and are unable to save ourselves, Christ came to die in order to solve the problem of sin for us. His love has accomplished something substantial, and this has been put before us. Now we can see His love in a substantial way. His love is no longer merely a feeling. It has become a thoroughly manifested act.

In this great matter of God's love, we must take note of three things: the nature of God's love, the action of God's love, and the expression of God's love. Thank and praise God! His love is not only a feeling within Him. It is also an action, and even an expression and manifestation. His love made Him do what we cannot do by ourselves. Since He is love and since He has loved the world, salvation has been produced. Since man has sin and since God is love, a lot of things follow. If you are not poor, you will have no need of me. But if I do not love you, even if you are extremely poor, I will not be concerned at all. The situation today is that man has sinned and God has loved; therefore, things begin to happen. Hallelujah, a lot is happening because man has sinned and God has loved. When you put the two things together, the gospel comes into being. *(The Gospel of God,* Vol. 1, pp. 26–31)

Righteousness

What is God's righteousness? God's righteousness is the principle by which God works. When God works, He must operate according to righteousness. Everything that God accomplishes is accomplished according to righteousness. The Bible shows us that there are three items specially related to God: glory, holiness, and righteousness. God's glory is God Himself; God's holiness is God's nature; and God's righteousness is the method, the way, in which God works. Every time we read about God's glory in the Bible, we should realize that it refers to God Himself. Every time we read about God's holiness, we should realize that it refers to God's nature. Every time we read about God's righteousness, we should realize that it refers to the method or the way in which God works. God is righteous, and the procedure by which He works also has to be righteous. Hence, God's salvation of man must also be righteous. God can save man in many ways, but no matter which way He takes, He has to do it according to righteousness. This is the most difficult problem in God's salvation of man. If God were not strict, He could resort to any kind of method. But it is a challenge for God to do things without conflicting with His righteousness. A sinner only cares to be saved; he does not care about the method which is used. But God cannot be unrighteous in saving man. Righteousness is the foundation of God's throne (Psa. 89:14). God cannot do something that is unrighteous. God wants to save man, but He also wants to maintain His own righteousness. Hence, God has a problem. He must find a way to save man that is righteous, a procedure that is compatible with His righteousness, which also will enable Him to save man.

Two years ago the father of one of our coworkers was imprisoned for violating the law of the country. He had indeed violated the written regulation. But the sin he committed was forgivable because he was forced by others to do it and did not commit the crime intentionally. The law he violated carried a very severe punishment. I felt that, under the circumstance, the offense he committed should be pardoned. Moreover, he was advanced in age and was the father of one of my coworkers. He was quite close to several coworkers, and we all treated him as our own father. Because of my family connections, I knew some prominent persons in the government, and I promised to try my best to help him. We went to a prominent one in the Nanking government, and said to him, "Our friend is an upright person. We can guarantee that he did not commit the crime. We only need a statement to be issued in order for him to be released." But he replied, "I believe what you said. In my heart I also want to release him. In the last ten days, I have solicited the help of some influential people, but I still do not have a way. This is not just a matter of personal influence. I could release a statement immediately, but I must have the proper basis before I can issue the statement. I cannot transgress against the state through my act. I will try to think of a way to release him, but I have to use a method that is legal and proper. I cannot incriminate myself by releasing him." Do you see this? God was faced with a similar situation in order to save us. He wants to save us, but He must find a way that is righteous and that will also save at the same time. God's righteousness is manifested in the fact that when He saves man, He does so by not making Himself unrighteous.

Here we see the problem that God has in saving man. On the one hand, He must satisfy His love, and on the other hand, He must satisfy His righteousness. He cannot sacrifice love for the sake of fulfilling His righteousness. He also cannot become unrighteous for the sake of love. Neither of the two can be sacrificed. The Bible says that unrighteousness is a sin (1 John 5:17). God cannot do anything that is not according to righteousness. God wants man to know that he is saved through righteousness; it is a salvation that is lawful, proper, and procedurally righteous. This is why God has to be careful in how He deals with the sins of the world. Now we have three facts: Man is a sinner, God is full of love, mercy and grace, and God is righteous. Romans 3:25 says, "God set forth [Jesus] as a propitiation place through faith in His blood, for the demonstrating of His righteousness." Verse 26 continues, "With a view to the demonstrating of His righteousness in the present time, so that He might be righteous and the One who justifies him who is of the faith of Jesus." This means that in reckoning those who believe in Jesus to be righteous, God demonstrates to man that He is righteous. Through His act of saving man, God wants man to know that He is righteous. God cannot violate the law. He cannot make Himself unlawful just because He wants to save man.

Romans 3:21 says that God's righteousness has been manifested apart from the law. If God's righteousness was manifested according to the law, we would have to die because the law says that all who sin must die. Therefore, if God's righteousness was according to the law, all sinners would have to die, and there would be no gospel to preach. God's righteousness is apart from the law; therefore, man can be saved, and God is still righteous.

How does God preserve His righteousness and save us at the same time? This was accomplished by the cross of Christ and the precious blood of Christ. Friends, I do not know whether or not it has ever occurred to you that without God's righteousness, there would be no need for Christ to die. Why was the cross needed? It was so troublesome. Jesus had to go from Bethlehem to Calvary to be crucified on the cross. Why did God go to such lengths? He could have declared to the world that everyone was forgiven and could go away free. This would only involve God's forgiveness. Would this not be the simplest thing to do and the most efficient way to take? However, if He took such a simple and efficient way, His righteousness would be sacrificed. This is why God cannot be so free. He needed the Lord Jesus to come as a man and put on a body of flesh and blood. One day He was crucified on the cross and shed His precious blood so that all those who believe in Him could have their sins forgiven. This is how God fulfilled His righteousness and accomplished His goal of saving man. In God's righteous salvation, He sent the Lord Jesus to die on the cross and to accomplish the work of redemption on our behalf. This satisfied the love that God has toward man and also fulfilled His own righteous require-ments. Hallelujah for God's wonderful love, mercy, grace, and righteousness! Praise Him! *(The Collected Works of Watchman Nee,* Vol. 43, pp. 564–567)

Mercy

The outlet of love is either grace or mercy. Mercy is negative, and grace is positive. Mercy is related to the present condi-tion, and grace is related to the future condition. Mercy speaks of the poverty of your present condition, and grace speaks of the bright condition that you will be saved into in the future. The feeling that God has toward us when we are sinners is mercy. The work that God does upon us to make us the children of God is grace. Mercy arises from our exist-ing condition; grace arises from the work that we will receive.

I do not know if you are clear about this or not. Suppose there is a destitute person here with us. You love him and have pity upon him. You feel sorry for his difficult situation. If you did not love him, you would not suffer and grieve for him. But by doing so, you are having mercy on him. But such mercy is negative. Your mercy on him is in sympathy for his present condition. But when is grace accomplished? It is accomplished when this person is rescued today out of his poor condition to a new position, to a new realm and a new environment. Only then does your love to him become grace. This is why I say that mercy is negative and for today, while grace is positive and for the future. The future I am talking about is the future in this age, rather than the future in the coming age. I do not mean that the Old Testament speaks only about mercy. The Old Testament speaks about grace, too. It is not true that we no longer need mercy. No, we still need mercy. God was merciful in the time of the Old Testament, because His work was not yet completed. Therefore, the Old Testament was full of mercy. God showed mercy for four thousand years. But today, in the New Testament age, we have grace because the Lord Jesus has accomplished His work. He has come to bear our sins. Hence, what we have received today is not mercy, but grace. Hallelujah! Today is not a day of mercy, but a day of grace.

If there were only mercy, we could only have hope. In the Old Testament, there was only hope; hence, the Old Testament speaks of mercy. But thank the Lord, today we have obtained what was hoped for. There is no need to hope for it anymore.

Mercy comes from love and issues in grace. If mercy has not come from love, it will not issue in grace. Since it originates in love, it arrives at grace. In the Gospels there is the account of a blind man receiving his sight (Mark 10:46–52). When he met the Lord, he did not say, "Lord, love me!" or "Lord, be gracious to me!" Rather, he said, "Son of David, have mercy on me!" (v. 48). He asked for mercy because of his present condition, his present difficulty, and his present pain. He knew that if the Lord Jesus were to sympathize with him, He would not stop at showing mercy to him; He would surely do something.

In the New Testament there are also a few places where mercy is mentioned. In most cases, mercy is mentioned in reference to the situation at the time. Some may ask, "Since the love of God is so precious, why must there be mercy? Love is very good as the source, and grace is also very good as the result. Why then is there the need for mercy?" It is because man is destitute. We have no courage to go to God and ask for His love. We are of the flesh and do not know God well enough. Although God has revealed Himself to us in the light, we still do not dare come close to Him. We feel that it is impossible for us to go to God and ask for love. At the same time, we do not have the adequate faith to go to Him and ask for grace, telling Him that we need such and such a blessing. We have no way to ask for God's love, and we do not have enough faith to ask for God's grace.

But thank the Lord. Not only do we have love and grace; we also have mercy. Love is manifested in this mercy. Because God is merciful, if you hear the gospel and are still unable to believe, you can cry, "Son of David, have mercy on me!" You may be afraid to ask about other things, but you need not be afraid to ask this one thing. I dare not ask the Lord to be gracious to me. I dare not ask Him to love me. But I can ask Him to be merciful to me. For other things we dare not ask. But we can be bold to ask for mercy. God is pleased with this. God has placed His love among us so that we would have the right to come to Him. But if there were only love, we would still be afraid to come to God. Since God is also merciful, we are able to come to Him. I dare not ask God to love me, nor do I dare ask Him to show grace. But I can ask God for mercy. I can at least ask for that.

Last year I met a man who was very old and was suffering from a serious illness. When he saw me he cried. He told me that he was not bitter toward God, but that he was, indeed, in much pain. I told him that he should ask God to love him and be gracious to him. He said that he could not do this. When I asked him why not, he answered that for sixty years he had been living for himself and not for God. Now that he was dying, he would be ashamed to ask God to love him and be gracious to him. Had he not been so far away from God, had he drawn closer to God during the past few decades, had he developed some affection for God, it would have been easier for him to ask for love and grace. But such as he was, away from God his whole life, how could he ask God to love him as he lay on his deathbed? In spite of my persuasion, he would not believe my words. I told him that God could grant grace to him, that He could be gracious to him and could love him. But he simply could not believe it. I went to see him many times, but I could not get through. Then I prayed, "O God, here is a man who will not believe in You. Nor will he believe in Your love. I have no way to help him. Please open up a way for him in his last hour." Later I felt that I should not speak to him about grace, nor about love, but only about mercy. I went to him again rejoicingly. I said to him, "You should forget about everything now. Forget about the love of God or the grace of God. You should go to God and say to Him, 'God! I am suffering. I have no way to go on. Have mercy on me.' " Immediately he agreed. And as soon as he agreed, his faith came and he prayed, "God, I thank You that You are a merciful God. I am weak and suffering. Have mercy on me." Here you see a person being brought to the presence of the Lord. He realized his destitute situation and asked for mercy. In his present condition, he asked God to be merciful to him. *(The Gospel of God,* Vol. 1, pp. 33–36)

Mercy is God coming into our midst, whereas grace is God bringing us into His midst. In His incarnation as a man, God apprehended man's sufferings and bondage to sin, pain, and Satan. This is His mercy. When Christ came to the earth, He spoke mostly of mercy and not much of grace. The four Gospels rarely mention "grace." Grace came in only after He died on the cross, when God put man's sins upon Christ and Christ took our sins away. The Epistles frequently speak of grace because God's salvation has been accomplished. God loves us; His heart is filled with mercy toward our condition. Therefore, He accomplished something for us to save us. God's heart is full of mercy for us—this is the best factual basis for asking God to do something for us. When we pray that God would forgive our sins, what is God's basis for answering our prayer? We can say, "O God, I am evil. I am a sinner. I cannot save myself. I cannot even come to You for salvation. But the Bible says that You love mercy and not sacrifice. O God, please have mercy on me; forgive me." Both the New Testament and the Old Testament say that God desires "mercy and not sacrifice" (Matt. 9:13; Hosea 6:6). Mercy is God giving something to man, whereas sacrifice is man giving something to God. But God says, "I like to give something to you, but I do not like you to give anything to Me." We cannot perform any good. Even if there is some goodness in us, it is not perfect. We have nothing to depend on; we have nothing to rely upon. We can only depend on God's mercy. We can count on God's mercy and say, "God, unless You have become a merciless God, I am delighted and happy to seek Your mercy. I want to be a person on whom

You have mercy." *(The Collected Works of Watchman Nee,* Vol. 43, pp. 561–562)

Grace

But, brothers and sisters, God's love does not stop here. Since God is love, the matter of grace comes up. It is true that love is precious, but love must have its expression. When love is expressed, it becomes grace. Grace is love expressed. Love is something in God. But when this love comes to you, it becomes grace. If God is only love, He is very abstract. But thank the Lord that although love is something abstract, with God it is immediately turned into something substantial. The inward love is abstract, but the outward grace has given it substance.

For example, you may have pity on a pauper, and you may love him and have sympathy for him. But if you would not give him food and clothing, the most you could say is that you love him. You could not say that you are grace to him. When can you say that you have grace toward him? When you give him a bowl of rice or a piece of clothing or some money, and when the food, clothing, or money reach him, your love becomes grace. The difference between love and grace lies in the fact that love is within and grace is without. Love is primarily an inward feeling, while grace is an outward act. When love is turned into action, it becomes grace. When grace is traced back to its feeling, it is love. Without love, grace cannot come into being. Grace exists because love exists.

The definition of grace is not just the act of love. We must add something else to this. Grace is the act of love upon the destitute. God loves His only begotten Son. But there is no element of grace in this love. One cannot say that God deals with His Son in grace. God also loves the angels, but that cannot be considered as grace either. Why is not the Father's love toward the Son and God's love toward the angels grace? The reason is that there is no destitution and deprivation involved. There is only love; there is no thought of grace. Only when there is deprivation and destitution, when there is no way for one to solve his problems on his own, is love realized as grace. Since we are sinners, we are those with problems; and we have no way to solve our problems. But God is love, and His love is manifested to us as grace.

Hence, when love flows on the same level, it is simply love. But when it flows down, it is grace. Therefore, those who have never been on the low end can never receive grace. Love can also flow up. But when it does, it is not grace. Love can also flow between equal heights. When it does, it is not grace either. Only when love flows downward is it grace. If you want to be above God, or if you want to be equal with God, you will never see the day of grace. Only those who are below God can see the day of grace. This is what the Bible shows us about the difference between love and grace.

Although the Bible mentions the love of the Lord Jesus, it pays more attention to the grace of the Lord Jesus. The Bible also speaks of the grace of God, but it pays more attention to the love of God. I am not saying that there is no mention of the love of the Lord Jesus and the grace of God in the Bible. But the emphasis in the Bible is on the love of God and the grace of the Lord Jesus. How did Paul greet the church in Corinth? "The grace of the Lord Jesus Christ and the love of God and the fellowship of the Holy Spirit be with you all" (2 Cor. 13:14). You cannot change the sentence to read, "the grace of God and the love of the Lord Jesus Christ and the fellowship of the Holy Spirit be with you all." You cannot do this, because the emphasis of the Bible is on the love of God and the grace of the Lord Jesus. Why is this so? Because it was the Lord Jesus who accomplished salvation. It was He who substantiated love and accomplished grace. The love of God became grace through the work of the Lord Jesus. Therefore, the Bible tells us that the law was given through Moses, but grace came through Jesus Christ (John 1:17). *(The Gospel of God,* Vol. 1, pp. 31–32)

Authority

First, we must know that God's acts are based upon His throne, and His throne is built on authority. All things were created through God's authority. All natural laws function according to God's authority. God did not create the universe with power, but with authority. He does not uphold the natural laws by power, but by authority. Scientists today have discovered atomic power. Actually, what they have discovered is God's power. Their discovery is merely an unveiling of the laws of nature. According to Hebrews 1:3 God upholds all things by His word, which relates to His authority. God upholds all things by His authority, not by His power. God's authority ensures the constancy of the natural laws in this universe. He created the universe with His authority, and He rules the universe with His authority. God's authority represents God Himself. Looking at the matter in another way, we can say that God is the embodiment of authority. God is also the embodiment of power; He is the embodiment of authority as well as power. It is easy for man to be forgiven when he only offends God's power. It is not easy for him to be forgiven if he offends God's authority. It is a serious thing for a man to offend God's authority. Brothers and sisters, we have to see that authority is the unchanging factor that rules and stabilizes the universe from the beginning of time to its end. Everything in the universe, from the highest design to the lowest form, is upheld by God's authority. From creation, only one thing involves man all the time—authority.

God's Greatest Requirement
Being Submission to Authority

Of all the commandments which the Bible places before men, the greatest is not the bearing of the cross, offerings, consecration, or sacrifices. The greatest and highest demand in the entire Bible is the demand for submission to authority. Man regards such things as offerings, consecration, and sacrifices as the greatest things, considering them to be the most that a Christian can offer. When many people meet young Christians, their natural inclination is to exhort the latter to give themselves to these things, but please remember that the greatest demand in the Bible is the demand to submit to authority. First Samuel 15:22b says, "To obey is better than sacrifice, And to heed, than the fat of rams." This means that the most basic requirement in the Bible is obedience. Obedience is more basic and crucial than sacrifice. The other side of obedience is authority. Offerings, consecration, and sacrifices may all be contaminated by self-will. Only obedience is not contaminated by self-will because obedience shuts out the self. We should obey whether or not things go our way. We should submit whether or not we are willing. We have to see that the bearing of the cross is not our highest obligation to God's will; submission to authority is.

The Lord's Prayer
in the Garden of Gethsemane

A few years ago I spoke in Shanghai on the Lord's prayer in the garden of Gethsemane. Today I would like to speak on this again. Some have the thought that the Lord's prayer, in which His sweat became like great drops of blood falling down upon the ground, was the result of the weakness of His flesh (Luke 22:44). They have the thought that He acted in this way because He was afraid of the cup. Nothing can be further from the truth. While He was praying in the garden of Gethsemane, the cup and God's will were two different things. This is the reason He prayed, "My Father, if it is possible, let this cup pass from Me" (Matt. 26:39). He did not say that He would not do the Father's will. He only asked that the "cup" be removed from Him if possible. He did not ask for God's will to be removed. At this point God's will was something absolute, while the cup was not yet something that was absolute. God's will is an expression of His authority. Before the Father revealed Himself clearly to the Lord, the Lord did not equate the cup with His will. Obedience is not the same as sacrifice, and taking heed is not the same as the fat of rams. There was a time when the cup and God's will were two things. This is the reason the Lord prayed to know God's will. He did not drink the cup simply because it was the cup. He had to wait until the cup and God's will became one thing before He could say, "The cup which the Father has given Me, shall I not drink it?" (John 18:11). Once He became clear that the cup was God's will, He readily drank it. Therefore, the Lord's prayer in the garden of Gethsemane was for the purpose of determining the relationship between the cup and God's will. The Lord wanted to know if it was God's will for Him to go to the cross. He did not hold to the cross;

He held to God's will. The prayer in Gethsemane contains a very deep thought, much deeper than human apprehension. The Lord went to the cross for the sake of accomplishing God's will. His crucifixion was the highest expression of His submission to authority. We have to realize that even with the cross, there was the possibility of a mistake. However, there could never be any mistake with God's will. When the Lord became clear that the cross and God's will were one and the same, He chose the cross without hesitation. Therefore, His crucifixion was an act of submission to God's will. Here we find the Lord upholding God's authority. He was not upholding His act of crucifixion. Crucifixion is not the highest goal; the accomplishment of God's will is. This is the reason Hebrews 10:7 tells us that when Christ came to the earth, He said, "I have come. . .to do Your will, O God." The Lord is truly our pattern! In our service to the Lord, we should act according to God's will, not according to our will.

The Need for God's Servant to Have a Genuine Touch with Authority

In working for the Lord, we are God's servants. As servants, the first thing we should touch is the authority of the Master. Those whose eyes are set on men have never touched authority. As ministers of God, being in line with the authority of the Head is the first principle we have to keep. Naturally, we were all under the principle of rebellion. In order to serve God, we have to be confronted by His authority in a definite way. We have to come into His presence and meet His authority face to face. We have to be wounded and defeated by this encounter. We have to be humbled by authority and face it in a genuine way. This experience has to be as real as our experience of salvation. This is the only way for us

50

to be ushered into His service. Before we can participate in His work, we must touch authority in a definite way once. In our relationship with God, one controversy—whether or not we have touched His authority—remains. Once we touch authority, we will sense it everywhere. We do not ask others to obey us. Those who know authority will never have a problem with men. *(The Collected Works of Watchman Nee, Vol. 59, pp. 97–98, 101–103)*

CHAPTER 2

THE ETERNAL PLAN OF GOD

MADE IN ETERNITY PAST ACCORDING TO
HIS GOOD PLEASURE

With this understanding of eternity, we can consider God's eternal will. According to Ephesians 3:11, God has an eternal purpose, that is, an eternal will. In Greek the word *purpose* has the same root as the word *purposed* in Romans 1:13. God has an eternal will. This means that God made a decision in the first eternity. According to Ephesians 1:9, God's decision is according to His good pleasure; it is purposed in Himself; and it is for the purpose of making known to us the mystery of His will. In Greek the words *good pleasure* mean "joy" or "delight." Since God has a *delight,* He purposed a *will.* Since God has a *will,* He made a *plan.* Based on His plan, God has a *mystery* to fulfill this plan.

God's will is something that is hidden in God's heart, but His plan is something that is manifested to others. God's plan is God's center, which is also God's goal. God's eternal plan spans from eternity to eternity; it begins with His purpose and will in the first eternity and ends with its full consummation in the second eternity.

GAINING MANY SONS FOR HIS GLORY

God's Original Purpose in Creating Man

Beginning from tonight we will study God's purpose in man in a systematic way and show how He accomplishes such a purpose. God's Word shows us that His purpose is to have many sons, that is, a group of men who will have the life of His Son (Heb. 2:10).

In Genesis we see God creating the heavens and the earth, and then creating man. After this He put the man He created in the garden of Eden. God's purpose in preparing the garden of Eden and putting man in it was not that man would merely be a gardener, but that he would eat the tree of life and receive His life. Human beings work according to a purpose and a plan. God, being much wiser than man, works even more according to a plan. God did all these things according to a plan. His plan is that man would have His life and become His many sons.

God wants many sons. Yet Adam did not have such a thought. Adam's goal might have merely been to become a perfect man. But even if he had become perfect, he would still have fallen short of God's purpose. A perfect man cannot fulfill God's purpose. In reality Adam did not become a perfect man; he became a sinner instead. Today man has two problems. First, he is a sinner, and second, he is a man. As a sinner, he needs salvation, and as a man, he also needs salvation. A person needs to be saved because he is a sinner.

A person also needs to be saved because he is a man. The forgiveness of sins merely recovers man to Adam's original position in the garden of Eden. As a "man," he still needs to receive God's life before he can become a son of God and before God's purpose can be accomplished in him. In order to accomplish His purpose in man, God has to do two things. First, He has to save the sinner and deliver him from sin. Second, He has to save the "man" himself. Since man fell through sin, he became a sinner estranged from God on the one hand, and a man who had fallen short of God's purpose on the other hand.

We are sinners, and as sinners we need forgiveness. We are also men, and as men we need God's life. Only when we have both of these things can God's purpose be fulfilled. Man's problem is not one of being good or bad, sinful or sinless, perfect or imperfect. Man's problem lies in what he is. As long as he is simply a man, he needs God's work, and he needs God to dispense His life into him. Only then will he be able to fulfill God's purpose. God's forgiveness of man's sin is an incidental work—it is not His goal. Man's sin is something negative, something incidental. In order for God to achieve His purpose in man, He first had to solve the problem of sin, but His ultimate goal is to dispense His life into man.

God's Purpose Being Frustrated

We know that Adam ate of the fruit of the tree of the knowledge of good and evil. As a result he became independent, knowing good and evil. There was no more need for man to ask God or to trust in Him; he became independent. Adam became an independent sinner estranged from God. What is a sinner? A sinner is simply one who is separated from God and independent of God. Being separated from God and independent of God is sin. Hence anything that originates from man is sin, and any act that is done independent of God is sin. A man does not have to commit fornication, robbery, murder, or arson. As long as he is separated from God, he is a sinner. Originally Adam was innocent. He was not able to differentiate good from evil. He had to ask God for everything and find out from God whether something was good or bad, right or wrong. After he ate of the fruit of the tree of the knowledge of good and evil, he was able to know good and evil by himself. There was no more need for him to seek after God or to trust in Him. He became independent from God. Through the knowledge he acquired, he became a man who was independent of God. In this way, God's purpose could not be fulfilled and His will was frustrated.

The Reason for Man's Fall

God created man's body from the dust of the earth so that man would be able to contact the physical world. After His creation He breathed into man's nostrils the breath of life, which gave man his spirit. Man's spirit is able to communicate with God. When God's breath of life came in contact with man's flesh, man became a living soul with his own personality, character, disposition, emotion, will, and volition.

However, God's purpose was not just to create such a man. After man was created, God placed the tree of life and the tree of the knowledge of good and evil in the midst of the garden of Eden, and He charged Adam not to eat the fruit of the tree of the knowledge of good and evil. It was almost as if God was telling Adam that He had to eat of the tree of life. But God did not force Adam to eat of the tree of life because He created man with a free will with a right to choose for himself. God's purpose was not fulfilled after the creation of Adam, because Adam did not have the life of God. If Adam had chosen the tree of life and eaten of its fruit, God's purpose would have been fulfilled.

God Accomplishing His Purpose through Christ

What is God's ultimate purpose? His ultimate purpose is to have many sons. What is a son? A son is not a chair; a chair is made by man. A son is not made, he is begotten. A son is not just something picked up from the street. Someone who is picked up from the street is not your son, because he has no life relationship with you. A son is one whom a person has begotten and who has a life relationship with that person. This is why the Gospel of John says that a man cannot enter the kingdom of God unless he is born of water and of the Spirit (John 3:5). If a man has not been born again and not received God's life, he cannot enter the kingdom of God. No lower forms of creatures can enter the kingdom of man, because they are too far apart from man; they do not have man's life. The distance between God and man is immeasurably greater than the distance between man and the lower creatures. As such, man cannot enter the kingdom of God if he does not have God's life. In order for man to enter God's kingdom and be a son of God, he must have the life of God.

The Lord Jesus was God's only begotten Son. Yet God is not satisfied with having only one Son; He wants to have many sons. This is why Christ is the only begotten Son as well as the firstborn Son. As the only begotten Son, He is unique, having no brothers. At the beginning of the Gospel of John, the Lord was the Word, the only begotten Son of God (1:18). But in Romans and Hebrews, He became God's firstborn Son (Rom. 8:29; Heb. 1:6). For God to have a firstborn Son means that He has other sons. The Lord Jesus is the firstborn Son, and He has many brothers. God calls those who have His life His sons. Man will not call a lower form of animal his son no matter how good that animal is. The matter is not about good or evil, but about whether one is of the same species with the same life.

In order for man to become God's son, he has to receive Christ. In the garden of Eden, God wanted man to eat of the tree of life. Today He wants man to receive Christ as life. There is a difference between a tree and fruit. A tree cannot be eaten, whereas fruit can be eaten. The fruit is the embodiment of the tree; it is the tree, but in an edible form. The substance of the fruit comes from the tree, and it shares the same life with the tree. God is the tree of life, while Christ is the fruit. Christ comes from God and shares the same life with God. He is God in a receivable form. On the one hand, God gave Christ to us to accomplish redemption so that we no longer have to be sinners. On the other hand, He gave Christ to us in order to dispense His life into us and make us His sons for the fulfillment of His purpose.

Romans 8 mentions conformation to the image of God's Son (v. 29). This conformation is not one man's imitation of another, moving when the other moves and stopping when the other stops. Conformation implies passing through the same mold. The Lord is a mold; He molds everyone who has believed and received Him into the same image. In Vietnam men make rice cakes by grinding rice into paste and pressing it with a mold. As a consequence, all the rice cakes bear the same image. Christ is our mold, and we will all be conformed to the same image. This is why some people say that Christians are in a class of their own, that they are all the same. This is true because we share the same life and are being conformed to the same image.

God's purpose is to have many men who share the same image as His Son so that they become His many sons and eventually be with Him in His glory in eternity. But something happened—man sinned and fell. Sin entered the world through one man (Rom. 5:12). But the Lord came as the world's Savior. He died on behalf of man and solved the problem of sin. Man has been recovered back to the point of being in the garden of Eden. Now this man must still choose the tree of life and receive Christ as life before he can become the son of God.

In this conference we want to see how God accomplishes His purpose in man. Tonight's word is merely a foundation. Starting tomorrow, we will begin to build the house. May the Lord be merciful to us so that we can clearly see God's purpose and the way to reach His purpose. *(The Collected Works of Watchman Nee,* Vol. 42, pp. 397–401)

THE CHURCH AS CHRIST'S COUNTERPART

In creation two persons were created: one was Adam and the other was Eve. Both were created human beings, but each typifies something different. First Corinthians 15 says that Adam was a type of the Lord Jesus, and Romans 5 says that Adam was a figure of the man who was to come. Adam, then, foreshadowed Christ; he portrayed Christ in figure. In other words, all that God purposed in Adam was to be achieved in Christ.

But besides Adam in the creation, there was also the woman, Eve. God very carefully recorded the creation of this woman in Genesis 2, and when we come to Ephesians 5 we are clearly told that Eve typifies the church. Therefore, we can see that God's eternal will is achieved partly through Christ and partly through the church. In order for us to understand how the church can achieve God's will on earth, we must learn from Eve. The purpose of this book is not to discuss the type of Adam. Therefore, we will not consider this matter here; rather, the emphasis is upon Eve. We are not focusing our thoughts upon the work of Christ, but upon the position the church occupies in relation to that work.

When we read Genesis 2:18–24 and Ephesians 5:22–32 we find that a woman is mentioned in both places. In Genesis 2 there is a woman, and in Ephesians 5 there is also a woman. The first woman is a sign typifying the church; the second woman is the first woman. The first woman was planned by God before the foundation of the world and appeared before the fall. The second woman was also planned before the foundation of the world, but was revealed after the fall. Although one appeared before the fall and the other after, there is no difference in God's sight: the church is the Eve of Genesis 2. God created Adam to typify Christ; God also created Eve to typify the church. God's purpose is not only accomplished by Christ but is also accomplished by the church. In Genesis 2:18, the Lord God said, "It is not good that the man should be alone; I will make him an help meet for him." God's purpose in creating the church is that she may be the help meet of Christ. Christ alone is only half; there must be another half, which is the church. God said, "It is not good that the man should be alone." This means that in God's sight Christ alone is not good enough. Genesis 2:18–24 reiterates the events of the sixth day of creation. On the sixth day God created Adam, but afterward it seems that He considered a little and said, "No, it is not good that the man should be alone." Therefore, He created Eve for Adam. By then, everything was completed, and we find that Genesis 1 ends with this record: "And God saw every thing that He had made, and, behold, it was very good" (v. 31). From this we realize that having Adam alone, or we may say, having Christ alone, is not enough to satisfy God's heart. With God there must also be Eve, that is, there must also be the church. Then His heart will be satisfied.

The Lord God said, "It is not good that the man should be alone." In other words, God desired to have both Adam *and Eve.* His purpose is to have a victorious Christ plus a victorious church, a Christ who has overcome the work of the devil plus a church which has overthrown the work of the devil. His purpose is to have a ruling Christ and a ruling church. This is what God planned for His own pleasure, and He has performed it for His own satisfaction. It has been done be-cause God desired to do it. God desired to have Christ, and God also desired to have a church which is exactly like Christ. God not only desired that Christ would have dominion, He also wants the church to have dominion. God allows the devil on earth because He said, "Let them," Christ and the church, "have dominion." God purposed that the church, as Christ's counterpart, should take part in dealing with Satan. If the church does not match Christ, God's purpose will not be fulfilled. In warfare Christ needs a help meet, and even in glory He also needs a help meet. God requires the church to be the same as Christ in every respect. It is God's desire that Christ should have a help meet.

Eve Came out of Adam

Adam needed a help meet. What did God do to meet this need? Genesis 2:19–20 says, "And out of the ground the Lord God formed every beast of the field, and every fowl of the air; and brought them unto Adam to see what he would call them: and whatsoever Adam called every living creature, that was the name thereof. And Adam gave names to all cattle, and to the fowl of the air, and to every beast of the field; but for Adam there was not found an help meet for him." God brought every kind of living creature before Adam, but Adam could not find his help meet among them. None of the living creatures made out of earth could be a help meet for Adam.

Therefore, "the Lord God caused a deep sleep to fall upon Adam, and he slept: and he took one of his ribs, and closed up the flesh instead thereof. And the rib, which the Lord God had taken from man, made he a woman, and brought her unto the man. And Adam said, This is now bone of my bones, and flesh of my flesh: she shall be called Woman, because she was taken out of Man" (vv. 21–23). This one was Adam's help meet and the figure of the church in Ephesians 5. The Bible says very clearly that all of the things made of earth and not taken out of the body of Adam could not be his help meet. All the beasts of the field, the cattle, and the birds of the air were made of earth. They were not taken out of Adam; therefore, they could not be the help meet to Adam. We must remember that Eve was formed out of a rib taken from Adam; therefore, Eve was the constituent of Adam. This means that the church comes out of Christ. Only that which is out of Christ can be the church. Anything that is not of Christ is not the church. *(The Glorious Church,* pp. 25–27)

GAINING A MAN TO EXERCISE GOD'S AUTHORITY
OVER THE EARTH

God's Purpose in Creating Man

Why did God create man? What was His purpose in creating man?

God has given us the answer to these questions in Genesis 1:26 and 27. These two verses are of great significance. They reveal to us that God's creation of man was, indeed, an exceedingly special one. Before God created man, He said, "Let us make man in our image, after our likeness: and let them have dominion over the fish of the sea, and over the fowl of the air, and over the cattle, and over all the earth, and over every creeping thing that creepeth upon the earth." This was God's plan in creating man. "God said, Let us. . ." This speaks of the kind of man God wanted. In other words, God was designing a "model" for the man He was to create. Verse 27 reveals God's creation of man: "So God created man in his own image, in the image of God created he him; male and female created he them." Verse 28 says, "God blessed them, and God said unto them, Be fruitful, and multiply, and replenish the earth, and subdue it: and have dominion over the fish of the sea, and over the fowl of the air, and over every living thing that moveth upon the earth."

From these verses we see the man that God desired. God desired a ruling man, a man who would rule upon this earth; then He would be satisfied.

How did God create man? He created man in His own image. God wanted a man like Himself. It is very evident then that man's position in God's creation is entirely unique, for among all of God's creatures, man alone was created in

God's image. The man that God's heart was set upon was completely different from all other created beings; he was a man in His own image.

It is by man that God's plan is fulfilled, and through man His own need is met. What, then, does God require from the man whom He created? It is that man should rule. When God created man, He did not predestine man to fall. Man's fall is in chapter three of Genesis, not chapter one. In God's plan to create man, He did not predestine man to sin, neither did He foreordain redemption. We are not minimizing the importance of redemption, but only saying that redemption was not foreordained by God. If it were, then man would have to sin. God did not foreordain this. In God's plan to create man, man was ordained to rule. This is revealed to us in Genesis 1:26. Here God unveils to us His desire and tells us the secret of His plan. "Let us make man in our image, after our likeness: and let them have dominion over the fish of the sea, and over the fowl of the air, and over the cattle, and over all the earth, and over every creeping thing that creepeth upon the earth." This is God's purpose in creating man.

Perhaps some may ask why God has such a purpose. It is because an angel of light rebelled against God before man's creation and became the devil: Satan sinned and fell; the Daystar became the enemy of God (Isa. 14:12–15). God, therefore, withdrew His authority from the enemy and put it, instead, into the hand of man. The reason God created man is that man may rule in the place of Satan. What abounding grace we see in God's creation of man!

Not only does God desire that man should rule, but He marks out a specific area for man to rule. We see this in Genesis 1:26: "Let them have dominion over the fish of the sea, and over the fowl of the air, and over the cattle, and over all the earth. . ." "All the earth" is the domain of man's rule. Not only did God give man dominion over the fish of the sea, the birds of the heavens, and the cattle, but He further required that man should rule over "all the earth." The area where God desired man to rule is the earth. Man is especially related to the earth. Not only in His plan to create man was God's attention focused upon the earth, but after God made man, He clearly told him that he was to rule over the earth. Verses 27 and 28 say, "So God created man in his own image, in the image of God created he him; male and female created he them. And God blessed them, and God said unto them, Be fruitful, and multiply, and replenish the earth, and subdue it. . . ." What God emphasized here is that man should "replenish the earth" and "subdue it"; it is of secondary importance that man should have dominion over the fish of the sea, the fowl of the air, and every living thing on the earth. Man's dominion over these other things is an accessory; the main subject is the earth.

Two words in Genesis are very meaningful. One is "subdue" in Genesis 1:28, which can also be translated "conquer." The other is "keep" in Genesis 2:15, which can also be translated "guard." We see from these verses that God ordained man to conquer and guard the earth. God's original intention was to give the earth to man as a place to dwell. It was not His intention that the earth would become desolate (Isa. 45:18). God desired, through man, to not allow Satan to intrude upon the earth, but the problem was that Satan was on earth and intended to do a work of destruction upon it. Therefore, God wanted man to restore the earth from Satan's hand.

Some may ask: Why doesn't God Himself cast Satan into the bottomless pit or the lake of fire? Our answer is: God can do it, but He does not want to do it Himself. We do not know why He will not do it Himself, but we do know how He is going to do it. God wants to use man to deal with His enemy, and He created man for this purpose. God wants the creature to deal with the creature. He wants His creature *man* to deal with His fallen creature *Satan* in order to bring the earth back to God. The man whom He created is being used by Him for this purpose.

Therefore, we must distinguish the difference between the work of saving souls and the work of God. Many times the work of saving souls is not necessarily the work of God. Saving souls solves the problem of man, but the work of God requires that man exercise authority to have dominion over all things created by Him. God needs an authority in His creation, and He has chosen man to be that authority. If we were here just for ourselves as mere men, then all our seeking and longing would be to love the Lord more and to be more holy, more zealous, and save more souls. All of these pursuits are good indeed, but they are too man-centered. These things are concerned simply with the benefit of man; God's work and God's need are entirely neglected. We must see that God has His need. We are on this earth not merely for man's need but even more for God's need. Thank God that He has committed the ministry of reconciliation to us, but even if we have saved all the souls in the whole world, we have not yet accomplished God's work or satisfied God's requirement. Here is something called God's work, God's need. When God created man, He spoke of what He needed. He revealed His need to have man rule and reign over all His creation and proclaim His triumph. Ruling for God is not a small thing; it is a great matter. God needs men whom He can trust and who will not fail Him. This is God's work, and this is what God desires to obtain.

We do not lightly esteem the work of gospel preaching, but if all our work is just preaching the gospel and saving souls, we are not causing Satan to suffer fatal loss. If man has not restored the earth from the hand of Satan, he has not yet achieved God's purpose in creating him. Saving souls is often only for the welfare of man, but dealing with Satan is for the benefit of God. Saving souls solves man's need, but dealing with Satan satisfies God's need.

Brothers and sisters, this requires us to pay a price. We know how the demons can speak. A demon once said, "Jesus I know of, and with Paul I am acquainted; but who are you?" (Acts 19:15). When a demon meets us, will he flee or not? Preaching the gospel demands that we pay a price, but a much greater price must be paid to deal with Satan.

This is not a matter of a message or a teaching. This requires our practice, and the price is extremely great. If we are to be men whom God will use to overthrow all of Satan's work and authority, we must obey the Lord completely and abso-lutely! In doing other work it matters less if we preserve ourselves a little, but when dealing with Satan, we cannot leave one bit of ground for ourselves. We may hold on to something of ourselves in our study of the Scriptures, in preaching the gospel, in helping the church or the brothers, but when we are dealing with Satan, self must be utterly abandoned. Satan will never be moved by us if self is preserved. May God open our eyes to see that His purpose demands that we be wholly and absolutely for Him. A double-minded person can never deal with Satan. May God speak this word to our hearts.

God's Rest

In all six days of God's work of creation, His creation of man was distinct. All His work throughout the six days was for this. His real aim was to create man. In order to do this, God first had to repair the ruined earth and heaven. (Genesis 2:4 says, "These are the generations of the heavens and of the earth when they were created, in the day that the Lord God made the earth and the heavens." "The heavens and the earth" refer to the creation in the beginning, since at that time it was the heavens that were first formed and then the earth. But the second part, "in the day that the Lord God made the earth and the heavens," refers to His repair and restoration work, since in this work the earth was cared for first and then the heavens.) After God restored the ruined earth and heaven, He created the man of His design. After the sixth day, there was the seventh day; on this day God rested from all His work.

Rest comes after work: work must be first, and then rest may follow. Moreover, work must be completed to entire satisfaction before there can be any rest. If the work has not been done completely and satisfactorily, there can never be any rest to the mind or heart. We should not, therefore, esteem lightly the fact that God rested after six days of creation. For God to rest is a great matter. It was necessary for Him to have gained a certain objective before He could rest. How great the power must be which moved such a Creator God to rest! To cause such a God, who plans so much and who is full of life, to enter into rest requires the greatest strength.

Genesis 2 shows us that God rested on the seventh day. How is it that God could rest? The end of Genesis 1 records that it was because "God saw every thing that he had made, and, behold, it was very good" (v. 31).

God rested on the seventh day. Before the seventh day, He had work to do, and prior to His work, He had a purpose. Romans 11 speaks of the mind of the Lord and His judgments and ways. Ephesians 1 speaks of the mystery of His will, His good pleasure, and His foreordained purpose. Ephesians 3 also speaks of His foreordained purpose. From these Scriptures we gather that God is not only a God who works, but a God who purposes and plans. When He delighted to work, He proceeded to work; He worked because He wished to work. When He found satisfaction with His work, He rested. If we desire to know God's will, His plan, His good pleasure, and His purpose, we have only to look at that which caused Him to rest. If we see that God rests in a certain thing, then we may know that is something He was originally after. Man, too, cannot rest in that which does not satisfy him; he must gain what he is after and then he will have rest. We must not regard this rest lightly, for its meaning is very great. God did not rest in the first six days, but He rested in the seventh day. His rest reveals that God accomplished His heart's desire. He did something which made Him rejoice. Therefore, He could rest.

We must note the word "behold" in Genesis 1:31. What is its meaning? When we have purchased a certain object with which we are particularly satisfied, we turn it around with pleasure and look it over well. This is what it means to behold. God did not just casually "look" upon all that He had made and see that it was good. Rather, He "beheld" everything which He had made and saw that it was very good. We need to take note that God was there at the creation "beholding" what He had made. The word "rested" is the declaration that God was satisfied, that God delighted in

69

what He had done; it proclaims that God's purpose was attained and His good pleasure was accomplished to the fullest. His work was perfected to such an extent that it could not have been made better.

For this reason God commanded the Israelites to observe the Sabbath throughout their generations. God was after something. God was seeking something to satisfy Himself, and He attained it; therefore, He rested. This is the meaning of the Sabbath. It is not that man should purchase fewer things or walk less miles. The Sabbath tells us that God had a heart's desire, a requirement to satisfy Himself, and a work had to be done to fulfill His heart's desire and demand. Since God has obtained what He was after, He is at rest. It is not a matter of a particular day. The Sabbath tells us that God has fulfilled His plan, attained His goal, and satisfied His heart. God is One who demands satisfaction, and He is also One who can be satisfied. After God has what He desires, He rests.

What then brought rest to God? What was it that gave Him such satisfaction? During the six days of creation there were light, air, grass, herbs, and trees; there were the sun, the moon, and the stars; there were fish, birds, cattle, creeping things, and beasts. But in all these God did not find rest. Finally, there was man, and God rested from all His work. All of the creation before man was preparatory. All of God's expectations were focused upon man. When God gained a man, He was satisfied and He rested.

Let us read Genesis 1:27–28 again: "So God created man in his own image, in the image of God created he him; male and female created he them. And God blessed them, and God said unto them, Be fruitful, and multiply, and replenish the earth, and subdue it: and have dominion over the fish of the sea, and over the fowl of the air, and over every living thing that moveth upon the earth." Now read Genesis 1:31 with Genesis 2:3: "And God saw every thing that he had made, and, behold, it was very good. . . . And God blessed the seventh day, and sanctified it: because that in it he had rested from all his work which God created and made." God had a purpose, and this purpose was to gain man—man with authority to rule over the earth. Only the realization of this purpose could satisfy God's heart. If this could be obtained, all would be well. On the sixth day God's purpose was achieved. "God saw every thing that he had made, and, behold, it was very good. . .and he rested on the seventh day from all his work." God's purpose and expectation were attained; He could stop and rest. God's rest was based upon man who would rule. *(The Glorious Church,* pp. 5–12, 20–23)

CHAPTER 3

THE INCARNATION OF GOD

THE EMBODIMENT AND EXPRESSION OF THE TRIUNE GOD

What did Jesus of Nazareth say about Himself? In John 10:30 He said, "I and the Father are one." We need some explanation here. In the Bible the invisible God is called the Father. The Son manifests and expresses the Father. What is hidden is the Father, and what is expressed is the Son. The Son is the One who can be seen and touched. Behind, you have the Father. In front, you have the Son. The two are actually one. They are the two sides of the same reality. When we talk about two, we refer to the fact that one is hidden while the other is revealed. When we talk about one, we say that the revealed One is just the hidden One in manifestation. This is the biblical interpretation of the Father and the Son.

Therefore, when Jesus of Nazareth one day said, "I and the Father are one," it was a statement that no one else could make. This man was saying, in reality, that He and the invisible God are one entity. He is God and God is He. God is the invisible Father, and He is the manifested Son. The

Father and the Son are one!

Perhaps we will go back a little bit to the earlier parts in the Gospel of John and see what it says there. John 1:18 says, "No one has ever seen God; the only begotten Son, who is in the bosom of the Father, He has declared Him." Why has no one seen God? It is because God is invisible. Jesus said that He was the only Begotten of the Father; He expressed the invisible Father. When you see the only Begotten, you see the Father.

John 5:17 says, "But Jesus answered them, My Father is working until now, and I also am working." He always put Himself in the same place as the Father. Verse 18 says, "Because of this therefore the Jews sought all the more to kill Him, because He not only broke the Sabbath but also called God His own Father, making Himself equal with God." When we read His words now, we may consider them to be ordinary remarks. But the Jews knew what He was saying. They knew that He was making Himself equal with God. The words, in fact, meant that God is His Father and He came to express God. The invisible One is God, and the visible One is He.

One of the disciples was confused. John 14:8 says, "Philip said to Him, Lord, show us the Father and it is sufficient for us." Philip was asking to be shown the Father who had been mentioned again and again by Jesus. Verse 9 says, "Jesus said to him, Have I been so long a time with you, and you have not known Me, Philip? He who has seen Me has seen the Father; how is it that you say, Show us the Father?" Here Jesus made it very plain that to see Him is to see God. He made no apology about it. He is God. There is no need to see the Father anymore. If you see Him, you see God!

The eternal, invisible God is now seen by us. There is no

need to conjure up an untouchable and far transcendent God or imagine what He is like; He has revealed Himself to us. He has dwelt in our midst and walked among us. Jesus of Nazareth is the very God dwelling among and with man. He has manifested God's nature and attributes to us. There is no need to search for God anymore because He has revealed Himself. Our mentality is too limited. Our hands are too short, and our viewpoint too narrow. If we were left to ourselves to study and search for God, we could only conclude that He is the unknown One. Now we know that God desires to reveal Himself. In fact, He has revealed Himself to us already. *(The Normal Christian Faith,* pp. 36–40, 52)

GOD UNITED WITH MAN

The Word becoming flesh is the first scene in the beginning of the redemptive work. In himself, man is extremely feeble and of the flesh. What is man? Man is just dust! Man is limited and bound; all of man's virtues (if there are any) have limitations which cannot be transcended. Man's thought, character, behavior, and ethics are completely from man; they can never be higher than this level. Weakness, degradation, and sin are man's common qualities. If there is any merit, it can never go beyond the human realm. However, if man remains man—weak, defeated, sinful—God will not be satisfied. God is perfect. He wants man to be perfect in character, morality, behavior, and thought, according to His own standard. Otherwise, God would never choose man for His companion, giving man eternal life and having man with Him in heaven. Unless man reaches God's level of perfection himself, he cannot receive these things. What hope does man

have? It is very important that God became a man. The birth
of Jesus is the mingling of divinity with humanity. The Lord
Jesus is God, yet He became a man. Therefore, He is God
and man; He is man as well as God. Originally there was a
chasm separating God and man. God could not *become* man,
nor could man become God. However, the Word became
flesh when the Lord Jesus came to this earth. He is a floating
pontoon bridge between God and man. God and man met
in the Lord Jesus. Man did not *become* just God, neither did
God become just man. The Lord Jesus expresses God, and
He also represents man. He is the unique God, and He is
also the unique Man. Because He is both God and man,
God is able to give grace to man in Him. Because He is both
man and God, man is able to draw near to God in Him. Now
there are men on earth who are filled with divinity. Man has
the possibility to receive God's life. God's life is able to enter
into the spirit of man. Originally, it was impossible for God
and man to be joined together; however, God and man have
been joined in the Lord Jesus. From this point there is the
possibility for God and man to be joined together. Incarnation is not the totality of the gospel. It is the very first step of
salvation; this step proclaims the nature and issue of the
coming salvation. *(The Collected Works of Watchman Nee,*
Vol. 3, pp. 77–78)

There is a doctrine in Christianity that speaks of the union
of God and man. It is a very important doctrine. If you open
the Bible to see how this can be, you will see that the source
of such a doctrine is the fact that God became a man—Jesus.
He is God mingled with man.

The Bible does not present a doctrine of God becoming
one with man. Rather, it shows Jesus of Nazareth, who is a

sample of God being one with man. Originally, God and man were separate; there was a wide gulf between them. There was no possibility of union. But the Nazarene came. He was God coming to be a man. He was the bridge between man and God, joining the two into one. This is not a doctrine that teaches people to be one with God. Here is the fact: henceforth, when a man is in Christ, he can be one with God. *(The Normal Christian Faith,* p. 72)

CHAPTER 4

CHRIST—THE SON OF GOD

THE ANOINTED ONE OF GOD

"Who Do You Say That I Am?"

Who do men say that the Son of Man is?" The Lord Jesus posed this question to the disciples. No doubt the Lord was the Son of Man. Everyone would admit that He was the Son of Man. The Jews admitted it, and so did the Gentiles. This was not the problem. The problem was not whether the Lord was the Son of Man, but who the Son of Man was. The Lord was not asking if others considered Him to be good or bad, but who did men say that He was. Those who opposed Him said that He was demon-possessed (John 7:20; 8:48, 52), a gluttonous man, and a drunkard (Matt. 11:19). We are not very concerned with these blasphemous remarks. But those who were favorable towards Him also had different views. Some said that He was John the Baptist; others said that He was Elijah. Still others said that He was Jeremiah or one of the prophets. Nicodemus said that He came from God as a teacher (John 3:2). The

Samaritan woman said that He was a prophet (4:19). Who really was this Son of Man? Everyone had their own view and own opinion.

But the Lord did not stop with this question. He wanted to know one thing: He wanted to know the difference between the disciples' view of Him and the view of other men. In particular, He wanted to know the difference between Peter's knowledge of Him and others' knowledge of Him. In effect, the Lord was saying, "Others have said that I am this and I am that. But who do you say that I am? You who are My disciples, who do you say that I am?" "Who do you say that I am?" (Matt. 16:15). This was the Lord's main question.

Simon Peter answered the Lord and said, "You are the Christ, the Son of the living God" (v. 16). Peter's word was clear: "You are the Christ, the Son of the living God." Peter acknowledged two things about the Lord. First, he acknowledged that He is the Christ. Second, he acknowledged that He is the Son of God. As far as the Lord's person is concerned, He is the Son of God. As far as His work is concerned, He is the Christ of God. His being the Son speaks of who He is, and His being the Christ speaks of what He does. His being the Son speaks of His relationship with God, and His be-ing the Christ speaks of His relationship with God's plan. As far as His person is concerned, He is the Son of the living God. As far as His work is concerned, He is the Christ, the Christ of the living God; He is the anointed One, the One set apart to accomplish God's plan. This was Peter's confession of the Lord Jesus. This is also our confession of the Lord Jesus.

The Rock Being Christ, the Son of the Living God

As far as His own person is concerned, He is the Son of God. This knowledge is indispensable to everyone. Our knowledge of the Lord does not depend on what the Gospels say that He has done; our knowledge of Him depends on our knowledge of Him as the Son of God. What man sees, hears, and touches are not enough. The Lord is much more than what man sees and touches. He is the Son of the living God. Everyone confesses Him as the Son of Man; both friends and foes acknowledged Him as the Son of Man. But only those who have received God's revelation know that He is the Son of God. In God's eyes, whether or not a man has life depends on whether he knows Jesus of Nazareth as the Son of God. The Bible says, "And this is eternal life, that they may know You, the only true God, and Him whom You have sent, Jesus Christ" (John 17:3). "That you may believe that Jesus is the Christ, the Son of God, and that believing, you may have life in His name" (20:31). "He who has the Son has the life; he who does not have the Son of God does not have the life" (1 John 5:12). Eternal life is knowing Jesus Christ, the One whom God has sent. Eternal life is knowing the Lord Jesus as the Son of God.

God is not only revealing the person of the Lord Jesus to us. He is also revealing His ministry to us. In His person, the Lord Jesus is the Son of God; in His ministry, He is the Christ of God. The word *Christ* is the same as the word *Messiah,* which means *the anointed One.* An anointed person is one who is joined to God's work. In the Old Testament, when a man was appointed by God to be a priest, a prophet, or a king, he was anointed with ointment. Hence, an anointed one is one who is commissioned and sent by God to accomplish His work and fulfill His plan. The Lord Jesus is the Christ of God. This means that God's eternal plan is accomplished through Christ. In eternity past, the Lord Jesus was the Son of God. But at the beginning of God's eternal plan, the Son of God became the Christ of God, for the purpose of accomplishing God's eternal plan. God's Christ is eternal, but He was there from the eternity which has a beginning, while the Son of God was there from the eternity that does not have a beginning. The Son of God does not have a beginning, in the same way that God does not have a beginning. But God's Christ came into being when God's eternal plan came into being. Christ was established for the fulfillment of God's plan. The anointed One was separated for God's special work. From that point on, God's Son became God's Worker, His Messenger, and His Christ. From that point on, all of God's work, all of His hopes, and all of His goals were centered on His Son. From that point on, God's Son is not only God's Son, He has also become God's Christ. God's Son became God's Christ and the anointed One for the purpose of accomplishing God's eternal plan.

A Christian must see God's eternal plan before he can become useful in God's hand. It is not enough for a Christian merely to know that he has sinned, that the Lord Jesus has accomplished redemption for him, and that he can be saved through receiving the Lord Jesus. This Christian will not perish and go into perdition, but he will be of no use in God's hand. God did not establish the church simply for the purpose of gaining a group of people. God established the church for the purpose of gaining a group of people who would know His purpose and plan in Christ. We must be clear about this. We need revelation from the Father who is in the heavens in order to know that the Lord Jesus is the

Christ of God and the anointed One, that Christ is the Head of the church, that the church is the Body of Christ, and that it shares in the anointing of Christ. Brothers and sisters, we have to confess that the Lord Jesus is the Christ, and we have to confess that we are Christians who belong to Christ and who share in the anointing. One day when God opens our eyes, we will realize how narrow our view has been during all the years we were Christians, and how small a realm we have covered in our work. One day God will place us under His anointing, and we will see the kind of work that He has done. It is amazing that some claim that they have received the outpouring of the Holy Spirit, and yet they have not entered into God's work or seen the purpose of the anointing. May the Lord open our eyes to see the purpose of the Lord Jesus' anointing and the purpose of the church's anointing. The anointing which the church receives is the same anointing the Head received, because the church is under the anointing of the Head.

Not only do we need to know the Lord Jesus as the Son of God, but we must know Him also as the Christ of God. Not only do we need to know that the Lord Jesus possesses God's life and nature, but we must know that He is the anointed One who accomplishes God's eternal plan. Through Him as the Son of God, we can know God Himself, and through Him as the Christ of God, we can know God's plan. If we only know the Lord Jesus as the Son of God without knowing Him as the Christ of God, we will not understand God's purpose in creating us and His purpose in saving us; we will not understand what God wants to gain from the church. We must have both kinds of knowledge—the knowledge of the Lord Jesus as the Son of God and the knowledge of the Lord Jesus as the Christ of God. *(The Collected Works of*

Watchman Nee, Vol. 36, pp. 109–112, 114–116)

THE CENTRALITY AND UNIVERSALITY OF GOD

Why are there all things? Why are there angels? Why are there human beings? Has God created these things without a purpose, or are they a part of God's plan?

Why did God choose man, commission the prophets, send the Savior, give us the Holy Spirit, set up the church, and establish the kingdom? Why would God want to spread the gospel to the uttermost part of the earth and save sinners? Why do we have to save sinners and edify the believers?

Some have considered baptism, speaking in tongues, forsaking the denominations, holiness, the keeping of the Sabbath, or other things as the center. But what is God's center?

God's work is with a goal. What is the goal of our work? We must first have a goal in our vision and then have a goal in our work. If we do not see God's center, our work will not have any goal.

God's truths are all systematic and interrelated. There is a center to God's truths, and everything else is auxiliary.

Some have determined the center of their work by basing it on their own inclinations and the need around them. But our center should be according to God's predestination and His need.

What is God's center? What is God's consistent truth? What is the one line in God's truth?

Who is the Lord Jesus? We all say that He is our Savior, but very few people can say as Peter did, that He is the Christ of God.

The center of God's truths is Christ. God's center is

Christ. "The mystery of God, Christ" (Col. 2:2). A mystery is something hidden in God's heart. God never told anyone why He created all things and why He created man. Hence, it was a mystery. Later He revealed this mystery to Paul and charged him to speak it out. This mystery is Christ.

The Lord Jesus is the Son of God; He is also the Christ of God. When the Lord was born, an angel told Mary that He is the Son of God (Luke 1:35), but the angels told the shepherds that He is Christ the Lord (Luke 2:11). Peter acknowledged Him both as the Christ and as the Son of God (Matt. 16:16). When the Lord resurrected, He was designated the Son of God (Rom. 1:4). Through His resurrection, God also made Him both Lord and Christ (Acts 2:36). A man receives life by believing that He is the Christ and the Son of God (John 20:31). In Himself, as far as His person is concerned, the Lord is the Son of God. In God's plan, according to His work, He was anointed by God and is, therefore, the Christ of God. He is the Son of God from eternity to eternity. He is the Christ since the beginning of God's plan. God's goal is for His Son to have "the first place in all things" (Col. 1:18). God's plan is focused on Christ. "Christ is all and in all" (Col. 3:11).

God created all things, and He created man for the purpose of expressing Christ's glory. Today believers express only a little of Christ. In the future all things will express Christ; the whole universe will be filled with Christ. God created all things so that all things will express Christ. God created man in order that man would be like His Son, having the life of His Son and the glory of His Son, so that the only begotten Son can become the firstborn Son among many sons. God created man and redeemed him for Christ. Redemption is for the purpose of reaching the goal of creation. Christ is the Bridegroom, and we are the friends of the Groom. He is the chief cornerstone, and each one of us is one of the millions of stones. God created us for the satisfaction of Christ's heart. We are thankful that we have seen the relationship between Christ and us. We praise Him because we have seen the relationship between God and Christ. God's center is Christ. God's goal is centered upon Christ. God's goal has two aspects: (1) that all things would express the glory of Christ and (2) that man would be like Christ, having the life of Christ and the glory of Christ. *(The Collected Works of Watchman Nee,* Vol. 11, pp. 731–733)

THE PREEMINENT ONE

In Creation

After the Father made a plan, the Son came to create. The Father planned creation according to His own will. The Son agreed with this and created, while the Spirit's power accomplished it. The Son is the One who created all things. In creation the Son is the Firstborn of all creation (Col. 1:15), and the beginning of the creation of God (Rev. 3:14). According to His eternal plan and before the foundation of the world, God ordained that the Son become flesh and accomplish redemption (1 Pet. 1:20). In God's plan the Son was the first in creation. Therefore, He is the Head of all creation. God planned, and the Son created. Creation was completed for the Son. God created all things in order to satisfy the Son's heart. Oh! The Lord is so great! He is the Alpha and the Omega! He is the Alpha because all things are of Him. He is the Omega because all things are unto Him. This is the meaning of the third group of verses.

God created man in order that man would be like Christ, having His life and His glory. God expresses Himself through Christ, while Christ expresses Himself through man. God called us to partake of His Son that we would become like His Son and that His Son would be the Firstborn among many brothers. From eternity past until the resurrection, the Lord was the only Begotten. When the Lord was resurrected from the dead, He became the Firstborn. This is why after His resurrection, He said, "Go to My *brothers* and say to them, I ascend to My Father and your Father, and My God and your God" (John 20:17). The many sons became sons in the only begotten Son. God caused the only begotten Son to die in order that many sons could be produced. God has made us not only the sons but the heirs as well. God has not only given us the life of the Son but has also caused us to inherit the inheritance with the Son. The Son was made a man, a little lower than the angels for a while. After that He received honor and glory as His crown and will lead many sons into glory. The reason God created man was that man would have the life of His Son and enter into glory with His Son, thus satisfying His Son's heart. Thank God that He created and redeemed us for the satisfaction of Christ's heart. *(The Collected Works of Watchman Nee,* Vol. 11, pp. 734–735)

In Redemption

A few days ago we saw that "Christ is all and in all" (Col. 3:11). What God planned before the foundation of the world is "that He Himself might have the first place in all things" (1:18). Today we want to see how Christ's redemption accomplishes God's plan.

God's plan has one goal with two aspects: (1) to have all things expressing Christ's glory, so that Christ may have the first place in all things, and (2) to have man conformed to Christ, having His life and His glory.

Colossians 1 tells us these two things: (1) Christ has the first place in all things, and (2) Christ is the Head of the church.

Ephesians 1 also tells us these two things: (1) Christ is heading up all things in the heavens and on earth, and (2) the church becomes His inheritance.

Revelation 4 and 5 also tell us these two things: (1) chapter four speaks of creation, and (2) chapter five speaks of redemption.

God's creation is for the carrying out of His plan. God's goal in creating all things and man, is to have all things express Christ and to have man conformed to Christ, having His life and glory. However, Satan rebelled and came in to interrupt, causing all things to become disjointed and causing man to fall. Therefore, God had to use redemption to achieve the goal of His creation. As a result, Christ's redemption must (1) reconcile all things to God, and (2) redeem fallen mankind and impart His life to them. To solve God's problems, Christ's redemption must also (3) deal with the rebellious Satan, and (4) take care of man's sin.

Christ's redemption indeed solved these four matters. It accomplished God's goals: (1) by reconciling all things to God, and (2) by dispensing His life to man. It also solved God's problems: (3) by dealing with the rebellious Satan, and (4) by taking care of man's sin. Two are positive and two are negative.

The goals of Christ's redemption are that we be His particular people (Titus 2:14) and living sacrifice (Rom. 12:1), that we would live to Him and die to Him (Rom. 14:7–9), that we would be the temple of the Holy Spirit glorifying God (1 Cor. 6:19–20), that we would live to Him (2 Cor. 5:15), and that whether through life or through death, Christ would be magnified in our body, so that for us to live is Christ (Phil. 1:20–21).

The goal of redemption is to give Christ the first place in all things. In order that Christ may have the first place in all things, He must first have the preeminence in us. We are the firstfruits among all things. First we must be subjected to Christ, then all things can be subjected to Christ. The cross enables God to reach this goal in us. The cross makes us decrease and makes Christ increase. The cross will find room for Christ and will ensure that Christ has the first place. God works through the cross, which in turn works through the environment to dig into us deeply, causing us to know Christ and be filled with Him, so that Christ may have the first place in us. Christ's redemption has accomplished God's plan before the foundation of the world. This plan is to give Him the first place in all things. We should forget about our personal interests and care only for the accomplishment of God's eternal destiny which is to have Christ gain the first place in all things. When we see the Messiah, we will cast away our waterpot! When we see God's Christ, we will cast away everything! *(The Collected Works of Watchman Nee,* Vol. 11, pp. 739, 742–743)

In Eternity

After the Lord's death and resurrection, "God highly exalted Him and bestowed on Him the name which is above every name, that in the name of Jesus every knee should bow, of those who are in heaven and on earth and under the earth, and every tongue should openly confess that Jesus Christ is Lord to the glory of God the Father" (Phil. 2:9–11). God has made Him both Lord and Christ (Acts 2:36) and has put all things under His feet (Eph. 1:20–22). Revelation 4 and 5 show the scene of the Lord's ascension into the heavens after His resurrection, in which He receives glory and praise. Chapter four shows the praise of all the creatures for creation. Chapter five reveals their praises for redemption. God wants to put the enemy underneath the Lord's feet (Matt. 22:44). Concerning this matter, the church today bears a great responsibility. God is waiting for the church to fulfill this work.

Since Satan's rebellion and the fall of man, all things have been subjected to vanity. This means that their former goal has been lost and that they have no definite direction. Today all things are subject to vanity and are waiting for God's sons to be manifested. In this waiting period, all creation is under the slavery of corruption. We see this in the decreasing intensity of sunlight and in the withering of plant life. However, all things have a hope that one day they will be freed from the slavery of corruption. While having this hope, all things groan and travail in pain. When God's children enter the freedom of the glory, all things will be freed. In the day of the redemption of our bodies, all creation will be set free. But today we can have a foretaste of the power of the coming age. (The church is a foretaste of the power of the coming age, while the kingdom is a foretaste of the power of eternity.) One day our bodies will be redeemed; we will receive full sonship and will enter into the freedom of the glory (Rom. 8:19–23).

When the Lord appears, we shall be like Him (1 John 3:2). On the one hand, we are His sons and have His life and nature. On the other hand, we are His heirs, inheriting God's inheritance in glory (1 Pet. 1:3–4).

Revelation 21 and 22 show us a picture of eternity, not of the millennium. These two chapters speak of four crucial points: (1) God; (2) the Lamb; (3) the city, the physical city with its citizens, the ones God had predestinated before the foundation of the world and whom He gained; these are also the thirsty ones mentioned in Revelation 7; and (4) the nations. God and the Lamb are the center of the city. Revelation 21:9–22 speaks about the city. Verse 23 speaks about the center of the city. God's glory is the light, and the Lamb is the lamp. Light comes through the lamp, signifying God being revealed through the Lamb. The center of the new creation is the New Jerusalem which is composed of God's sons. The center of this city is God and the Lamb. The glorious light of God is in the Lamb. The Lamb lights the city, and the bright city shines on the nations. In the city there is only one street and one river. There is only one street, so no man will become lost. This street must be shaped like a spiral. The river is in the middle of the street and flows along with the street. Both the street and the river proceed out of the throne of God and of the Lamb. Thus God and the Lamb are the center.

After all things have been subjected to the Lord, He Himself will willingly be subjected to God (1 Cor. 15:28). This is the meaning of the fifth group of verses.

Therefore, we see that from eternity to eternity, all the things God has done are for His Son to have the first place in all things. God's goal is to make His Son the King over all things. *(The Collected Works of Watchman Nee,* Vol. 11, pp. 737–738)

In the Christian Life

The life of a Christian is Christ (Col. 3:4). Christ being our life and Christ being our power are two different things. How can we be holy? How can we be victorious?

(1) Many think that holiness and victory mean being delivered from the little sins and dealing with the temper.

(2) Some think that holiness and victory mean being patient, humble, and meek.

(3) Some think that holiness and victory mean putting the self and the flesh to death.

(4) Some think that holiness and victory mean studying the Bible more, praying more, being careful, and trusting in the Lord for one's strength.

(5) Some know that power is with the Lord, that our flesh has been crucified on the cross, and that by faith, we should claim the Lord's power to overcome and be holy.

None of the above five cases is right. The fifth case may seem to be right, but actually it is not for the following reason:

Christ is our life. This is victory! This is holiness! The victorious life, the holy life, the perfect life, are all Christ. From beginning to end, everything is Christ. Outside of Christ, we have nothing. Christ must have the first place in all things. The victorious life God has given us is not a thing, such as patience or meekness, but the living Christ. Christ never mends our wrongs. What we lack is not patience but a living Christ. God will never tear a piece of cloth from Christ to mend our hole. To be short of patience is to be short of Christ, because God wants Christ to have the first place in all things. Therefore, to put the self to death is not holiness. Holiness is Christ. Christ must have the first place in all things.

If God were to cause us to have power, it would only make us powerful persons; Christ would not have the first place in us. Christ is my power; it is Christ who holds the first place in me. We do not have power because we are not weak enough. The power of Christ "is made perfect in weakness." It is not that the Lord *makes* me powerful; but it is the Lord who is the power in my stead.

Mr. Hudson Taylor saw that "You *are* the branches." The author of *The Victorious Life* saw that victory is just Christ. It is not that I draw power from Christ to help me be a man; rather, it is Christ who is the man *in my place.* It is not that Christ gives me the power to be patient; rather, it is Christ who lives the patience out from me. "Lord, I allow You to live out from me!" We do not overcome by the Lord; rather, it is the Lord who overcomes through us! It is not us overcoming through Him; rather, it is Him overcoming through us. By faith I commit myself to the Lord and allow the Lord to live Himself out of me. I do not live by Christ; rather, "it is Christ who lives in me" (Gal. 2:20). I live because of the life of Christ and also because of "the faith in the Son of God" (v. 20b). When we believed and received the Son of God, not only did His life enter into us, but His faith also entered into us. Therefore, we can live because of His faith.

Victory is Christ! Patience is Christ! What we need is not patience, meekness, or love, but Christ. Christ must have the first place in all things. From within us, Christ lives out patience, meekness, and love. Man deserves only to die. There is nothing else that he deserves. After God created Adam, He had a will, and Adam had to obey this will. But when God re-created us, it was not like this. He put us in death, and God Himself lives out His will from within us. We should not only see a substitutionary Savior on Mount Golgotha, we should also see a Lord within us who lives in our stead. Christ is our wisdom. In the past He was our righteousness for our salvation. In the present He is our sanctification for us to live a holy life. In the future He will be our redemption that our body may be redeemed (1 Cor. 1:30). He holds the first place in all things!

How can we enter into this victorious life? We must do the following things:

1. Have Absolutely No Hope in Our Self:
    We must know the self thoroughly. We must see that the self deserves only to die; any hope in the self must come to an end. Our end is God's beginning. We cannot receive the victory of Christ if we still have hope in our self. Christ is living in us, but we have not given Him the ground to rule over us and reign within us.

2. Have a Full Consecration:
    We must consecrate wholeheartedly. If we do not see our utter weakness, we cannot accept the cross and fully consecrate ourselves, nor hand over all our rights to the Lord's hand to allow Him to be the Lord.

3. Believe:
    After consecration we have to believe that Christ is being lived out in us and that He has taken over our rights.

Christ is to be lived out in our flesh in the same way that

He was lived out of the flesh given Him through Mary. Christ today wants to live Himself out on the earth through our flesh as He did in His own flesh while on earth. Christ has to be lived out in our lives. Our victory is based on our yielding to Christ the first place in all things and allowing Him to be the Lord in all of our living.

The Old Testament tells us how God's chosen people lived on the earth. There was first the tabernacle as the center of the twelve tribes. Later the temple was their center. The center of the temple was the ark. The tabernacle, the temple, and the ark all typify Christ. When the relationship between the Israelites and the tabernacle or the temple was proper, they were victorious; no nation could overcome them. Although their enemies had learned warfare and they had not, they still overcame all their enemies. When something was wrong between them and the temple, they were carried away. It did not depend on whether or not they had a competent king; neither did it depend on whether or not they were clever and able. It depended only on whether or not something was wrong between them and the ark in the temple. We must allow the Lord to have the first place. Only then will we be victorious. We must be concerned about the Lord's victory before we can have the victory. Once the hair of separation is shaven, there can be no victory. The same is true with us today. If we do not give Christ the highest place, we cannot be victorious. If Christ does not have the first place in our heart, we cannot be victorious. *(The Collected Works of Watchman Nee,* Vol. 11, pp. 743–746)

In the Christian Experience

The experience of a Christian has two sides: one is sweet, the other, painful. God causes us to experience a sweet and suffering life in order that Christ may have the first place in all things.

The Experience on the Sweet Side

The goal of prayer to let Christ have the first place in all things must be reached, before it will be answered. Seek first God's kingdom and God's righteousness, then God will add to us all that we need. (To add is not to give but to add to something that is already there; while to give is to give something that is not there.) To ask in the Lord's name is to ask the Father on behalf of the Lord that the Lord may gain something. According to this principle, those who care for the flesh have nothing to pray. They must let the cross cut away the flesh before they can become the Lord's intercessors, praying in His will rather than praying for their own purpose. Only those who let Christ have the first place in all things can enter into the Holy of Holies. We should turn the time we pray for our own need into the time we pray for God's business. God will listen both to the prayers that we utter (the prayers we pray that are for God's business) as well as the prayers that we do not utter (the prayers we pray that are for our own affairs). We should let the Lord gain something first. Afterward, the Lord will let us gain something. The sweetest part of the Christian life is to receive answers to prayer continually. But God's purpose in answering our prayers is that Christ may have the first place in all things.

Growth is also a sweet side of the Christian life. We should be like children but not be childish. Growth is not having biblical knowledge but having more of Christ, to be filled with Christ. Growth is less of self, even none of self. It is to think less of self, even to think nothing of the self. Humility is to not look at the self. To see oneself is to be relatively humble; not to see oneself is to be absolutely humble. To grow is to let Christ have the first place in us. "He must increase, but I must decrease" (John 3:30). It is not how much biblical knowledge we have, but how much consecration we have, how much we have put in God's hand, and how much we have allowed Christ to have the first place. The real growth is to let Christ be magnified.

There is also the receiving of light from God—spiritual vision—which is another sweet side of the Christian life. Revelation is something given to us by God objectively. Light is the revelation God shows to us subjectively. Vision is what we see when we are enlightened by God's light; it includes light and revelation. First there is the enlightening, then the faith. To be continually under the enlightening we must allow Christ to have the first place in all things continually. "If therefore your eye is single, your whole body will be full of light" (Matt. 6:22). It is not that we do not understand, but that we cannot understand, because the eye is not single. "The pure in heart. . .shall see God" (Matt. 5:8). The heart must be pure. "If anyone resolves to do His will, he will know" (John 7:17). Only those who let Christ have the first place can have light.

Power is also a sweet side of the Christian life. In order to have power, we must let Christ be enthroned. When He increases, we have the power. Without separation, there can be no power. To be separated is not only to come out, but to come in—to be in Christ. We are different from others because we are in Christ and have put on Christ. Christ is our power.

The Experience on the Suffering Side

In general all believers have financial difficulties. Perhaps this is because the things they formerly did were improper, things they now can no longer do. Or perhaps it is because of spiritual reasons, where God is behind the scene directing matters with some specific goal. God takes away our material possessions so that we will seek Christ that He may have the first place in all things. It is not impossible for a rich man to enter the kingdom of God, but it is difficult. It is not impossible for him to serve the Lord, but it is difficult. Cast your treasure in the dust, and Jehovah will be your treasure (Job 22:24–25). In the wilderness God dealt with the children of Israel by stripping them of all the earthly supply of food and clothing in order that they might know God's riches. When the earthly supply stops, the heavenly supply comes. Difficulty in material supplies comes for the purpose that we may seek to have Christ take the first place in all things and learn the lessons of faith. When difficulty comes, we should believe that it is from God and rejoice. But we should not hope for difficulties to come. If we do, Satan also can cause difficulties to be added to us.

The reason we lose our parents, husband, wife, children, and relatives is that God wants us to take Christ as our satisfaction. God takes these away from us in order that we would take Christ as Lord and allow Him to have the first place in us. God has no intention to deal with us severely; His intention is only for us to take Christ as Lord. To weep before the Lord is more precious than to be happy before men. What we find in the Lord is what cannot be found in our parents, wife, and children. Both in creation and in His dealing with the believers, God wants His Son to have the first place. If we offer up Isaac, we will receive back Isaac. God does not let us have anything outside of His Son.

God allows sickness and weakness to come to our body in order that we may learn to (1) pray at night, (2) be watchful as sparrows on the rooftop, (3) know that the Lord makes our bed for us, (4) deal with sin, (5) wait quietly, (6) touch the hem of the Lord's garment, (7) know that the Lord sent His word to heal us, (8) know that through sickness God causes us to become useful persons, (9) know that holiness is healing, and (10) know that the Lord's resurrection power removes our weakness, sickness, and death. Through sicknesses, God causes us to learn to trust, rely, and obey, so that Christ may have the first place in us.

After a person is saved, he always exercises his natural virtues. But after some time, perhaps a few years, the Lord will remove his natural virtues. This will make him suffer. The Lord deprives us of our virtues in Adam that we may see our own corruption. God takes away our goodness that we may be filled with Christ.

God deprives us of our possessions, relatives, health, and goodness in order that we would take Christ as our satisfaction, be filled with Christ, and allow Him to have the first place in all things.

Whatever God gives to us, whether it be a sweet life or a suffering life, is for the purpose of making Christ the One who occupies the first place in us. *(The Collected Works of Watchman Nee,* Vol. 11, pp. 746–750)

In Christian Work and Messages

Christ Having the First Place in Christian Work

Christ should have the first place in our work. "Good works, . . .that we would walk in them" (Eph. 2:10). "Good works" are just Christ. The goal of God's work is Christ, and we should walk in this work. All believers, no matter what profession they hold, are doing the work of God and should walk in God's good works. To serve God and to work for God are two vastly different matters. Many work for God but do not serve God. Whether or not a work is of faithfulness depends upon the intent, motive, and purpose and if the goal is for Christ. In doing God's work, although there is suffering, there is also joy; although there is difficulty, there is also comfort. There is also the attraction to God's work. We often work because of our interest, not because of Christ. Many times men run to and fro to work for a name for themselves. They have worked, but they have not served God. God's work from eternity to eternity has always been with the view that His Son would have the first place in all things. Therefore, our work should also be for Christ. If God does not purify our intent and motive, we cannot receive God's blessing. We work not for sinners but for Christ. How successful our work is depends on how much Christ is in it. We should allow the Holy Spirit to discern our intention right from the beginning, to see if it belongs to the spirit or to the soul, and to see if it belongs to this side or to that side. Our work should not be for our own increase, our own group, or our own message; rather, we should work for Christ. As long as God gains something, we should rejoice. When we see God gaining something, even if it is not through our hands, we should be happy for it. We are not saving our message but saving sinners; we are not here to gain our own heart but Christ's heart. When things go our way and we gain something, it means that the Lord gains nothing and nothing goes His way. If we would take God's gain as our satisfaction, we would not be proud or jealous. Many times we seek God's glory as well as our own glory. God saves men for Christ, not for us. Paul planted, and Apollos watered. It was not accomplished by one person, lest anyone would say, "I am of Paul," or "I am of Apollos." All the things concerning the work are for Christ, not for the worker. We are the loaves in the Lord's hand. When people eat the loaves, they thank the one who gives them the loaves; they do not thank the loaves, which are we. The work from its beginning to its end is all for Christ, not for us. We should be satisfied with the work allotted to us by the Lord and with the position the Lord arranged for us. We should not be "in another man's rule" (2 Cor. 10:16). We like very much to leave our own lot to tread on another's lot. The question is not whether we can do it or know how to do it, but whether God has commanded it. Sisters should stand in the sisters' position (1 Cor. 14:34–35). Sisters should not be teachers, making judgments concerning God's word (1 Tim. 2:12). In all the work, we should let Christ have the first place.

Christ Having the First Place in Christian Messages
Christ should also have the first place in our messages. We "preach. . .Christ Jesus as Lord" (2 Cor. 4:5). "For I did not

determine to know anything among you except Jesus Christ, and this One crucified" (1 Cor. 2:2). Christ is the center of God's plan and the center of God's goal. The cross is the center of God's work. The work of the cross is to accomplish God's goal. The cross works to eliminate all that issues from the flesh in order that Christ may have the first place. Our central message should not be the dispensations, the prophecies, the types, the kingdom, baptism, forsaking denominations, speaking in tongues, keeping the Sabbath, or holiness, etc. Our central message should be Christ. The centrality of God is Christ. Therefore, we should take Him as the center.

After a person is saved, we should help him to consecrate himself to be a slave of Christ, so that he receives Christ as his Lord in all things.

All the truths in the Bible are related like a wheel with spokes and a hub, having Christ as the center. We are not neglecting the truths outside the center; rather, we need to link these truths with the center. Concerning any truth we should know two things: (1) we should know about this truth, and (2) we should know how this truth relates to the center. We should pay attention to the center. Of course, this does not mean we do not speak of other truths. Paul said, "I did not determine to know anything among you except Jesus Christ, and this One crucified" (1 Cor. 2:2). Later he also said, "But we do speak wisdom among those who are full-grown" (2:6). It is only after a person has consecrated himself and received Christ as his Lord that we can speak to him the truths concerning his building up. In our work we should continually draw people back to the center and let them see that "Christ is Lord." We cannot do this work in an objective way. We ourselves must be the first to be broken by God and allow Christ to have the first place in us, before we can lead others to receive Christ as Lord and allow Christ to have the first place in them. We must live out a life of giving Christ the first place before we can spread this message. Our message is just our person. We should allow Christ to have the first place in the small things in our daily life before we can preach the message of the centrality of Christ. I only wish that every one of us would give the Lord Jesus His place on the throne! If the will of God is to be accomplished, what does it matter if I am put in the dust? The Lord's "well done" surpasses all the praises of the world. The smiling face of heaven surpasses all the angry faces of the earth. The comfort of heaven surpasses the tears of the earth. The hidden manna is enjoyed in eternity. May the Lord bless His word that He would gain us and others also. *(The Collected Works of Watchman Nee,* Vol. 11, pp. 750–753)

CHAPTER 5

THE DEATH OF CHRIST

THE REDEEMING ASPECT—
CRUCIFYING ALL NEGATIVE AND OLD THINGS

The greatest negative in the universe is the cross, for with it God wiped out everything that was not of Himself: The greatest positive in the universe is the resurrection, for through it God brought into being all He will have in the new sphere. So the resurrection stands at the threshold of the new creation. It is a blessed thing to see that the cross ends all that belongs to the first regime, and that the resurrection introduces all that pertains to the second. Everything that had its beginning before resurrection must be wiped out. Resurrection is God's new starting point.

We have now two worlds before us, the old and the new. In the old, Satan has absolute dominion. You may be a good man in the old creation, but as long as you belong to the old you are under sentence of death, because nothing of the old can be carried over to the new. The cross is God's declaration that all that is of the old creation must die. Nothing of the first Adam can pass beyond the cross; it all ends there.

The sooner we see that, the better, for it is by the Cross that God has made a way of escape for us from that old creation. God gathered up in the Person of His Son all that was of Adam and crucified Him; so in Him all that was of Adam was done away. Then God made, as it were, a proclamation throughout the universe saying: "Through the Cross I have set aside all that is not of Me; you who belong to the old creation are all included in that; you too have been crucified with Christ!" None of us can escape that verdict. *(The Collected Works of Watchman Nee,* Vol. 33, pp. 58–59)

Removing Our Sins

The blood is toward God, man, and Satan. Primarily, the blood is for God, not for man. It is required by God, but if we do not realize the value of the blood to God, we will not realize its value to us. In the Old Testament the blood is mentioned over four hundred times, and in each case, it is always for God Himself. On the day of Atonement the blood was sprinkled before the Lord seven times, and no *man* except the high priest, typifying the Lord Jesus, was allowed to draw near to the Lord. In Egypt the blood was smeared on the outside of the door for *God* to see; those who were in the house could not see it. The *life* is in the blood, and God requires blood to satisfy His righteousness. The blood was God's portion and was never allowed to be eaten. Sometimes we feel our sins are more real than the blood, yet we have to accept God's valuation. We have to believe that the blood is precious to God. If God accepts it for our redemption, then we can believe that the debt is paid. First John 1:7 says, "The blood of Jesus His Son cleanses us from every sin." In the business world, if I pay a debt, the one to whom I pay the money has to see that the money is good! If God says the blood is enough to satisfy His requirements, then it must be. Our valuation of the blood must be in accordance with His valuation. The result will be that our hearts will be purified from an evil conscience (Heb. 9:14). (The blood cleanses our conscience, not our hearts.) We know how important it is to have a clear conscience, because without this we are unable to believe. If our conscience condemns us, faith leaks out. The temptation to many is to think they must live up to what they regard as God's standard before they can come with confidence to God. But the blood is the way of access, and our approach is always with boldness because it has nothing to do with our attainment or holiness. The blood is the only thing that is needed; it is absolutely sufficient. The first time we came to the Lord, we were made near by the blood, and every subsequent time that we come to Him, we are made near by the blood. Penance will not make our approach any easier. The blood is our only plea. Since our conscience is cleansed before God we have "no more conscience of sins." From this ground we can face the enemy and all of his efforts to bring us under condemnation. The blood puts God on our side, and we can be fearless. The fall brought in something which gave Satan some footing. Furthermore, man was put outside the garden, and God was outside of man. The blood restores us to God and God to us.

The blood of the Lord Jesus cleanses us not only from sin but from *every* sin. As He is in the light, we can walk in the light, and the blood will cleanse us from every sin—those which we think are unforgivable and even those which we are not conscious of. It is only as our conscience is clear that we can overcome Satan. His attacks are based on his accusations, and if we accept these accusations we will go down. Why do we come under his accusations and believe them? It is because we still hope to have some righteousness of our own. We often may be disappointed in ourselves, but God is never disappointed with us because He expects *nothing* from us! If we accept God's verdict that *no* good thing dwells in us, and judge ourselves to be worthy of nothing but death, and if we see that the blood more than pays every time, Satan will have no ground of attack. Our attitude only will be, "Lord, I cannot hope to be any better, but Your blood is always sufficient." *(The Collected Works of Watchman Nee,* Vol. 46, pp. 1258–1260)

The precious blood is the basis for spiritual warfare. If we do not know the value of the blood, we cannot fight. Once our conscience is weakened, we are finished. Therefore, if we do not maintain a blameless and clean conscience, we will have no way to deal with Satan. Satan can use thousands of reasons in his accusations against us. If we accept them, we will fall. But when Satan speaks to us, we can reply to all his reasons with the one answer of the blood. There is not a single reason which cannot be answered by the blood. Spiritual warfare requires a conscience without offense, and the blood alone can give us such a conscience.

Hebrews 10:2 says, "Because those worshipping, having once been purified, would have no longer had the consciousness of sins. . . ." When a Christian's conscience no longer has the sense of sin, it is because of the blood. Once we stand on the ground of the blood, once we believe in the blood, Satan can no longer work upon us. We often like to reason that we can no longer fight because we have sinned. But the Lord knows that we are sinful, so He has prepared the blood. The Lord has a way for sinful man, because the

Lord has the blood. But He has no way for one who willingly receives Satan's accusations. Anyone who accepts the accusations of Satan denies the power of the blood. No one who believes in the precious blood can receive Satan's accusations at the same time. Either one or the other must go. If we accept the accusations, the blood has to go; if we accept the blood, the accusations have to go.

The Lord Jesus is the High Priest and Mediator for us (see Heb. 2:17–18; 4:14–16; 7:20–28; 8:6; 9:15; 1 John 2:1). He is always serving in this position—the High Priest and the Mediator. The purpose of His serving is to keep us from Satan's accusations. It takes only a moment of time for man to receive Him as Savior, but it is a lifelong matter to face the accusations of Satan. The word *mediator* in Greek means "an appointed defender." The Lord is our Mediator, our Defender. The Lord speaks for us. But do we stand on the side of the Mediator or on the side of the accuser? It would be ridiculous if we believed the words of the accuser while our Mediator is in the very act of defending us. If an attorney continually proved that a defendant was not guilty and defendant persisted in believing the accuser, would that not be quite absurd? Oh, may we see that the Lord Jesus is our Mediator and that He is defending us. May we see that the blood is the basis for us to deal with Satan. We should never answer Satan's accusations with good conduct; we should answer with the blood. If we realized the value of the blood, there would be a great increase of peaceful and joyful Christians on the earth today.

"They overcame him because of the blood of the Lamb" (Rev. 12:11). How precious are these words! The brothers overcame him not because of their merit, their advancement, or their experience. They overcame him because of the blood of the Lamb. Whenever accusations come from Satan, we need to deal with them by the blood. Once we accept the blood, Satan's power will be nullified. All that we are depends on the blood, and we need the blood every day. Just as we depended upon the blood and trusted in the blood on the day we were saved, we must continue to depend upon the blood and trust in the blood from that day forward. The blood is our only foundation. God desires to deliver us from many senseless accusations. He wants to break these chains. We must never feel that we are being humble by receiving accusations day after day. We must learn to overcome these accusations. If we do not overcome accusations, we can never be the overcomers. The overcomers must know the value of the blood. Although we do not know the immense value of the blood, we can still say to the Lord, "O Lord, apply the blood on my behalf according to Your evaluation of it." We should deal with the power of Satan according to God's valuation of the blood, not according to our valuation of the blood. *(The Glorious Church,* pp. 89–90)

Terminating the Old Man

The Cross Dealing with the Sin within Man

In the Bible there are two different ways of dealing with sin: The sins before God are taken away by the blood, but the sin in the flesh must be dealt with by the work of the cross. The effect of the blood and the effect of the cross are entirely different. The blood is for God. It is outward and objective. The cross is for man. It is inward and subjective. The Bible only speaks of man being crucified with Christ; it does not speak of man shedding blood with Christ. Only Christ can deal with outward sins. Man cannot do this. However, in order to deal with inward sin, the old man has to be annulled by the power of the cross (Rom. 6:6). The old man is the old "I."

Romans 6:6 speaks of three things: the old man, the body of sin, that is, the body that belongs to sin, and sin itself. First, there is sin, then there is the old man, and finally there is the body. What does it mean for a person to no longer be a slave to sin? Sin is the lord and master, the one who has the power over man. In the original Greek, as well as in English translations, the word "sin" is singular in this verse. This is the inward sin, the motivating power that urges and compels us to sin. Some have been serving this sin for decades, and they are still not free from it. Sometimes they resist a little, but they are always defeated. Even though sin is powerful, we cannot blame it for our acts of sins. The one to blame is our old man. The old man is the one that has descended from Adam's fall.

Brothers and sisters, what happens when we sin? When we are about to sin, something in us tells us that it is wrong to sin. However, a power within compels us and causes us to sin. Suppose someone says something that is not very nice about us. Something within urges us to argue with him. The thing that is urging us to commit a sin is the inward sin. We are Christians, and we know that it is wrong to argue with others, but if we do not argue, we feel unhappy. After we argue, we feel better because we have vented our anger. It seems as if a company director is giving us all kinds of instructions, while a company executive is ratifying all his instructions. The result is the actual carrying out of the sinful actions.

Sin is a power that induces us to sin. It is our old man that determines to sin because it likes to sin. One brother told me that if he tried to be patient, he would get an ulcer.

Can you see how powerful the inward temptation is? Sin gives the suggestion, and the old man gives the consent. One does the persuading, and the other performs the actions. The body is merely the acting faculty. No sin can be carried out without the body. The body is like a puppet. When you tell it to sin, it sins. When you tell it to act, it acts. The Bible calls it the body of sin. All evil things come from the body. The eyes behold evil things, the mind thinks evil things, the hands perform evil things, and the legs walk on evil paths. All the evil things are done by the body. According to the Bible, sin proposes, the old man consents, and the body acts. When these three work together, man sins.

The Way of Deliverance from Sin Being the Crucifixion of the Old Man

How can we be delivered? The holiness group says that once a person has uprooted sin, he will never sin again. The Chinese say that since all the evil things come from the evil body, we should practice asceticism to buffet the body so that it will see no evil, hear no evil, speak no evil, and act no evil. In this way the body can be fully brought under control. But this is useless. Many people who are well-behaved outwardly are corrupt in their heart.

Once two Christians lived together. One was an aunt, and the other was the niece. One day someone rebuked the aunt for no apparent reason. She smiled and did nothing. The niece who was watching admired the aunt's reaction. After the person left, she said to her aunt, "He was scolding you, not me, but I was burning." Her aunt said, "Do you think that I was not burning? I was burning, but the burning was inside." Many think that as long as they have not

112

committed any sin outwardly, they have overcome. How wrong this is!

God does not deal with the body of sin, nor does He crucify the root of sin. God's work is not carried on outwardly, but inwardly; He deals with the old man. The old man likes to be a slave to sin, so God crucified him. Sin entices, tempts, and coerces, while the old man likes being a slave to sin. As a result, it urges the body to sin. Paul said, "Knowing this, that our old man has been crucified with Him" (Rom. 6:6). The one being crucified is the old man. The word "crucified" in the original Greek is a verb in the past tense. It is something that has been accomplished forever. It does not say that the old man intends to be crucified with the Lord, nor that the old man will be crucified with the Lord, but that the old man has been crucified with the Lord. When Christ was crucified, our old man was also included in this crucifixion. When Christ died, the old man died as well.

Suppose a sinner wants to be saved tonight and prays, "O God, please have mercy on me! May the Lord shed His blood for me to redeem me." We will certainly tell him that it is wrong to pray this way. He should not ask the Lord to shed His blood again, because the Lord's blood was shed for him long ago. All he has to do is ask God to give him faith. Once he believes, he is saved. He should not ask the Lord to shed His blood for him or to redeem him from his sins before God. Instead, he should believe that Christ's blood has already been shed. Once he believes, he is justified. The same is true of our dealing with the old man. We do not have to ask God to crucify our old man. The Word says that the old man was crucified on the cross long ago. Just as forgiveness and redemption are facts of the past, the crucifixion of the old man is also a fact of the past.

Through faith we see forgiveness as a work that is entirely of the Lord. In the same way, through faith we see the accomplishment of the crucifixion of the old man. By faith we believe that the old man has been crucified with the Lord. If we look in the Greek text, we will see that the crucifixion of the old man is something that happened in the past. It is not enough to know this; we must believe it. By faith we see that the old man has died, and we should praise God, saying, "Praise God, I am already dead."

The Old Man Crucified, the Flesh Unemployed

Once the old man is crucified, the body of sin is annulled. The word *annulled* in the original Greek means "unemployed." Originally, the job of the body of sin is to sin. The mouth slanders, and the mind engages itself in filthy thoughts. But when the old man dies, the mouth no longer slanders and the mind no longer wanders. In this way, the mouth and the mind become unemployed. Even though sin continues to urge us to sin, the old man is gone. The new life of the Lord within does not sin. It does not like to sin, and as a result, the body becomes unemployed.

There was a person in Tientsin who loved to play mahjong. His two hands were almost made for mahjong. But after he believed in the Lord, his two hands became unemployed. Paul said that once the old man within is crucified, the body outside becomes unemployed. The result is that one no longer sins and is no longer a slave to sin. Even though the sin within continues to tempt us and even though temptations continue, the old man is dead and no longer has any feeling or response. This is the work of the cross as revealed in the Scriptures.

The work of the cross and the work of the blood are completely different. The Lord's blood was shed by Him alone to remove our sins before God; we have no part in this work. But our crucifixion with Christ is different. Crucifixion is not for dealing with sins but for eliminating the old man. First John 1:7 says, "The blood of Jesus His Son cleanses us from every sin." The Bible says that the blood of Christ washes us of our sins; it does not say that the blood washes away the old man, the self, or the flesh. These can only be dealt with by the cross (Gal. 2:20). These are not washed away by the blood; they are crucified. "But they who are of Christ Jesus have crucified the flesh with its passions and its lusts" (5:24). The flesh cannot be washed away by the blood; there is no way to wash it away. The filth on the outside can be washed away by the blood, but the flesh and the old man cannot be washed away; they can only be crucified by the cross (6:14).

Every time the Bible speaks of crucifixion, it is in reference to the self and the old man, not to sins. Sins must be washed away by the blood; the old man must be dealt with by the cross. Brothers and sisters, do you see the full salvation? In China opium is forbidden. Even the sale of opium is illegal. Opium is a product of the opium factory. Our old man is like the opium factory which produces goods daily. One can eliminate the opium, but as soon as it is eliminated more goods will come out of the factory. Our outward sins are washed away by the precious blood. But after they are washed away, the old man can produce more sins. This is why, in addition to the blood dealing with the sins that have been committed, there is a need for the cross to eliminate the old man that sins. It is not enough to eliminate the opium that is produced daily; one has to destroy the opium factory. Once the factory is destroyed, no opium will be produced.

Once the cross eliminates the old man, we will no longer sin.

What is the meaning of the cross? When the Jews rejected the Lord, the crowd cried, "Crucify! Crucify!" (John 19:6). Then they said, "Take Him away!" (v. 15). The cross is a big taking away. The Jews took away the Lord by the cross. Today the Lord is taking away our old man by the cross. The blood is for redeeming us; the cross is for taking away the old man. After the old man is taken away, there is complete salvation. The blood is objective; it redeems us from the sins that are before God. The cross is subjective; it takes away the old man so that we can be released from sin.

Everything hinges on *faith*. Everything has been accomplished by God. We are already crucified with Christ (Gal. 2:20). Perhaps we do not have the faith; perhaps there is doubt in our heart that there is such a thing: "I am still I. I do not feel like I am crucified." The sins of a sinner are washed away by the blood of the Lord as soon as he believes. Do you remember the story of how you were saved? If you believe now, you will praise God in a similar way, saying, "Thank the Lord! My old man is dead!" *(The Collected Works of Watchman Nee,* Vol. 43, pp. 611–616)

Destroying the Devil

The reasons that the Son of God "Himself. . .partook of the same [blood and flesh]" are (1) "that through death He might destroy. . .the devil"; and (2) "release those [men]" (Heb. 2:14–15). All have sinned, and the wages of sin is death. The one who has the power of death is the devil. Sin leads man to death, and through death due to sin, the devil dominates man. Therefore, for God to save man, He had to solve the problem of the penalty of sin by destroying the power of death, which is under the command of the devil. The penalty of sin is death, but death requires a physical body. Thus, the Lord Jesus "partook of the same [blood and flesh]." Since He had a physical body, He was able to die and redeem man. Therefore, God had "a body. . .prepared" for Him "to do Your will, O God"; this will is "the offering of the body of Jesus Christ once for all. . .having offered one sacrifice for sins, sat down forever" (Heb. 10:5, 7, 10, 12). The devil had the power of death. Since no man could overcome death, Jesus obtained a human body, died, and also resurrected. He overcame all the power of the devil and destroyed him. *(The Collected Works of Watchman Nee,* Vol. 3, p. 78)

Judging the Satanic World

Our deliverance from the world begins, not with our giving up this or that but with our seeing, as with God's eyes, that it is a world under sentence of death as in the figure with which we opened this chapter, "Fallen, fallen is Babylon the great!" (Rev. 18:2). Now a sentence of death is always passed, not on the dead but on the living. And in one sense the world is a living force today, relentlessly pursuing and seeking out its subjects. But while it is true that when sentence is pronounced death lies still in the future, it is nevertheless certain. A person under sentence of death *has* no future beyond the confines of a condemned cell. Likewise the world, being under sentence, has no future. The world-system has not yet been "wound up," as we say, and terminated by God, but the winding up is a settled matter. It makes all the difference to us that we *see* this. Some folk seek deliverance from the world in asceticism, and like the Baptist, neither eat nor drink. That today is Buddhism, not Christianity. As Christians we both eat and drink, but we do so in the realization that eating and drinking belong to the world and, with it, are under the death sentence, so they have no grip upon us.

Let us suppose that the municipal authorities of Shanghai should decree that the school where you are employed must be closed. As soon as you hear this news you realize there is no future for you in that school. You go on working there for a period, but you do not build up anything for the future there. Your attitude to the school changes the instant you hear it must close down. Or to use another illustration, suppose the government decides to close a certain bank. Will you hasten to deposit in it a large sum of money in order to save the bank from collapse? No, not a cent more do you pay into it once you hear it has no future. You put nothing in because you expect nothing from it.

And we may justly say of the world that it is under a decree of closure. Babylon fell when her champions made war with the Lamb, and when by His death and resurrection He overcame them who is Lord of lords and King of kings (Rev. 17:14). There is no future for her.

A revelation of the cross of Christ involves for us the discovery of this fact, that through it everything belonging to the world is under sentence of death. We still go on living in the world and using the things of the world, but we can build no future with them, for the cross has shattered all our hope in them. The cross of our Lord Jesus, we may truly say, has ruined our prospects in the world; we have nothing to live for there.

There is no true way of salvation from the world that does not start from such a revelation. We need only try to escape the world by running away from it to discover how much we love it, and how much it loves us. We may flee where we will to avoid it, but it will assuredly track us down. But we inevitably lose all interest in the world, and it loses its grip on us, as soon as it dawns upon us that the world is doomed. To see that is to be automatically severed from Satan's entire economy.

At the end of his letter to the Galatians, Paul states this very clearly. "Far be it from me to glory, save in the cross of our Lord Jesus Christ, through which the world hath been crucified unto me, and I unto the world" (6:14). Have you noticed something striking about this verse? In relation to the world it speaks of the two aspects of the work of the cross already hinted at in our last chapter. "I have been crucified unto the world" is a statement which we find fairly easy to fit into our understanding of being crucified with Christ as defined in such passages as Romans 6. But here it specifically says, too, that "the world has been crucified to me." When God comes to you and me with the revelation of the finished work of Christ, He not only shows us ourselves there on the cross. He shows us our world there too. If you and I cannot escape the judgment of the cross, then neither can the world escape the judgment of the cross. Have I really seen this? That is the question. When I see it, then I do not try to repudiate a world I love; I see that the cross *has* repudiated it. I do not try to escape a world that clings to me; I see that by the cross I *have* escaped.

Like so much else in the Christian life, the way of deliverance out of the world comes as a surprise to most of us, for it is so at odds with all man's natural concepts. Man seeks to solve the problem of the world by removing himself physically from what he regards as the danger zone. But physical separation does not bring about spiritual separation; and the reverse is also true, that physical contact with the world does not necessitate spiritual capture by the world. Spiritual bondage to the world is a fruit of spiritual blindness, and deliverance is the outcome of having our eyes opened. However close our touch with the world may be outwardly, we are released from its power when we truly see its nature. The essential character of the world is Satanic; it is at enmity with God. To see this is to find deliverance.

Let me ask you: What is your occupation? A merchant? A doctor? Do not run away from these callings. Simply write down: Trade is under the sentence of death. Write: Medicine is under the sentence of death. If you do that in truth, life will be changed for you hereafter. In the midst of a world under judgment for its hostility to God you will know what it is to live as one who truly loves and fears Him. *(The Collected Works of Watchman Nee,* Vol. 39, pp. 90–93)

Annulling the Separating Ordinances

Ephesians tells us about a wall between the Jews and the Gentiles. The two are separated. But the cross has broken down the middle wall of partition. There is no longer any distinction or separation. If we meet someone who is in Christ, we should not say that he is Chinese; he is a person in Christ. We should not say that someone is an Englishman; we should say that he is in Christ. We have all become one in Christ.

Never think of having a Chinese church or a Chinese testimony. This is a great mistake, and the idea should not even cross our mind. Please remember that in Christ, there is no distinction between Greeks and Jews. There is no such thing. If a brother or a sister introduces such a thing among us, it means that he or she is bringing in a foreign element. The result will be corruption within. We do not have any distinction between Jews and Greeks. In Christ we are all joined together. We have to eradicate all nationalistic notions from our heart. The moment we bring such a thing into the church, the church becomes an organization of the flesh and no longer the Body of Christ.

Some people are so strong in their nationalistic feelings that they cannot be Christians in a proper way. Though we are Chinese and under the jurisdiction of our country, this relationship ceases when we are in Christ. Whenever we come before the Lord, we do not come as a Chinese person. Such a consciousness should be kept outside the door. We hope new believers will see from the very beginning that we are linked together in the life of Christ. I have received the life of Christ, and a brother in England or a brother in India or Japan has also received the same life of Christ. We are united according to the life of Christ, not according to our nationalities. We must have a very clear vision about this. In the Body, in Christ, and in the new man, nationality does not exist. That distinction has been totally abolished.

After the First World War, a few brothers from England went to Germany for a conference. During the conference, a brother stood up and introduced the British brothers with the words, "The war is over, and some English brothers are here to visit us. We warmly welcome them." After this introduction, a brother from England stood up and said, "We are not English brothers; we are brothers from England." This is a marvelous word. There are no English brothers; there are only brothers from England. How can there be an English brother, an American brother, a French sister, or an Italian sister in the house of God? Thank God, there are no national distinctions in Christ.

THE RICHES OF WATCHMAN NEE

Brothers and sisters, we are all part of the church. We have received the laying on of hands already. Now we must see that all distinctions between Greeks and Jews have been abolished. There are no longer any such distinctions in Christ. This is a glorious fact, a truly glorious truth. In the church there is only Christ. Christ is all and in all. There is nothing besides Christ. *(Messages for Building Up New Believers,* Vol. 1, pp. 116–118)

*Satisfying the Requirements of
God's Holiness and Righteousness*

It is God's holiness, God's righteousness, which demands that a sinless life should be given for man. There is life in the Blood, and that Blood has to be poured out for me, for my sins. God is the One who requires it to be so. God is the One who demands that the Blood be presented, in order to satisfy His own righteousness, and it is He who says: "*When I see the blood,* I will pass over you" (Exo. 12:13). The Blood of Christ wholly satisfies God.

Now I desire to say a word at this point to my younger brethren in the Lord, for it is here that we often get into difficulties. As unbelievers we may have been wholly untroubled by our conscience until the Word of God began to arouse us. Our conscience was dead, and those with dead consciences are certainly of no use to God. But later, when we believed, our awakened conscience may have become acutely sensitive, and this can constitute a real problem to us. The sense of sin and guilt can become so great, so terrible, as almost to cripple us, by causing us to lose sight of the true effectiveness of the Blood. It seems to us that our sins are so real, and some particular sin may trouble us so many times, that we come to the point where to us our sins loom larger than the Blood of Christ.

Now the whole trouble with us is that we are trying to sense it; we are trying to feel its value and to estimate subjectively what the Blood is for us. We cannot do it; it does not work that way. The Blood is first for God to see. We then have to accept God's valuation of it. In doing so we shall find our salvation. If, instead, we try to come to a valuation by way of our feelings we get nothing; we remain in darkness. No, it is a matter of faith in God's Word. We have to believe that the Blood is precious to God *because He says it is so* (1 Pet. 1:18–19). If God can accept the Blood as a payment for our sins and as the price of our redemption, then we can rest assured that the debt has been paid. If God is satisfied with the Blood, then the Blood must be acceptable. Our valuation of it is only according to His valuation—neither more nor less. It cannot, of course, be more, but it must not be less. Let us remember that He is holy and He is righteous, and that a holy and righteous God has the right to say that the Blood is acceptable in His eyes and has fully satisfied Him. *(The Collected Works of Watchman Nee,* Vol. 33, pp. 10–11)

THE LIFE-RELEASING ASPECT— IMPARTING THE DIVINE LIFE INTO THE BELIEVERS

The Redemptive and Non-Redemptive Aspects of Christ's Death

Before man sinned, God had a goal and a plan. He wanted man to receive His life—His uncreated life—and become

His sons. This is why He created man. After man was created, God placed him in front of the tree of life, implicitly indicating that man should eat of the tree of life, that is, man should receive God's uncreated life into him. Man did have life, but the life he had was only a created life. God is uncreated, and His intention is that the created man would receive His own uncreated life and be uplifted from the level of man to one that is before God. This does not mean that man would become God. It only means that man would share the life of God and live by God. This is God's original intention. But Adam fell and failed God's purpose. God then sent His own Son to die for us on the cross. In this way all our sins are dealt with through the blood and the cross of Christ.

The Lord also shows us in His Word that there is another aspect to the death of His Son. This is the non-redemptive aspect of His death. We all know that His death is for redemption. But there is another aspect—a non-redemptive aspect to His death, which is spoken quite a number of times in the Bible. One great mistake that men make today is in thinking that the cross of Christ was solely for the accomplishment of redemption. But the Bible shows us that there is another aspect to the work of the cross. Through the cross, Christ released His life and dispensed it into men.

In Genesis 3:21 we see a type of the death of Christ. God killed a lamb and gave its skin to Adam for a covering. But in Genesis 2:21 there is another type of the death of Christ—Adam's sleep. Regarding Adam's sleep, the Bible does not speak of the shedding of blood. It only says that God took a rib from him and made Eve.

The killing of the lamb and the covering of Adam's body with the skin refer to the redemptive aspect of the death of

Christ. After He accomplished the work of redemption, He clothed us with the garment of righteousness. We were naked before God, but the Lord died for us and put a garment of righteousness on us. All those who are in Christ and who have come to God are accepted by Him. They are accepted by Him in the same way that Christ is accepted. God receives all those who come to Him through putting on the skin of the Lamb. God receives them in the same way that He received the lamb. Today every saved person comes to God by trusting in the work of the Lord's redemption and by putting on the Lord as their righteousness.

God caused a deep sleep to fall upon Adam, took a rib from him, and made Eve out of it. Adam's sleep is a type of the non-redemptive aspect of the death of Christ. Out of His death, God took out something to build up the church. God took life out of Christ and gave this life to man, a life which is the same as God's, divine and uncreated.

We know from Genesis that God created many animals, and He created Adam. The animals are lower than man. When God wanted to prepare a mate for Adam, He did not look among the lower animals. Rather, He took a rib out from Adam and made Eve, whose life, like Adam's, was different from the lower forms of life. Similarly, man's life is on one level, while Christ's life is on a higher level. God took the life of Christ and created us in a fresh way. In this way we received the life of Christ to fulfill God's goal. This is the church, which is built up with all the saved ones. The life of the church is the same as the life of Christ. The life which we received at the time of salvation and regeneration is higher than any other form of life. Originally, our life was fleshly and earthly. But God has given Christ's life to us. By this life we are built up as the church.

Adam's sleep in Genesis 2:21 is not a type of the redemptive death of Christ, because at that time man had not yet sinned. Without sin there was no need of redemption. The death of the lamb in Genesis 3:21 is a type of the redemptive death of Christ. The covering of skin became necessary after man fell. Without sin there was no need and use for the skin. The skin signifies the coming redemptive death of Christ; it is entirely different from the sleep in Genesis 2:21. Adam's sleep in Genesis 2:21 typifies another aspect of the death of Christ. It is not an ordinary sleep. It is a sleep that has nothing to do with death. It is the kind of sleep that a saved person goes through when he departs from this world. We no longer have to go through death, which comes as a result of sin. The Lord said that those who believe in Him will have eternal life and will not see death (John 6:47). The death of a Christian is a sleep and has nothing to do with death or sin.

If we want to understand the Bible and trace its outlines, we have to differentiate between the redemptive aspect and the non-redemptive aspect of the death of Christ. The non-redemptive aspect on the positive side brings forth Christians, who are bone of His bone and flesh of His flesh. They are a new man created with His life. When the Lord Jesus was on earth, He spoke of the non-redemptive aspect of His death, which would give life to men and enable them to overcome the old creation to become the new creation. Salvation brings the forgiveness of sins. When a man is forgiven, he is like a criminal who is pardoned while on death row. This takes care of the negative need, and Christ has accomplished this for us. But there is the non-redemptive aspect of His death, in which He dispenses His life into us and through which we inherit a life we did not previously possess. The death of Christ delivers us from death on the negative side and dispenses life to us on the positive side. These two aspects are absolutely different.

The Lord Casting Fire on the Earth

Verses 49 and 50 of Luke 12 are two of the most precious verses in the Bible. They are also among the hardest verses to understand. If we were to nominate four or five of the most puzzling passages in the New Testament, these two verses would be among them. In verse 49 the Lord said, "I have come to cast fire on the earth." The Lord told His listeners that He came to the earth with a specific purpose—to cast fire on the earth. What is this fire? This is not a fire that is produced by ordinary matches, but a fire that is apart from the earth. For example, I may throw my hymnbook on the chair. This means that the hymnbook was not on the chair but was thrown onto it from elsewhere. The Lord said that He came to cast fire on the earth. Where did this fire come from? It came from heaven. What is this fire? The book of Hebrews tells us that our God is a consuming fire (12:29). In many instances in the Bible, fire signifies God's life. His life is righteous and holy, and it is like a fire.

The Lord Jesus said that His purpose for coming to the earth was to cast God's life on it and to give God's life to man. At the time He spoke such a word, man did not have His life. This is why He said, "How I wish that it were already kindled!" (Luke 12:49). This means that He wished that man would receive His life that very day. Yet man did not receive it, because "I have a baptism to be baptized with, and how I am pressed until it is accomplished!" (v. 50). The Lord told us that the fire was not kindled because He still had a baptism to be baptized with. This is puzzling. Was not

Christ already baptized? Luke 3 clearly records that He was baptized. What does baptism in this verse mean? In reading Romans 6 and Colossians 2, we see that this baptism signifies death. For Christ to say that a baptism was still waiting to be accomplished meant that He had not yet died. Luke 12:50 does not say that He had not been baptized; rather, it says that there was a baptism which still needed to be accomplished. Why did such a baptism need to be accomplished? To accomplish something means that there is a goal. Suppose you want to do a certain work. After you have done the work, you have accomplished it. Christ's death was for the purpose of accomplishing one thing—God's purpose. Since He had not yet died, the fire was not yet kindled.

These two verses tell us that Christ came to cast God's life to the earth and to give man His life. Before Christ died, man had not received that life. After He died, man received this life. Without His death, this life could not have been released, and man could not have received it. Why did Christ have to die before man could have His life? The reason is provided in the following words: "How I am pressed." The word *pressed* in the original language means "squeezed, constrained." Christ said that He had a baptism to be baptized with, and He was pressed, or constrained, until it was accomplished. Why was He constrained? He was the divine life itself, and He was like the fire. This life filled the universe and was not bound or restricted by time and space. His life was omnipresent and omnipotent. It was everywhere and existed at all times. This life was like a fire. It kept on spreading; no one could lock it up, and no place was big enough to contain it.

Although Christ was equal with God, He became a man and confined this great life to the flesh. Such a tremendous life was contained in the flesh, which was limited by time and space. When He was in Caesarea Philippi, He could not be in Capernaum; He could not be everywhere at the same time. This flesh might have appeared in Galilee one day and in Judea the next, but it could not be in both places at the same time. God's life was restricted by time and space. This is why He felt pressed. His outward flesh had locked up His omnipresent and omnipotent life like a prisoner; it was no longer free. How pressed the omnipresent life was! What could the Lord do but be pressed? He was pressed because He had not died. After He died and resurrected, He was no longer pressed. Hence, there is a different aspect to the death of Christ, one in which He shed His body and released God's life. This is the baptism He was about to go through. This aspect of the Lord's death freed Him from the outward prison and released the fire, through which man received His life. This is the non-redemptive aspect of His death. It is different from the blood and the crucifixion. In the Bible this aspect of His death is signified by His flesh (John 6:54). Because of the limitation of time, I can only give a brief foundational word to show you the aspect of Christ's death which involves the release of His life.

One Grain Falling to Produce Many Grains

John 12:24 touches the mystery of the gospel. This is the highest and most crucial passage in the Bible because it touches God's goal. The Lord compared His death to a grain of wheat. The Bible never uses wheat as a type of redemption, because wheat has no blood. The death of the grain of wheat refers to the non-redemptive aspect of Christ's death. Christ is the one grain of wheat. On the outside of the grain, there is a glossy shell, which locks the life of the grain inside.

In order for the life to be released, the grain must first be buried into the ground.

The Lord said, "Unless the grain of wheat falls into the ground and dies, it abides alone; but if it dies, it bears much fruit." The Lord's life is like a grain of wheat. The life of this grain is bound by its outward shell, and unless the outward shell is removed by the grain passing through death, the wheat will never grow. When the grain is buried in the ground, the moisture and humidity of the earth act on the shell and break it. In a few days the grain sprouts, and after a few months, hundreds of grains are produced.

The Lord said that He was like a grain of wheat. Life was in Him, but unless He died, He would forever be the only One, because God had only one Son; He was the only Begotten of God. He was the only One who had life. When He became flesh and came to the earth, His life was bound by the flesh even though He was God's Son and had God's life. Men could not receive His life, and He could not bring forth many grains. Suppose one hundred grains are harvested from one grain. How many grains would there be? There would be one hundred and one. Because the one grain has died, one hundred grains are produced. Originally, there was only one unique grain, who is God's only begotten Son. But after death and resurrection, He brought forth many grains. What happened to the original one grain? It became the first grain. Originally, it was the unique one; now it has become the first of one hundred and one grains. Originally, He was God's only begotten Son. Now through death and resurrection, He has become God's firstborn Son. Before the Lord Jesus died, He was God's only begotten Son. After resurrection, He became God's firstborn Son. *(The Collected Works of Watchman Nee,* Vol. 43, pp. 652–658)

CHAPTER 6

THE RESURRECTION OF CHRIST

OVERCOMING DEATH

Our Lord was resurrected. While the disciples were gathering together behind closed doors, the Lord came into their midst and appeared to them. He came in without opening the door (John 20:19, 26). He appeared to the two disciples who were on their way to Emmaus. When they recognized Him, He disappeared suddenly (Luke 24:31). This is the wonder of resurrection. He transcends over time and space. Within a second, He can travel from here to the end of the earth. He does not have to wait for three or five years to accomplish something. We do not have to pray for eight or ten years to receive something. Here is One who has transcended over time and space. This One is the resurrected Lord. The Lord was on earth for over thirty years. Humanly speaking, His wisdom and stature grew (2:52). But after His resurrection He manifested the full power of God. This power broke through the greatest barrier, death. His life transcended over time and space; His life broke through death. Therefore, our Lord is the eternal One. Man is limited by death, but our Lord is not limited by death. This is the resurrection of our Lord.

We all know that death is a great limitation. All living creatures come to their end at death. The greatest limitation to all living things, whether blades of grass or large trees, is death. A cat or a dog may follow us for three or five years; they may be very clever and useful. But they cannot live forever; their lives are limited. Once they die, they are through. The same is true with man. The foolish rich man might be very good at planning, but "God said to him, Foolish one, this night they are requiring your soul from you; and the things which you have prepared, whose will they be?" (Luke 12:20). Once death comes, everything is over. As long as a man is in his body, he can do many things and be very useful. But his usefulness stops at death. However, with our Lord, death no longer exists. Death has been shattered by our Lord. Death cannot hold Him. Holding is to limit, and resurrection has broken through the greatest limitation. No gate, city, or mountain can stop resurrection. No problem of yesterday, today, or tomorrow can stop Him. He is not only living, but He will not die. He not only will not die, but He has no possibility of death. He is the living one. He became dead, but He is alive, and He will live forever and ever (Rev. 1:18). In Him, all barriers have been broken.

Resurrection is the power of God. Ephesians 1:20–21 says, "Which He caused to operate in Christ in raising Him from the dead and seating Him at His right hand in the heavenlies, far above all. . .not only in this age but also in that which is to come." After the Lord resurrected, He sat on the right hand of God and was far above all things. Everything that can be named is under Him, not only in this age, but in that which is to come. In creation God did not gain the man He was after, but after the Lord's resurrection God gained such a man. God wanted to gain a created man who is the same as He is. If He cannot gain a created man who is the same as He is, He has not gained what He is after. Only the self-existing and ever-existing God is above all things. However, God wants man, who is neither self-existing nor ever-existing, to also transcend over all things. There must be one created man who is transcendent over all things before God's goal can be attained. When the Lord resurrected from the dead and was received to the right hand of the Father, He annulled all the limitations of death, as well as all other restrictions, and God gained the man that He was after. *(The Collected Works of Watchman Nee,* Vol. 19, pp. 590–591)

CHRIST IS THE RESURRECTION

Let us consider again what resurrection is. Whatever encounters death and still exists is resurrection. Resurrection is that which withstands death and endures death. After man ate the fruit of the tree of the knowledge of good and evil, death came in and man died. Those who enter the grave never come out again. Once they go in, they never return. In the whole universe, of all men, only one came out of death. This One is our Lord. The Lord said, "I am. . .the living One; and I became dead, and behold, I am living forever and ever" (Rev. 1:17–18). The Lord is the resurrected Lord. Resurrection is that which passes through death but is not imprisoned by death. In the Bible, the authority of death is described as a kind of imprisonment. To imprison someone is to confine him and not release him. Once man enters death, he cannot come out anymore. Death imprisons everyone who enters it. But death cannot imprison Him. This is the meaning of life, and this is the meaning of resurrection. Resurrection is the life that passes through death and rises above death. Our Lord Jesus is the life. He became dead and was in Hades. He was in the deepest place of death. But death could not imprison Him. Death was unable to detain or keep Him. He came out of death! When life passes through death and is not imprisoned by death, this is resurrection.

Resurrection means that a life bears the mark of death, yet still lives; it is living, yet it also bears the mark of death. This is what is meant by resurrection.

Many people ask why is it that after His resurrection in John 20, the Lord Jesus left the mark of the nails in His hands and the mark of the spear in His side for Thomas to touch (v. 27). We have to realize that this is what is meant by resurrection. The Lord Jesus was not showing Thomas one who had never been wounded and one who had never died; He wanted Thomas to see that He was wounded but now alive. He wanted Thomas to see that He had died but now lived. The Lord has the mark of death in His body, yet He is now living. This is what is meant by resurrection.

We can apply this principle to ourselves. There are many things in us that do not have the mark of death; they cannot be considered as resurrection. Resurrection must be something that has the mark of death and yet is still living. Do not think that as long as you have eloquence, cleverness, and talent, everything will be all right. It is possible for you to have eloquence without the mark of death. It is possible for you to have wisdom without the mark of death, and it is possible for you to have talent without the mark of death. Whether or not others see the mark of death in our eloquence, cleverness, and talent determines whether we have resurrection. A brother may be very competent, capable, and apparently lively. However, he is too self-confident and self-assured. He thinks that everything put in his hands will be handled well. There is no mark of death with this person; one does not see any mark of death in his competence. Although he is self-confident, self-trusting, self-assured, and very energetic, the mark of death cannot be found in him. This does not mean that a person who has passed through resurrection has no ability in himself. It merely means that with such a person, there is the mark of death. He can still do things, but he dares not trust in himself anymore, and he has lost all confidence. His own energy has been weakened. This is resurrection.

Paul wrote to the church in Corinth and said, "I was with you in weakness and in fear and in much trembling" (1 Cor. 2:3). This was spoken by a man who knew God. What a pity that among Christians, there are too many strong and self-confident ones! However, here is a man who said that he was "in weakness and in fear and in much trembling." His body bore the mark of death, the seal of death.

Therefore, resurrection can never be separated from the cross. The cross removes something from us. Many things that originate from the self will not rise again once they have passed through the cross; they are lost in death. Whatever remains after it has passed through death, and whatever has the mark of death and is still living is resurrection. Resurrection must be something that has passed through death and whatever has passed through death must have suffered deprivation and loss. Brothers and sisters, if you really see what resurrection is, you will see what the cross is. You will see the stripping power of the cross. If you really know what resurrection is, you will find many things removed from you as you pass through the cross. If you really know what resurrection is, you will become another person; many things will be stripped from you. Only those things that have life will resurrect. Without life there is no possibility of resurrection. Suppose we cut a piece of wood into small segments and bury them into the ground. After some time, they will decay and become worthless. However, if we cut down a branch from a tree and plant it in the ground, after some time, it will germinate. In one case the sticks become rotten. In the other case the branch germinates. Anything that is dead rots, and anything that has life resurrects after it passes through death. Hence, the Lord's resurrection was based upon His life. Because there is an incorruptible life in Him, death cannot imprison Him. Since there is something in Him which cannot die, death was cast away even while He was put into death. When we go through the cross experientially, many things will remain in death and not come out. Only the things which are of God will resurrect. When we touch the cross, we ourselves will be eliminated. The cross is a big minus; it subtracts many things.

Many brothers and sisters often ask, "How do I know whether I am dead or not? How do I know that the Lord has done something within me through the cross?" It is quite easy to answer this question. If the Lord has done something within, you should have lost many things. But if you have been the same since the day you were saved, and if you are still as full as you were before, the cross has not done anything within you. If the cross has truly done something within, you will find that a great elimination work has been done; you will find that the Lord has done a thorough cleanup job in you. The result of this elimination is that you can no longer do what you could do before, and you are no longer capable of the things you were once capable of. You are no longer sure of what you had such assurance of before.

Where you were bold before, now you become fearful. This proves that the Lord has done something within you. If resurrection is within you, many things have been left behind in the grave, because these things could not pass the test of death. Nothing in Adam can live once it passes through death. Anything that belongs to resurrection belongs to the Lord's life, the life which has passed through death and which has come out of death. Some things are lost through death, but are given back to us by the Lord. This is like the cutting of a branch from a tree. The branch seems to be dead. But when it is planted in the ground, after a period of time, it grows up again. This is resurrection. When we speak of having the mark of death on our body, it does not mean that we cannot speak or move anymore. Instead, it means that when we speak and move, we will not be as loose and self-confident as before. If a man has been touched by the Lord and dealt with by the cross, he will be weak, fearful, and trembling. He will not say, "I will do it," "I can do it," or "I can make it." From that time on, he will still work, but he will be very fearful of God when he works. He will still walk, but his walk will be a walk after God just as Abraham walked step by step with God. You will see the mark of the cross on such a man. Such a man will have been penetrated and pierced by God. He will not be as whole as he was before. There will be the mark of death on his body. This is resurrection. *(The Collected Works of Watchman Nee,* Vol. 36, pp. 77–80)

MAKING CHRIST THE FIRSTBORN SON OF GOD

"Whom he foreknew, he also foreordained to be conformed to the image of his Son, that he might be the firstborn among many brethren; and whom he foreordained, them he also called: and whom he called, them he also justified: and whom he justified, them he also glorified" (Rom. 8:29–30). What was God's objective? It was that His Son Jesus Christ might be the firstborn among many brethren, all of whom should be conformed to His image. How did God realize that objective? "Whom he justified, them he also glorified." Thus God's purpose in creation and redemption was to make Christ the firstborn Son among many glorified sons. That may perhaps at first convey very little to many of us, but let us look into it more carefully.

In John 1:14 we are told that the Lord Jesus was God's only begotten Son: "The Word became flesh, and dwelt among us (and we beheld his glory, glory as of the only begotten from the Father)." That He was God's only begotten Son signifies that God had no other Son but this one. He was with the Father from all eternity. But, we are told, God was not satisfied that Christ should remain the only begotten Son; He wanted also to make Him His first begotten. How could an only begotten Son become a first begotten? The answer is simple: by the Father having more children. If you have but one son, then he is the only begotten, but if thereafter you have other children, then the only begotten becomes the first begotten.

The divine purpose in creation and redemption was that God should have many children. He wanted *us,* and could not be satisfied without us. Some time ago I called to see Mr. George Cutting, the writer of the well-known tract *Safety, Certainty and Enjoyment.* When I was ushered into the presence of this old saint of ninety-three years, he took my hand in his and in a quiet, deliberate way he said: "Brother, do you know, I cannot do without Him? And do you know, He cannot do without me?" Though I was with him for over an hour, his great age and physical frailty made any sustained conversation impossible. But what remains in my memory of that interview was his frequent repetition of these two questions: "Brother, do you know, I cannot do without Him? And do you know, *He cannot do without me?*"

In reading the story of the prodigal son, most people are impressed with all the troubles the prodigal meets; they are occupied in thinking what a bad time he is having. But that is not the point of the parable. "My son. . .was lost, and is found"—there is the heart of the story. It is not a question of what the son suffers, but of what the Father loses. *He* is the sufferer; *He* is the loser. A sheep is lost: whose is the loss? The shepherd's. A coin is lost: whose is the loss? The woman's. A son is lost: whose is the loss? The Father's. That is the lesson of Luke 15.

The Lord Jesus was the only begotten Son, and as the only begotten He has no brothers. But the Father sent the Son in order that the only begotten might also be the first begotten, and the beloved Son have many brethren. There you have the whole story of the Incarnation and the Cross; and there you have, at the last, the purpose of God fulfilled in His "bringing many sons unto glory" (Heb. 2:10).

In Romans 8:29 we read of "many brethren"; in Hebrews 2:10 of "many sons." From the point of view of the Lord Jesus they are "brethren"; from the point of view of God the Father they are "sons." Both words in this context convey the idea of maturity. God is seeking full-grown sons; but He does not stop even there. For He does not want His sons to live in a barn or a garage or a field; He wants them in His home; He wants them to share His glory. That is the explanation of Romans 8:30: "Whom he justified, them he also glorified."

139

Sonship—the full expression of His Son—is God's goal in the many sons. How could He bring that about? By justifying them, and then by glorifying them. In His dealings with them God will never stop short of that goal. He set Himself to have sons, and to have those sons, mature and responsible, with Him in glory. He made provision for the whole of heaven to be peopled with glorified sons. That was His purpose in the redemption of mankind.

The Grain of Wheat

But how could God's only begotten Son become His first begotten? The method is explained in John 12:24: "Verily, verily, I say unto you, Except a grain of wheat fall into the earth and die, it abideth by itself alone; but if it die, it beareth much fruit." Who was that grain? It was the Lord Jesus. In the whole universe God put His one grain of wheat into the ground and it died, and in resurrection the only begotten grain became the first begotten grain, and from the one grain there have sprung many grains.

In respect of His divinity the Lord Jesus remains uniquely "the only begotten Son of God." Yet there is a sense in which, from the resurrection onward through all eternity, He is also the first begotten, and His life from that time is found in many brethren. For we who are born of the Spirit are made thereby "partakers of the divine nature" (2 Pet. 1:4), though not, mark you, as of ourselves but only, as we shall see in a moment, in dependence upon God and by virtue of our being "in Christ." We have "received the spirit of adoption, whereby we cry, Abba, Father. The Spirit himself beareth witness with our spirit, that we are children of God" (Rom.

8:15–16). It was by way of the Incarnation and the Cross that the Lord Jesus made this possible. Therein was the Father-heart of God satisfied, for in the Son's obedience unto death the Father has secured His many sons.

The first and the twentieth chapters of John are in this respect most precious. In the beginning of his Gospel John tells us that Jesus was "the only begotten from the Father." At the end of his Gospel he tells us how, after He had died and risen again, Jesus said to Mary Magdalene, "Go unto my brethren, and say to them, I ascend unto my Father and your Father, and my God and your God" (John 20:17). Hitherto in this Gospel the Lord had spoken often of "the Father" or of "my Father." Now, in resurrection, He adds, ". . .and your Father." It is the eldest Son, the first begotten speaking. By His death and resurrection many brethren have been brought into God's family, and so, in the same verse He uses this very name for them, calling them "my brethren." By doing this He affirms that He "is not ashamed to call them brethren" (Heb. 2:11). *(The Collected Works of Watchman Nee,* Vol. 33, pp. 74–77)

MAKING CHRIST THE LIFE-GIVING SPIRIT

In the Gospel of John, the Lord Jesus reveals that He is now in the Holy Spirit and that He is ready for us to receive Him. Paul knew of Christ according to the flesh, but in 2 Corinthians 5:16, he said that "now we know Him so no longer." Christ was God putting on the flesh. He was the Word incarnated on the earth to become a man. The flesh was like a garment to the Lord. In His incarnation, He put on the flesh. After His death and resurrection, He put on the Holy Spirit. He put on the flesh; then He put on the Holy Spirit. Before His death the

Holy Spirit was in Him; after His resurrection, He was in the Holy Spirit. When He was on the earth, the Holy Spirit was present with the disciples through Christ; after His resurrection, Christ was present with the believers through the Holy Spirit. First, the Holy Spirit came through Christ. Now Christ has come through the Holy Spirit. First, Christ was in the flesh. Now Christ is in the Holy Spirit. Paul knew of Christ according to the flesh. This means that he only knew of the Christ who had put on the flesh. But in 2 Corinthians, he no longer knew of Him in this way. This means that he knew the Christ who had put on the Holy Spirit.

There is a big difference between putting on the flesh and putting on the Holy Spirit. When Christ was living in the flesh, He was always limited by time and space. When He was in Galilee, He could not be in Bethsaida. If He was in one place, He could not be in another place at the same time. By putting on the flesh, Christ became a Savior outwardly. If He was by the sea, He could not be in an inland region. The disciples were at times close to Him and at times far away from Him; they could not be with Him all the time. If Christ were in Judea and we were in Singapore, we could not follow Him every day. When He became Christ in the flesh, He became a Savior outwardly. If He had remained this way, what could we do? We could go to worship Him in Jerusalem three times a year. We could draw near to Him in this way, but once we left Jerusalem, we would be far away from Him again. When we were in the right place, we could be with Him, but when we were not in the right place, we could not be with Him. This is the Christ in the flesh.

But Christ is no longer in the flesh. Through His death He put off the flesh, and in resurrection He took on a spiritual body. After His resurrection, He put on another garment; He put on the Holy Spirit, and He is now in the Holy Spirit. His birth in Bethlehem was His first coming. During the first coming He put on the flesh. After His death and resurrection, He put on the Holy Spirit, and He is now living within us. The Holy Spirit is Christ. At one time the Holy Spirit lived in the earthly Christ; now the resurrected Christ lives in the Holy Spirit. The Spirit is not physical; He is omnipresent. Since Christ is in the Spirit, He can live in us. Since Christ resurrected for us, we can receive Him through faith and regeneration.

Brothers and sisters, have you seen this? The tree of life has now produced fruit. Originally, it was a tree; there was life, but no one could eat it. No one can take in the life of a tree. But once a tree bears fruit, the life of the tree gets into the fruit, and when one eats the fruit, he takes in the life of the tree. When the Lord was a man, we could not receive Him into our spirit. But now that He is in the Holy Spirit, we can receive Him into us as our life. Thank the Lord that Christ is no longer an outward, objective Savior; He is our life within. The descending of the Holy Spirit is crucial. Without the descending of the Holy Spirit, Christ could not be in the Spirit, and man could never be one with Him. Thank the Lord that today we are in Christ and that we are one spirit with Him. God's salvation is complete. He caused Christ to die and resurrect. Now Christ can live within us. This completes what He did not complete in Adam.

This is the meaning of "another Comforter" (John 14:16). What does the word *another* mean? It means that there is a second one. It implies that there is a first and a second. The Lord was the first Comforter, and the Holy Spirit is another Comforter. Christ has become our Comforter in the Holy Spirit.

We no longer have to be orphans (vv. 17–18). He has given us the strength for our journey and has made us sons of God. Today every believer can be in Christ and receive God's life into him. Not only have we been forgiven and not only has the old man been crucified, but God's life is now living within us. In the Bible this life is represented by the flesh. *(The Collected Works of Watchman Nee,* Vol. 43, pp. 661–663)

REGENERATING THE BELIEVERS

First Peter 1:3 mentions a very wonderful thing. It says that we have been regenerated through the resurrection of Jesus Christ from the dead. Many people in the church today talk about regeneration, but they do not understand how regeneration occurs. Many say that we have been regenerated through the cross. But Peter said that we have been regenerated through the resurrection of Jesus Christ from the dead. We have been regenerated through Christ's resurrection. In other words, if Christ had not resurrected, we would not have been regenerated. When Christ died and resurrected, we died and resurrected with Him as well (Eph. 2:6), and we received His life into us. Regeneration brings us the life of Christ. This life was imparted to us at the time of Christ's resurrection. He first had to die before He could resurrect. If He had not died, He could not have resurrected and would not have been able to impart His life to us. Thank the Lord that He has died and lived again. Therefore, He can dispense His life to us.

We need to consider Christ's death and resurrection before we can understand the overcoming life that we have received in Christ. When the Lord was on earth, He spoke of the parable of the wheat. This is recorded in John 12:24. The Lord said that if a grain of wheat does not fall into the ground and die, it abides alone. But if it dies, it bears many grains. Verse 33 shows clearly that the death of the grain of wheat, as mentioned by the Lord, refers to His death. A grain of wheat is different from a grain of sand. A grain of wheat has life, whereas sand does not have life. But if the grain of wheat does not fall into the ground and die, it will remain as grain even after millions of years. The Lord Jesus as the grain of wheat fell into Bethlehem and died at Golgotha. Then He resurrected, and in resurrection He regenerated us, giving us the same life as His. If Christ had not left heaven to come to earth, there would only be one person, Himself, today. The Bible says that Christ is God's only begotten Son (1:18). This means that He is the unique Son. God loves His only begotten Son, but He wants to have many sons (Heb. 2:10). He desires to see His only begotten Son become the firstborn Son so that He can have many sons.

In the Gospel of John, Christ is God's only begotten Son. But in Romans 8 and Hebrews 2, He has become God's firstborn Son. We cannot call a person a firstborn son and an only begotten son at the same time. Being a firstborn son means that there are other sons to follow, but being the only begotten son means that there are no more sons. Yet God wants His only begotten Son to become the firstborn Son. How can Christ as the only begotten Son of God become God's firstborn Son? If the only begotten Son remained in heaven all the time, there would forever be an only begotten Son. In order for Him to become the firstborn Son, there is a need for Him to "fall" from heaven to the earth. One day Christ "fell" from heaven to Bethlehem and later died. There are two aspects to His death: the first is the redemptive aspect, which is for the purpose of taking away our sins. The second is the non-redemptive aspect, which is for the purpose of releasing His life.

God's Life Being Released through Death

Let us read Luke 12:49. This is the deepest verse in the Gospel of Luke. The Lord said, "I have come." He does not mention anything about redemption. He merely came "to cast fire on the earth, and how I wish that it were already kindled!" This verse speaks of a fire being cast on the earth. This means that the fire is not from the earth, but from heaven and from God. Fire signifies the life in the Spirit. The Lord came to cast fire on the earth, that is, to release God's life to the earth. Following this the Lord said, "But I have a baptism to be baptized with, and how I am pressed until it is accomplished!" (v. 50). The word "pressed" in Greek means "bound" and "confined." The Lord was saying that He came to release the life of God. Yet He was still in the flesh and could not release such a life. He felt bound and confined. Because of His flesh, God's life could not be released; His life was limited by the flesh. This is why He felt bound and confined.

The Lord spoke of a baptism which He had to be baptized with, which was not yet fulfilled. Since He had already been baptized in chapter three, why did He say that He had another baptism to be baptized with? We must note that the Lord did not say that He had not been baptized. He was saying that there was a baptism that had not yet been accomplished. "Baptism" in this verse clearly refers to His death on the cross (Mark 10:38). The death of Christ was His great release. If Christ had not died, the divine life within Him would have been imprisoned and bound. But once He died, the divine life was released and ready to be received by man. This is what He wished to see.

The phrase *in Jesus* is not in the Bible. The Bible only says "in Christ." We cannot be in Jesus, because Jesus was a man. He was God's only begotten Son, and we have no part in Him. No one can be in Jesus of Nazareth. But one day this man who was in the flesh, this individual man, was crucified on the cross. Although His flesh died, this death released His life. When He resurrected from the dead, He became Christ Jesus; He became the One whom we can get into. When we are in Christ, we receive His life; we die and are raised up together with Him. This is what Christ's resurrection has accomplished.

Let us now turn back to John 12:24. The grain of wheat in this verse refers to Christ, the only Begotten of God. When Christ died, the grain of wheat died. The shell of the grain was broken, and the life of the grain was released. After some time, the one grain became many grains. All the grains come from the one grain. Originally, there was only one grain. Now it has become many grains. The one grain becomes many grains by falling to the ground to die. Christ, the one Man, died; His body was broken, and His life was released. In resurrection, the one grain becomes us; we become the many grains. Our life has its origin in Christ, the one grain. Our life is derived from Christ. In this way, we know what it means for Christ to be the Head and for us to be His members. Although this life is in us today, this life comes from Christ. This is the process through which Christ regenerated us.

Having the Same Life

The Lord was first the only begotten Son. After His death and resurrection, He brought forth many grains and became God's firstborn Son. As the many grains, we have now become God's many sons. On the day of resurrection the Lord said to Mary, "I ascend to My Father and your Father" (John 20:17). The Lord could not have said this three days before. But on the day of resurrection, He could say this. Before His death, He did not have such a relationship with us, but through His death and resurrection, He released His life to us. We have all received the same life and become the sons of God. Before our regeneration, we were different in Adam in many ways. Now, in Christ, we become the same. We have the same life and share the same nature. *(The Collected Works of Watchman Nee,* Vol. 42, pp. 368–371)

CHAPTER 7

THE DIVINE LIFE

THE ETERNAL LIFE

What is the meaning of eternal life? It simply means a life of eternity. Man's life is transient; it will not survive in eternity. Only the life of the Son of God can exist there. If I put my own life in eternity, it would shrivel up immediately. It would not last! It would perish as a fish in air or a bird in water. Man's life can only carry him through a temporary existence on this earth. It will not make it through eternity. Only an eternal life can survive in eternity.

First John 5:11–12 says, "And this is the testimony, that God gave to us eternal life and this life is in His Son. He who has the Son has the life; he who does not have the Son of God does not have the life." Here we are told that this life of eternity is in the Son. It is found in no other place. Whoever does not have this life in the Son is merely a human; he can only exist on earth, but not survive in eternity. He does not have that life which qualifies him for eternity.

After the Son of God passed through death and resurrection and became the Holy Spirit, He is no longer limited by time and space. We can now receive Him anytime and anywhere. Hitherto, whoever received the Son of God received God. In the same way, whoever receives the Holy Spirit receives the Son. First Corinthians 15:45b says, "The last Adam became a life-giving Spirit." This enables all those who have received Christ to obtain a new life. Not only are their sins forgiven, but they inherit an eternal life from God as well. *(The Normal Christian Faith,* p. 141)

God's life is most often called "eternal life" in the Bible. This word "life" is *zoe* in the original language, which means higher life or spiritual life. Everyone who believes in the Lord Jesus is regenerated and receives eternal life as soon as he believes. What is the function of the eternal life? "And this is eternal life, that they may know You, the only true God, and Him whom You have sent, Jesus Christ" (John 17:3). Therefore, eternal life is not only a later blessing for believers' enjoyment but also a spiritual ability. Without eternal life we do not know God, neither can we know the Lord Jesus. Knowing the Lord by intuition comes after man receives God's life. This tiny bit of God's life within man can eventually develop and grow into a spiritual man. *(The Spiritual Man,* Vol. 2, p. 222)

THE OVERCOMING LIFE

The Life That God Has Ordained for a Christian

The Bible shows us that God has ordained for every Christian a life that is filled with joy. This life is completely at peace, has no barriers in its fellowship with God, and is not contrary to His will in any way. The life that God has prepared for a

Christian is one that does not thirst after the world. It walks apart from sin and is victorious over sin. It is holy, powerful, and victorious. It knows the will of God and fellowships with God without interruption. This is the life that God has ordained in the Scripture for a Christian.

God has ordained a life that is hidden with Christ in God. What can touch this life? What can affect or shake this life? Just as Christ is unshakable, we also are unshakable. Just as He is transcendent over all things, we also are transcendent over all things. Our standing before God is the same as Christ's standing before God. We should never consider that we are destined for weakness and failure. There is no room for such a thought for a Christian in the Bible. Colossians 3:4 says, "Christ our life." Christ is far above everything. Nothing can touch Him. Hallelujah! This is the life of Christ!

A Life That Is Free from All Sins

Matthew 1:21 says, "And she will bear a son, and you shall call His name Jesus, for it is He who will save His people from their sins." When I was in Chefoo and Peking recently, a few brothers remarked that in the past they loved calling the Lord the Christ, but that now they like calling Him "Jesus, my Savior!" He is called Jesus because He "save[s] His people from their sins." We have received Jesus as our Savior. We have obtained the grace of forgiveness. Thank and praise the Lord that Jesus is now our Savior and our sins are forgiven. But what has Jesus done for us? "He. . .will save His people from their sins." This is God's ordination. This is Jesus' accomplishment. The question now is whether we are still living in sin or whether we are delivered from it. Does our old temper come back to plague us? Are we still bound by our sins and entangled by our thoughts? Are we still as proud as before? Are we still as selfish as before? Or have we been delivered from our sins? I have mentioned one illustration many times, and I will mention it again: There is a difference between a life-saving ring and a life raft. When a man falls into the water and is thrown a life-saving ring, he will not drown if he holds onto the ring, but neither will he be delivered out of the water. He will not sink, but neither will he be lifted out. He is neither dying, nor is he living. It is different with a life raft. In the case of a life raft, the drowning person is lifted out of the water into the raft. Our Lord's salvation is not the salvation of a life-saving ring but the salvation of a life raft. He will not stop halfway between dying and living. He will save His people from their sins. He does not leave us in sins. Therefore, biblical salvation saves us from sin. However, even though we have believed, we are not yet saved from sin; we still live in sin. Is the Bible wrong? No, there is nothing wrong with the Bible; it is our experience that is wrong.

What else did Jesus do when He came to us? What does the Bible say about His work? Let us go on.

A Life That Is in Intimate Fellowship with God
Luke 1:69 says, "And raised a horn of salvation for us in the house of David His servant." Verses 74 and 75 say, "We, having been delivered out of the hand of our enemies, might serve Him without fear, in holiness and righteousness before Him all our days." God has raised up a horn of salvation for us in the house of David. We have this horn of salvation already. What has this horn of salvation done for us, and to what degree has it delivered us? He has delivered us out of the hand of our enemies. What kind of life does He want us

to live after we are delivered? After we are delivered out of the hand of our enemies, is He only interested in our serving Him in holiness and righteousness? Is that all He wants? If this is true, we will only serve Him in righteousness and holiness sometimes. But thank and praise the Lord, His Word says that we should serve Him in holiness and righteousness *all our days.* We should serve Him in holiness and righteousness for as long as we live on earth. This is the kind of life that God has ordained for us. We should serve Him in holiness and righteousness all our days. Of course, to our shame, we must admit that we have not served Him in holiness and righteousness all our days, even though God has delivered us from the hand of our enemies. Either the word of the Bible is wrong or our experience is wrong. The only way our experience can be right is for the Bible to be wrong. In the past, I always wondered what kind of life the Bible expects from a Christian. According to the Bible, everyone who is saved by the Lord should serve Him in holiness and righteousness all his days. If the Bible is wrong, our experience can be justified. But if the Bible is not wrong, our experience must be wrong.

A Life That Is Fully Satisfied in the Lord

John 4:14 says, "But whoever drinks of the water that I will give him shall by no means thirst forever; but the water that I will give him will become in him a spring of water gushing up into eternal life." How precious is this word! It does not speak of a special kind of Christian. It does not say that only those who have received special grace from the Lord can have a spring of water gushing up into eternal life. The Lord said this to a Samaritan woman whom He previously had never met. He said that if she believed, she would receive living water. This living water would be in her a spring that gushes up into eternal life. Brothers and sisters, what is the meaning of being thirsty? When one is thirsty, it means that he is not satisfied. Those who drink of the water that the Lord gives will never thirst again. Thank and praise the Lord! A Christian is not only a contented person but a person who is forever satisfied! It is not enough for a Christian to merely be contented. Everything that God gives to us makes us eternally satisfied. But how many times have we crossed the main streets without feeling thirsty? When we pass by the great department stores, are we thirsty? If we crave for this or that, is this not being thirsty? Are we thirsty when we consider our classmates or colleagues and envy their possessions? Yet the Lord said, "Whoever drinks of the water that I will give him shall by no means thirst forever; but the water that I will give him will become in him a spring of water gushing up into eternal life." What He gives to us is one kind of life, yet we experience something else. The Lord says that He is all we need, but we say that He is not enough. We need this and that before we can be satisfied, but He said that He alone is enough. Is what we received from the Lord wrong or is our experience wrong? One of the two must be wrong. The Lord cannot possibly write us a bad check. Whatever He promises, He will surely give. Our experience in the past was, in the words of one hymn, "a half salvation" (*Hymns,* #513, stanza 2). Why does the Lord say that a believer will not be thirsty again? This is because he has become different inside. Within him, there are new demands and new satisfactions. Brothers and sisters, are we living before God and serving Him in holiness and righteousness all our days? Are we living before God every day in holiness and righteousness, as the priest Zachariah spoke of in Luke 1:75? Do we have something within that gushes forth all the time to quench others' thirst? The Chinese have an expression, *wu-wei,* which means "to do nothing." Christians have to be those who are asking for nothing. We can say that the Lord is enough for us. Are we satisfied with just the Lord? Are we really satisfied with the Lord Jesus alone? If we are not satisfied, it means that there is something wrong with our living.

A Life That Affects Others

John 7:37 and 38 say, "Now on the last day, the great day of the feast, Jesus stood and cried out, saying, If anyone thirsts, let him come to Me and drink. He who believes into Me, as the Scripture said, out of his innermost being shall flow rivers of living water." Rivers of living water will flow out of whose innermost being? They will not flow out of only special Christians or the apostles Paul, Peter, or John, but out of all those who believe, out of ordinary men like us. It is out of the innermost being of men like us that rivers of living water will flow. When men touch us, they should be satisfied and cease from their thirst. I had a friend whose simple contact with others made them feel the banality of the world, the foolishness of ambition, and the tastelessness of greed. Someone might feel dissatisfied about something. But as soon as he contacted her, he would find that the Lord is enough to satisfy. On the other hand, one might feel satisfied about something, but as soon as he contacted her, he would find these things to be worthless. The Lord said those who believe Him will have rivers of living water flowing out of their innermost being. This should be the common experience of all ordinary Christians. What I am talking about is not the experience of special Christians but the experience of all common

Christians. Brothers and sisters, do others stop thirsting when they touch us? Or do they continue in their thirst? If others complain about their sufferings and we also complain, if others feel sorrowful and we also feel sorrowful, and if others confess their failures and we also confess our failures, we are not rivers of living water but dry deserts. Even the grass of others will be dried up by us. When this happens, either God is wrong or we are wrong. God cannot be wrong, so it must be we who are wrong.

A Life That Is Free from the Power of Sin

Let us see what happens in Acts. Verse 26 of chapter three says, "God, having raised up His Servant, has sent Him to bless you in turning each of you away from your wicked deeds." Peter's message at the portico of the temple still speaks of our condition today. The Lord Jesus' accomplishment is more than able to deliver us from sin. One basic experience of a Christian should be deliverance from sin. As Christians, we should at least overcome the known sins. We may not overcome the sins that we do not know about. But we should overcome by the Lord all the sins that we know about. We may have many besetting sins that have plagued us for years. By the power of the Lord, we should overcome all these sins. This is the biblical standard. A man should only be occasionally overtaken by offenses. But our experience is that we only occasionally overcome. How abnormal is our experience!

Romans 6:1–2 says, "What then shall we say? Should we continue in sin that grace may abound? Absolutely not! We who have died to sin, how shall we still live in it?" Every person who has believed in the Lord Jesus and has become a

Christian is dead to sin. No one who has believed in the Lord Jesus and has become a Christian should live in sin any longer. But how do we know that we are dead to sin? The next verse provides the answer.

Verse 3 says, "Or are you ignorant that all of us who have been baptized into Christ Jesus have been baptized into His death?" In other words, everyone who is baptized and saved is dead to sin. When a person is baptized, he becomes dead in Christ Jesus.

Verse 4 says, "We have been buried therefore with Him through baptism into His death, in order that just as Christ was raised from the dead through the glory of the Father, so also we might walk in newness of life." This should be the daily life of every Christian. Everyone who is baptized should walk in newness of life. This is not a verse for some special Christians; it is for Christians who are saved and baptized. We all have been baptized; therefore, we all should walk in newness of life. This is the experience that God has ordained for every Christian. Are we those who walk in newness of life?

Romans 6:14 says, "For sin will not lord it over you, for you are not under the law but under grace." I treasure this verse very much! Brothers and sisters, who is not under the law but under grace? Is Andrew Murray the only one? Are Paul, Peter, or John the only ones? Or are all those who have believed not under the law but under grace? How many of you sitting here today are under grace? Thank and praise our God, we are all under grace! None of us is under the law.

However, there is another sentence prior to this sentence: "Sin will not lord it over you." Thank and praise the Lord, sin will not lord it over us! Thank and praise Him that victory is not only the experience of some special Christians. Thank and praise God that victory is the experience of ordinary

Christians. Thank and praise Him that every saved Christian is under grace. When I was first saved, I saw this verse and treasured it very much. I realized that I had experienced many victories and had overcome many sins. I realized that God had graced me. But there was still one sin which lorded it over me. In fact, a few sins always came back to visit me. I had overcome several sins, but a few other sins often came back to visit me. This was like my experience with a brother one day. I met him on the street and nodded to him. Then I went into a shop to buy something. When I came out, I met him coming my way, and I nodded to him again. Then I went into a second store and bought something else. When I came out, I met him yet again and nodded to him once more. When I turned to the next street, I met him and nodded to him again. I turned on to a second street and met him once again and nodded to him yet another time. In all I met and nodded to him five times that day. We encounter sins the same way that I encountered this brother. It seems that sin purposely tries to meet us. We are always running into it; it seems that it is constantly following us. Temper seems to follow some all the time. Pride and jealousy seem to follow others all the time. Laziness seems to follow one, and lies seem to follow another. One finds himself always having an unforgiving spirit while another is plagued continually by base desires or selfishness. Some find unclean thoughts following them all the time, while others find unclean lusts following them all the time. Everyone seems to have at least one sin which follows him all the time. I had a few sins which continually plagued me. I had to admit that sin lorded it over me! God says that sin will not lord it over me, but I had to confess that something was wrong with me. I had to admit that the mistake was in me and not in God's Word. Brothers and sisters, if we are living a defeated life, we should know that this is not what God ordained for us. We have to know that it is not God's intention for sin to lord it over us. His Word says that sin will not lord it over us!

Romans 8:1 says, "There is now then no condemnation to those who are in Christ Jesus." I have expounded on the word *condemnation* many times. About twenty years ago someone discovered some ancient manuscripts and found that there were two meanings to this word. One is used in a civil context and the other in a legal context. According to its civil application, it can be translated "impotence." Hence, this verse can be translated, "There is now then no impotence to those who are in Christ Jesus." Brothers and sisters, how wonderful this is! But for whom is this verse written? Is it only for John Wesley? Is it only for Martin Luther or for Hudson Taylor? What does the Bible say? It says, "There is now then no impotence to those who are in Christ Jesus." Who are these ones? They are Christians. Every Christian is a person who is in Christ Jesus, and every one of them is no longer impotent.

Verse 2 says, "For the law of the Spirit of life has freed me in Christ Jesus from the law of sin and of death." I will repeat a hundred times that it is not special Christians only who are delivered from the law of sin and of death. Every Christian should be delivered from the law of sin and of death. What is the meaning of being impotent? According to Romans 7, it means doing what one hates and not practicing what one wills. It is finding that "to will is present with me, but to work out the good is not." The meaning of impotence is being unable to do anything. The history of many Christians is one of constant resolutions and constant breaking of resolutions. They continually resolve to do something and continually fail. But thank and praise the Lord, God's Word says that no Christian is impotent any longer.

What is a law? It is something that happens again and again. With a law, the same action produces the same result under whatever circumstances the action is performed. A law is a steady phenomenon; it is a constant tendency, a condition that continues to come back. For example, there is the force of gravity. Whenever an object is dropped, gravity will draw it downward. This gravitational force is a law. With some people, losing their temper is a law. They may hold back once or twice, but they are provoked the third time. By the fourth time, they lose their temper. This happens to one brother after another. One may hold back at the beginning, but eventually his temper breaks out. Every time a temptation comes, the same result occurs. We observe that the same is true with the matter of pride. When others say one good word about you, you may not be moved. But when they say a second good word about you, your expression immediately changes and your face shines. A law is anything that gives the same result when it goes through the same steps. Sin has become a law for us. Many brothers are agreeable in some things, but they are provoked as soon as they are stirred up in other things. They can overcome many things, but as soon as they encounter certain other things, they are provoked.

Brothers and sisters, it does not take special Christians to overcome the law of sin. No Christian has to remain impotent. Every Christian can be delivered from the law of sin. All of the above verses are facts; they are not commands. Every Christian should have these experiences. Yet our experience does not quite match God's Word. How sad this is!

A Life That Overcomes All Environments
Romans 8:35 says, "Who shall separate us from the love of

Christ? Shall tribulation or anguish or persecution or famine or nakedness or peril or sword?" Verse 37 says, "But in all these things we more than conquer through Him who loved us." Oh, our Lord who loves us has more than conquered all these things! This should be the Christian experience. But in our case, we do not need tribulation or swords to come upon us; as soon as someone gives us a bad look, we lose the love of Christ. However, Paul said that he more than conquered in all these things. This should be the common experience of all Christians. Victory is the normal experience of a Christian; defeat should be the abnormal experience. According to God's ordination, every Christian should more than conquer. Whether we encounter tribulation, anguish, persecution, famine, nakedness, peril, or sword, we should not only conquer it but more than conquer it! It does not matter whether there are difficulties. Outsiders may think that we Christians have gone mad. Hallelujah, others can say that we are mad. We are not concerned about these things any longer, and we have more than conquered them because of the love of Christ. Thank and praise the Lord, this should be the experience of a Christian; it is the experience that God has ordained for us. But what is our actual experience? The Bible has not kept these experiences from us, but we often do not find the way to enter such a life. Before tribulation even comes in abundance, we are already shouting, "I need patience! I am suffering!" If we find the way to this life, we will more than conquer in all these things.

Second Corinthians 2:14 says, "But thanks be to God, who always leads us in triumph in the Christ and manifests the savor of the knowledge of Him through us in every place." Brothers and sisters, a Christian life is not one that overcomes sometimes and is defeated at other times. It is not one that overcomes in the morning and is defeated in the afternoon. A Christian life is one that overcomes all the time. If you encounter a temptation today and you overcome it, you should not be so happy about it that you can hardly sleep at night. Only the experience of not overcoming should be uncommon. Overcoming should be common and frequent.

A Life with the Ability to Do Good

Ephesians 2:10 says, "For we are His masterpiece, created in Christ Jesus for good works, which God prepared beforehand in order that we would walk in them." Brothers and sisters, remember that Ephesians 2:10 comes after verses 8 and 9. In the preceding verses, it says that we are saved by grace. Here it says that we are His masterpiece, created for good works which God has prepared beforehand for us to walk in. This is not a special experience for some Christians; rather, it should be the common experience of every saved Christian. God saves us in order that we may do good. Brothers and sisters, are our good works according to God's ordination, or are we always complaining while we are doing good? Suppose you are mopping the floor. While you are mopping, you may complain that only one or two people are helping and that others are not helping. This will either result in boasting or murmuring. This is not doing good. Every good work of a Christian should be accompanied by an overflow of joy; we should not be stingy, boastful, or selfish, but generous and ready to give to others. It would be a pity if only the best Christians could do good. God's ordination is that doing good should be the common experience of every Christian.

A Life Filled with Light

John 8:12 says, "Again therefore Jesus spoke to them, saying, I am the light of the world; he who follows Me shall by no means walk in darkness, but shall have the light of life." This is the life that God has ordained for a Christian. Those who can stay away from darkness and who can walk in the light of life are not special Christians. Every Christian who follows Christ should not walk in darkness and should have the light of life. A Christian who is full of light is nothing more than a normal Christian, while a Christian who does not have the light is an abnormal Christian.

A Life That Is Wholly Sanctified

First Thessalonians 5:23 says, "And the God of peace Himself sanctify you wholly, and may your spirit and soul and body be preserved complete, without blame, at the coming of our Lord Jesus Christ." This is the apostle Paul's prayer for the Thessalonian believers. Since he said "sanctify you wholly," there must be the possibility of being sanctified wholly. It is possible to find no fault in a Christian. God will sanctify us wholly, and He will preserve us complete and without blame.

We are speaking of the Lord's provision for a Christian. The Lord's salvation has given every Christian the power to fully overcome sin, to be fully delivered from the bondage of sin, to trample sin underfoot, and to have unhindered fellowship with God. This is the life that the Lord has ordained for us. This is not merely a theory but a fact, because this is the Lord's provision. *(The Overcoming Life,* pp. 1, 17–28)

The Overcoming Life Being Christ Himself

God's provision for us in the gospel is for Christ to become our life. What does it mean to say that our life is Christ? Galatians 2:20 says, "I am crucified with Christ." This word is not a goal for us to attain. We could never accomplish this goal, because this is something that only the Lord Himself can do. This verse goes on to say that "it is no longer I who live, but it is Christ who lives in me." In other words, Christ is living within us instead of us living by ourselves. Our heart is deceitful above all things and very evil. Unless Christ lives within us, there is no way for us to not sin. Since man's heart is evil and beyond any remedy, God must set man aside and install Christ His Son within him to be his life.

What is the overcoming life? The overcoming life is simply the Son of God living within us to overcome sin on our behalf—this is the overcoming life. The overcoming life is not the Lord giving us the strength to be holy or pure in our thoughts. No! The overcoming life is Christ being obedient in our place, Christ praying in our place, and Christ being humble in our place. Christ lives in us to do everything for us. There is a world of difference between these two things. Have we seen the difference between applying Christ's power to act in a humble way and having Christ within us as our humility? If we see the difference, we will be blessed.

Last year when I was conducting a conference in Chefoo, Mrs. Witness Lee said to me, "I have overcome in many areas. I have made confessions to my mother-in-law, and my mother-in-law has said that there is no longer any problem between us. But I still have two little children who are quite rowdy. It is difficult for me to overcome in this matter. I try to be patient whenever they are noisy. I can overcome the first five or six times, but I lose my patience when they become rowdy for the seventh or eighth time. Can you pray for me that God would give me a better environment so that I can overcome?" I answered, "No. I cannot ask God to make you overcome; God will not make you overcome, He will only make you fail. Victory is something that only God can accomplish. Christ within you is your victory. God does not help you overcome. If it were up to you to overcome, you might overcome when your children shout four times, but by the fifth time you will fail. But if the Lord takes care of your children in your place, would you lose your patience? You would not lose your patience after they shouted five or ten times. In fact, after fifty or a hundred times, you would still come out more than a conqueror."

Victory Being Christ Living in Us

Victory is the Lord Jesus living in us. Because the Lord lives in us, He overcomes for us. No temptation is so great that He cannot overcome it. God has not given us Christ to be our example. He has given us Christ to be our life. Four years ago I was in New York, and I met a Presbyterian medical doctor with his wife and four children. The wife was about forty years old, and she was very humble. She came to me and said, "You have to pray for me. Pray that God would give me patience. My four children are driving me crazy. I can tolerate one being rowdy, and I can tolerate two being rowdy. But when three start to become rowdy, my temper begins to flare up. If all four become rowdy, I completely lose control of my temper." I asked, "What do you lack?" She said, "Patience, of course!" I then asked, "Has the Lord ever answered your prayer for patience?" She said, "No." I then said to her, "The Lord has not answered this kind of prayer before, and He will not answer this kind of prayer in the future. You cannot be patient, and you will not be patient. What you lack is not patience." She said, "What do you mean? If I do not lack patience, what do I lack?" I said, "What you lack is Christ, not patience, meekness, or quietness." Patience is Christ. True humility, meekness, and holiness are just Christ.

A brother said to me in Shanghai, "I cannot be patient. What do I have to do before I can have patience?" I told him that there is a toothbrush factory in Shanghai that sells toothbrushes wholesale; it does not sell toothbrushes retail. This is what our God does—He is in the wholesale business; He does not care for retail business. If you want a little patience from Him, He will not give it to you. He has put all virtues in Christ. When you believe and receive Him, Christ becomes yours, and all the virtues also become yours. First Corinthians 1:30 says that God has given Christ to us to be our sanctification. I cannot be sanctified in myself; rather, Christ is my sanctification in me and for me. You may not realize how precious this substitution is. God has given Christ to us to be our sanctification. He is living out a life of sanctification within us and for us. If anyone sees this to-night, I will shake his hand and congratulate him; he is the most blessed man on earth. If you are living by yourself, you cannot be sanctified. But if Christ is living in you, you can make it. This is the victory that God has given us.

Christ's Indwelling Being Our Overcoming Life

When God's life comes into us, it enables us to live a life on earth that is just the same as the one His Son lived in Nazareth. God is raising up a new race—those who have God's Son as their life and who live out the life of His Son. Philippians 4:13 says, "I am able to do all things in Him who empowers me." The Lord in you is empowering you. You have to see that nothing is too difficult for you because the One within you is empowering you. This One is omnipotent. The Lord does not want you to be an ordinary person; He wants you to live a life that God lives, to speak what no man can speak, to do what no man can do, to experience what no man can experience, and to face what no man can face. When Christ lives in you, you can live such a life.

I want to say one word that may offend some people. Many people who go to church are quite dispensable. Whether or not they are around does not mean much, and whether or not they are gone does not mean much either. God can never use such people, because they have not lived the overcoming life. They cannot testify to the world of the life of Christ and cannot help others overcome. We have to ask the Lord to enlighten us and show us the characteristics of the overcoming life. Thank God that our salvation is a full salvation. God has not only saved us from the judgment of sin, but also from the bondage of sin. God's way of salvation is for Christ to suffer sin's punishment on our behalf, to crucify our old man with Him, and to release His life and dispense it to us. Today He dwells within us. His indwelling constitutes our overcoming life.

Thank the Lord that His throne is in the heavens as well as in man's heart. Thank the Lord that He lives in the heavens as well as within us. He can accomplish God's desire within us. All the great and difficult commandments in the Bible are not for man to keep. They are meant for the Lord to keep. The harder the commandments are, the more they prove that only the Lord can fulfill them. Miss Barber once wrote the following words in her Bible beside the passage in Matthew that says we should love the Lord our God with our whole heart, soul, and will: "Lord, I thank You for this commandment." She knew that the Lord was the One who could accomplish this. The commandments in the Bible can only be fulfilled by Christ. Thank and praise the Lord. Christ is our life, and He is our victory. *(The Collected Works of Watchman Nee,* Vol. 42, pp. 448–450, 457–458)

CHAPTER 8

THE SPIRIT

THE CONSUMMATION OF THE
TRIUNE GOD

Another Comforter

Now we come to another problem. How does God dispense His life to us? We have to read John 14:16–20: "And I will ask the Father, and He will give you another Comforter, that He may be with you forever, even the Spirit of reality, whom the world cannot receive, because it does not behold Him or know Him; but you know Him, because He abides with you and shall be in you. I will not leave you as orphans; I am coming to you. Yet a little while and the world beholds Me no longer, but you behold Me; because I live, you also shall live. In that day you will know that I am in My Father, and you in Me, and I in you." The word "another" means that there was one already, and that this one is now another. The first Comforter was Christ. The second Comforter is the Holy Spirit. The word "comforter" is *paracletos* in the original language; it means a helper. The prefix *para* means to be alongside, just as the words *parallel lines* mean two lines that are alongside one another. This can be seen from two railway tracks which run alongside one another. Being parallel means maintaining the same distance all the time and being alongside all the time. God has given us a second Comforter, who will be alongside of us forever and help us all the time.

The word "another" also means another in kind, and not just another in number. Another Comforter does not mean the same kind of comforter. The kind that the disciples knew could die and leave them; He could not be with them forever. But the other kind would not be the same as this kind; the other Comforter would be with them forever. Verse 17 tells us who the other Comforter is. The other Comforter is the Holy Spirit, the Spirit of reality, whom the world cannot receive, because it does not behold Him or know Him. Hence, it was impossible for the world to receive Him. The other Comforter was different from the Lord, because the other One could be with us forever. John 14:17 reveals the difference between the Old Testament and the New Testament. In the Old Testament, the Lord could be present with men, but His presence was outward; it was not the kind of presence depicted in the New Testament. In the New Testament, the Lord is present within man; He brings His presence into man. Indeed, this is the real gospel! You and the Lord were two persons. But now you and He have become one, because He is present within you.

The Lord Being the Holy Spirit

The most mysterious part of this portion of the Word lies in the pronoun *He* in verse 17, which is changed to the pronoun

I in verse 18. Why is this? Please remember that the *He* is the *I* and the *I* is the *He*. The Lord Jesus is the Holy Spirit. I am not denying the doctrine of the Trinity. I am merely saying that the Lord Himself says that He is the Holy Spirit. Today the Lord Jesus is the Holy Spirit. This is like me saying, "A certain man is traveling to Pu-Chien-Ding to preach." Then I may go on to say, "I am preaching in Pu-Chien-Ding." What does this mean? This clearly means that the "He" in the first sentence is the "I" in the second sentence. Hallelujah! The Lord Jesus is now the Holy Spirit. Paul said that from now on he would no longer know Christ according to the flesh (2 Cor. 5:16). When the Lord Jesus was incarnated and put on flesh, He was immediately limited by time and space. Suppose the Lord was still in the flesh today, He would not be able to be in Tien-An Chapel if He was in the Savior's Church. If He was in the meeting in Ho-si Street, He could not be in the meeting behind the football field. If He was in London, He could not be in New York. If He was with the three disciples, He could not be with the other nine. If He was with the twelve disciples, He could not be with the other fifty-eight disciples. If He was with the seventy disciples, He could not be with the one hundred and twenty disciples. If He was with the one hundred and twenty, He could not be with the five hundred.

If the Lord was in Jerusalem, Christians would have to save money to make a pilgrimage once every three or five years to Jerusalem to see Him, just as Muslims make pilgrimages to Mecca. But today the Lord is no longer in the flesh. Before His death, He was in the flesh. He put on a human body in the same way that a man puts on a garment. But after His death, He put off the body of flesh and put on the Holy Spirit. The Lord has put off the flesh and put on the Holy Spirit. Today He is in the Holy Spirit. This is why He can be in us. I have often pondered the completeness of God's salvation. It is so complete that He Himself has become available to us. Today the Lord is in the Spirit, and the Spirit is omnipresent. Therefore, we can all receive Him. In Acts 2 the apostle Peter quoted the last verse of Joel 2, saying, "And it shall be that everyone who calls on the name of the Lord shall be saved" (v. 21). Paul even said that the Lord is near us, in our mouth and in our heart (Rom. 10:8). Please remember that the Lord can be such because He is in the Spirit. This is why He can be omnipresent today. John 14:18 says, "I am coming to you." This does not refer to His future coming, which will be visible; rather, it refers to His coming in the Spirit. Today the Lord has come to us in the Spirit, and He is even dwelling within us.

Knowing Christ According to the Spirit

Some regret that they were born too late. They think that it would be wonderful if they had been born two thousand years ago because they could have seen Jesus. But I tell such ones that I would not exchange places with Peter even if I could. Although I am quite insignificant, I can say humbly that I know much more than Peter. Peter only knew a Christ in the flesh. But I know the Lord who lives within me. When I was in Europe, I passed through the Mediterranean Sea and was approaching Egypt. A friend invited me to visit the holy land, but I declined the invitation. I asked myself, "Can a man increase his knowledge of Christ by visiting Golgotha, the garden of Gethsemane, or Sychar? No! Absolutely not!" That was why I declined to go. Paul said, "Even though we have known Christ according to the flesh, yet now we know Him so no longer" (2 Cor. 5:16). Today we do not know Christ according to the flesh or outward appearance, but according to spirit. *(The Collected Works of Watchman Nee,* Vol. 42, pp. 432–435)

The Holy Spirit Communicating God's Work to Us

There is another matter related to faith in God's Word. How can God's work become ours? The key is the Holy Spirit. The Holy Spirit has come. The Holy Spirit is the keeper of God's Word. The Word of God is living because the Holy Spirit is keeping watch over it. God has placed all His works in His Word. The Holy Spirit is keeping watch over it on the side. Whenever man receives God's Word by faith, the Holy Spirit comes and applies all of God's works to him. Here we see how complete the work of the Triune God is. It is God who has loved us and who has purposed the work of redemption. It is the Son who has accomplished the work of redemption. It is God who has placed the work of the Son in the Word, and it is God who communicates to us through the Holy Spirit all the works of the Son contained in the Word. The greatest problem of man, and his most foolish thought as well, is to be confused about the condition for the Holy Spirit's work. Man thinks that if he repents, God will work, or if he is baptized, God will work, or if he confesses his sins or does good works, God will work. But there is not such a thing. The Bible tells us clearly that only the Holy Spirit can communicate the Lord's work to us. The characteristic of the Holy Spirit's work is fellowship. After the Lord Jesus accomplished all the work, the Holy Spirit came and communicated this work to us. If there were only the accomplished work of the Lord Jesus without the fellowshipping work of the Holy Spirit, it would still be useless to us. Without the Father, man cannot be saved. Without the Son, man cannot be saved. Likewise, without the Holy Spirit, man cannot be saved. Although there is the work of the Father and the Son, there is still the need of the Holy Spirit to communicate these works to us and to cause the objective matters to become subjective. *(The Gospel of God,* Vol. 1, pp. 278–279)

The Spirit—The "Receivable" Lord

We have spoken of our being in Christ. Now we will speak on Christ being in us. How can Christ be in us? Christ is in us because of resurrection. Because the Lord Jesus has resurrected and because He is now in the Holy Spirit (He is not merely a man, but a man in the Spirit), He can be in us. The Lord said that His flesh is meat indeed and His blood is drink indeed. He can be eaten by us (John 6:53–56). If He were still a man like He was when He was on earth, He could not be eaten by us. We eat the fruit of the tree of life; we do not eat the tree of life itself. We cannot eat the tree; there is no way we can take the tree into us. When the Lord Jesus was on earth, He was like the tree of life; there was no way for us to take Him into us. In the same way, there is no way for us to take a person into us today. If the Lord Jesus were not a resurrected Lord, if He were only a Lord who once lived on the earth, He could only be Himself forever, while I could only be myself forever. There would be no way for us to receive Him. It would not matter how holy and lovely Jesus of Nazareth was; there would be no way for us to receive Him, because He would only be a man. But thank the Lord that He is not only a man today; He has died and resurrected. In the Holy Spirit, He has become the Lord whom we can receive. The Holy Spirit is the Lord's coming in another form (14:16–20). Another name for the Holy Spirit is "the Spirit of Jesus" (Acts 16:7). He is also called "the Spirit of Christ" (Rom. 8:9). When the Lord Jesus put on the Holy Spirit, He became a "receivable" Lord. If He had not become such a Lord, we would not be able to enjoy Him. Christ has resurrected and put on the Holy Spirit. When we receive the Holy Spirit, we receive Christ; in the same way, when we receive the Son, we receive the Father. When men in the past saw the Father, they saw the Son; in the same way, when men know the Spirit today, they know the Son. The Lord Jesus has resurrected, and He is in the Holy Spirit. Therefore, we can receive Him into us to be our life. All those who have received the Lord Jesus, whether they are clear or not, have received this experience from God. *(The Collected Works of Watchman Nee,* Vol. 36, pp. 170–171)

THE APPLICATION OF GOD'S SALVATION

The work of the Holy Spirit is fellowship. The characteristic of God is His love. The characteristic of the Lord Jesus is His grace, and the characteristic of the Holy Spirit is His fellowship. Second Corinthians 13:14 says, "The grace of the Lord Jesus Christ and the love of God and the fellowship of the Holy Spirit be with you all." God is love, and His characteristic is love. The Lord Jesus is grace, and His characteristic is grace. Lastly, the characteristic of the Holy Spirit is fellowship. The Holy Spirit has nothing in Himself. He brings the love of God and the grace of the Lord Jesus into you by the way of fellowship. This is the work of the Holy Spirit. The Holy Spirit has not accomplished a work of love. He has not accomplished a work of grace. The Holy Spirit conveys to you what God and the Lord Jesus have accomplished. Hence, the work of the Holy Spirit is fellowship. The Holy Spirit after the Lord's ascension is just filled with the work of the Lord Jesus. He is like the light. As long as there is a crack, He will come in. When He comes in, He will bring the grace of the Lord Jesus and the love of God into you. This salvation is surely complete.

Some time ago, a very famous servant of the Lord in England died. Of course, his death was under God's sovereignty. None of us can say anything about that. But humanly speaking, we can say something about his death. He was very weak and had been sick for years. The doctors had prescribed a kind of medicine for him. Whenever he inhaled that medicine, he became strong again. He put this medicine by his chest of drawers. Many times, when he suffered much and felt like dying, he would breathe in the medicine and become well. Although the medicine did not smell good, it was very effective. The night that he died he felt uncomfortable again. He tried to reach for the medicine but was too weak to open the drawer. The next morning others found him in his bed with his hand stretching for the medicine. He died there with half of his body outside his bed. It was not a matter of the lack of the best and most effective medicine. He had lived by that medicine for eight or nine years already. Every time he was about to die, he inhaled the medicine and became well again. Why did he die this time? It was not because there was no medicine, and it was not because he did not want the medicine. It was because the medicine did not get into his hand.

In the same way, we are those who are about to perish. The Lord Jesus has accomplished the work. God's medicine has been prepared. As long as we take it, we will be healed. But who will give this medicine to us? There is the doctor to prescribe the medicine. There must also be someone to apply the medicine. The work of the Holy Spirit is to convey the work of the Lord Jesus to us. The love of God is in the grace of the Lord Jesus, and the grace of the Lord Jesus is in the fellowship of the Holy Spirit. Hence, all those who have received the fellowship of the Holy Spirit receive the grace of the Lord Jesus, and all those who have received the grace of the Lord Jesus have a taste of the love of God. *(The Gospel of God,* Vol. 1, pp. 154–156)

In 2 Corinthians 13:14 Paul says, "The grace of the Lord Jesus Christ and the love of God and the fellowship of the Holy Spirit be with you all." God's heart is love. God purposed to save man. Love is something within. When it is expressed, it is grace. The outward expression of love is grace, and the inward reality of grace is love. Therefore, the grace of the Lord Jesus Christ is spoken of first because redemption was accomplished by Christ. God loves, and the love of God in the person of Christ results in grace. The Holy Spirit conveys Christ's accomplishments into us. This is the fellowship of the Holy Spirit. The Holy Spirit does not impart anything of Himself; rather, He flows what Christ has accomplished into us. It is impossible to receive the Lord's grace without the Holy Spirit. And if we only want the Holy Spirit without receiving what Christ has accomplished, it is also impossible to receive the Holy Spirit. A water pipe allows water to flow. Neither a pipe without water nor water without a pipe is effective. Therefore, the three parables in Luke 15 are not repetitious; they are a portrait of the sequence in God's way of redemption. Christ accomplished redemption, the Holy Spirit enlightens man, and God the Father receives us by His love. A proper understanding of these three parables will give us a balanced life, and we will not be biased in any way. *(The Collected Works of Watchman Nee,* Vol. 20, p. 142)

The Regenerating Spirit

At the time of man's regeneration, his spirit receives God's life and becomes enlivened. It is the Holy Spirit who actively accomplishes this work. It is the Holy Spirit who reproves man of sin, righteousness, and judgment. He prepares man's heart, causing him to willingly believe in the Lord Jesus as his Savior. The work of the cross is accomplished by the Lord Jesus. However, it is the Holy Spirit who applies this upon the sinner and within his heart. We must understand the relationship between the cross of Christ and the work of the Holy Spirit. While the cross has already accomplished everything, the Holy Spirit accomplishes within man what has been accomplished before. While the cross causes man to have the position, the Holy Spirit causes man to have the experience. While the cross achieves the "fact" for God, the Holy Spirit gives man the experience. While the work of the cross creates a position and achieves a salvation so that the sinner may have the possibility of being saved, the work of the Holy Spirit reveals to the sinner what the cross has created and accomplished so that he may receive and obtain it. The Holy Spirit does not work alone; rather, He works through the cross. Without the cross, the Holy Spirit has no ground to work. Without the Holy Spirit, the work of the cross is dead. Although it has already been effective toward God, it has no effectiveness toward man.

Although salvation is entirely accomplished by the cross, it is the Holy Spirit who works directly to cause people to receive. Therefore, the Bible says that our regeneration is the work of the Holy Spirit. "That which is born of the Spirit is spirit" (John 3:6). In verse 8, the Lord Jesus said again that regeneration is being "born of the Spirit." It is the Holy Spirit who applies the work of the cross to the believer and imparts God's life into the believer's spirit; thus, the believer is regenerated. The Holy Spirit is the executor of God's life. We "live by the Spirit" (Gal. 5:25). If man merely understands in his mentality and there is no Holy Spirit to regenerate him within his spirit, his understanding cannot help him. If what man believes in is of man's wisdom, not of God's power, he is merely stimulated in the soul and cannot last long, because he is not regenerated. Only those who believe with the heart (Rom. 10:10) can be saved and receive regeneration. *(The Spiritual Man,* Vol. 2, pp. 223–224)

THE INDWELLING SPIRIT AND THE COMING-UPON SPIRIT

What is the fundamental difference between the work of the Holy Spirit in the Old Testament and the work of the Holy Spirit in the New Testament? In the Old Testament the Holy Spirit gave new birth to people. He also gave new birth to the people of the New Testament. Regarding the matter of the new birth, there is no difference in the Old and New Testaments. All is the work of the Holy Spirit. We must not think of the new birth as something peculiar to the New Testament. The Lord told Nicodemus that as a teacher in Israel he should understand the new birth. What is the peculiar work of the Holy Spirit in the Old Testament? In the Old Testament one

179

thing is certain: we cannot find the Holy Spirit dwelling *in* human hearts. Of course, He worked in human hearts, but He never dwelt within them. We cannot find one verse in the Old Testament that says the Holy Spirit took up His abode in human hearts. In the Old Testament we find the Holy Spirit coming *upon,* but not *in,* human beings. In the Septuagint we find *epi,* upon, used continuously, but never *in.* In the New Testament we also find the Holy Spirit coming upon people. This aspect of the Holy Spirit continued, but the Holy Spirit did more than that. On the night the Lord was betrayed, He said, "He abides with you and shall be in you" (John 14:17b). This was something quite new. Thereafter men are said to be temples of the Holy Spirit. Being temples of the Holy Spirit means that the Holy Spirit lives within men.

In the New Testament we find two aspects of the Spirit's work: (1) His coming upon men, and (2) His dwelling within men. His coming upon men is still for power, miracles, and witness. His dwelling within men is for holiness. The indwelling of the Holy Spirit is to minister Christ to us, to make Christ ours, to make Him our life, and to make us bear the fruit of holiness.

If we carefully differentiate between the two, we can understand the many misconceptions regarding the Holy Spirit. Many think that if they can only have their "Pentecost," their problems would be settled. But now that you have had your "Pentecost," has it solved your problems related to holiness? Has it brought you victory over your temper, etc.? This has not settled the question of victory over sin. With this kind of "Pentecost," we find only gifts but not fruit.

When Paul saw the condition of the church in Corinth, he did not say, "Things are too bad here; we must stop everything." Many modern teachers would sweep everything away as carnal and devilish. Paul did not sweep everything away; rather, he brought something in to balance it. First Corinthians 3:16 says, "Do you not know that you are the temple of God, and that the Spirit of God dwells in you?" We must learn what it means to have the Holy Spirit dwelling *in* us.

Modern teachers teach us that the gifts are childish. They say, "We are grown up. We do not need toys like tongues. Our Christianity is far beyond that stage. We are far beyond the apostles. We can cast them away." However, those who stand for the gifts of the Holy Spirit have nothing in their mind except the gifts; they despise everyone who has not had a similar experience. They say, "On such and such a day I had the baptism of the Holy Spirit." Both of these parties are wrong.

In the New Testament we find these two aspects set before us. From the Lord's last supper until Pentecost, the Holy Spirit was spoken of *four times:* (1) During the Lord's supper, He was spoken of as the Paraclete, the Comforter. "He will give you another Comforter. . .He. . .shall be in you" (John 14:16–17). (2) After the Lord's supper the Holy Spirit was spoken of on the evening of His resurrection. He breathed into them and said, "Receive the Holy Spirit" (20:22). (3) Immediately before the Lord was taken up to heaven, He referred to the Holy Spirit when He said, "I send forth the promise of My Father upon you; . . .stay in the city until you put on power from on high" (Luke 24:49). (4) Finally, the Holy Spirit was referred to on the day of Pentecost.

People generally think that the promise of the Comforter was fulfilled at Pentecost, but this is not borne out by the Word of God. Both chapter fourteen and chapter twenty of the Gospel of John were written by John. In John 14 the Lord promised, "He will give you another Comforter" (v. 16). In John 20 this promise was fulfilled. There is no promise that the Holy Spirit would come upon men before the death of the Lord; before His death He only promised that the Spirit would dwell within men. On the day of His resurrection, He breathed into them and said, "Receive the Holy Spirit" (v. 22). What is a breath? A breath is life. If we give up breathing, we give up life. Christ breathed on the disciples and said, "Receive the Holy Spirit."

Did the Lord say, "You must wait another fifty days"? No. He breathed into them, and they received the Holy Spirit then and there. John 14 was fulfilled in John 20. The promise that was given at the Lord's supper was fulfilled on the day of resurrection. Then the Lord said to His disciples, "Stay in the city until you put on power from on high" (Luke 24:49). Pentecost was the fulfillment of Luke 24. Luke was written by Luke and Acts also was written by Luke! Acts 1 can be considered to be Luke 25 because it is the continuation of Luke. It is only natural that Luke would continue his own narrative.

Based on this we can see that the indwelling Holy Spirit, imparted by the Lord's breathing and based on His resurrection, is for life. The coming-upon Spirit, based on glorification of the Lord, is for service. *(The Collected Works of Watchman Nee,* Vol. 46, pp. 1141–1143)

THE INDWELLING SPIRIT

The Need for Revelation

"If so be that the Spirit of God dwelleth in you. . ." (Rom. 8:9). "If the Spirit of him that raised up Jesus from the dead dwelleth in you. . ." (Rom. 8:11).

As with the Spirit outpoured, so with the Spirit indwelling, if we are to know in experience that which is ours in fact, our first need is of divine revelation. When we see Christ as Lord objectively—that is, exalted to the throne in heaven—then we shall experience the power of the Spirit upon us. When we see Christ as Lord subjectively—that is, as effective Ruler within our lives—then we shall know the power of the Spirit within us.

A revelation of the indwelling Spirit was the remedy Paul offered the Corinthian Christians for their unspirituality. It is important to note that the Christians in Corinth had become preoccupied with the visible signs of the Holy Spirit's outpouring and were making much of "tongues" and miracles, while at the same time their lives were full of contradictions and were a reproach to the Lord's Name. Quite evidently they had received the Holy Spirit, and yet they remained spiritually immature; and the remedy God offered them for this is the remedy He offers His Church today for the same complaint.

In his letter to them Paul wrote: "*Know ye not* that ye are a temple of God, and that the Spirit of God dwelleth in you?" (1 Cor. 3:16). For others he prayed for enlightenment of heart, ". . .that ye may *know*" (Eph. 1:18). A knowledge of divine facts was the need of the Christians then, and it is no less the need of Christians today. We need the eyes of our understanding opened to know that God Himself, through the Holy Spirit, has taken up His abode in our hearts. In the person of the Spirit, God is present, and Christ is no less truly present too. Thus, if the Holy Spirit dwells in our hearts, we have the Father and the Son abiding in us. That is no mere theory or doctrine, but a blessed reality. We may perhaps have realized that the Spirit is actually within our hearts, but have we realized that He is a Person? Have we understood that to have the

183

Spirit with us is to have the living God within?

To many Christians the Holy Spirit is quite unreal. They regard Him as a mere influence—an influence for good, no doubt, but just an influence for all that. In their thinking, conscience and the Spirit are more or less identified as some "thing" within them, that brings them to book when they are bad and tries to show them how to be good. The trouble with the Corinthian Christians was not that they lacked the indwelling Spirit but that they lacked the knowledge of His presence. They failed to realize the greatness of the One who had come to make His abode in their hearts; so Paul wrote to them: "Know ye not that ye are a temple of God, and that the Spirit of God dwelleth in you?" Yes, that was the remedy for their unspirituality—just to know who He really was who dwelt within.

The Treasure in the Vessel

Do you know, my friends, that the Spirit within you is very God? Oh that our eyes were opened to see the greatness of God's gift! Oh that we might realize the vastness of the resources secreted in our own hearts! I could shout with joy as I think, "The Spirit who dwells within me is no mere influence, but a living Person; He is very God. The infinite God is within my heart!" I am at a loss to convey to you the blessedness of this discovery, that the Holy Spirit dwelling within my heart is a Person. I can only repeat: "He is a Person!" and repeat it again: "He is a Person!" and repeat it yet again: "He is a Person!" Oh, my friends, I would fain repeat it to you a hundred times—*The Spirit of God within me is a Person!!* I am only an earthen vessel, but in that earthen vessel I carry a treasure of unspeakable worth, even the Lord of glory.

All the worry and fret of God's children would end if their eyes were opened to see the greatness of the treasure hid in their hearts. Do you know, there are resources enough in your own heart to meet the demand of every circumstance in which you will ever find yourself? Do you know there is power enough there to move the city in which you live? Do you know there is power enough to shake the universe? Let me tell you once more—I say it with the utmost reverence: You who have been born again of the Spirit of God—you carry God in your heart!

All the flippancy of the children of God would cease, too, if they realized the greatness of the treasure deposited within them. If you have only ten shillings in your pocket, you can march gaily along the street, talking lightly as you go, and swinging your stick in the air. It matters little if you lose your money, for there is not much at stake. But if you carry a thousand pounds in your pocket, the position is vastly different, and your whole demeanour will be different too. There will be great gladness in your heart, but no careless jaunting along the road; and once in a while you will slacken your pace and slipping your hand into your pocket, you will quietly finger your treasure again, and then with joyful solemnity continue on your way.

In Old Testament times there were hundreds of tents in the camp of Israel, but there was one tent quite different from all the rest. In the common tents you could do just as you pleased—eat or fast, work or rest, be joyful or sober, noisy or silent. But that other tent was a tent that commanded reverence and awe. You might move in and out of the common tents talking noisily and laughing gaily, but as soon as you neared that special tent you instinctively walked more quietly, and when you stood right before it you bowed your head in solemn silence. No one could touch it with impunity. If man or beast dared to do so, death was the sure penalty. What was so very special about it? *It was the temple of the living God.* There was little unusual about the tent itself, for it was outwardly of very ordinary material, but the great God had chosen to make it His abode.

Do you realize what happened at your conversion? God came into your heart and made it His temple. In Solomon's days God dwelt in a temple made of stone; today He dwells in a temple composed of living believers. When we really see that God has made our hearts His dwelling-place, what a deep reverence will come over our lives! All lightness, all frivolity will end, and all self-pleasing too, when we *know* that we are the temple of God and that the Spirit of God dwells within us. Has it really come home to you that wherever you go you carry with you the Holy Spirit of God? You do not just carry your Bible with you, or even much good teaching about God, but God Himself.

The reason why many Christians do not experience the power of the Spirit, though He actually dwells in their hearts, is that they lack reverence. And they lack reverence because they have not had their eyes opened of the fact of His presence. The fact is there, but they have not seen it. Why is it that some of God's children live victorious lives while others are in a state of constant defeat? The difference is not accounted for by the presence or absence of the Spirit (for He dwells in the heart of every child of God) but by this, that some recognize His indwelling and others do not. True revelation of the fact of the Spirit's indwelling will revolutionize the life of any Christian. *(The Collected Works of Watchman Nee,* Vol. 33, pp. 95–98)

THE OUTPOURED SPIRIT OF POWER

Let us turn first to the Book of the Acts chapter two, verses 32 to 36 and consider this passage briefly:

*This Jesus did God raise up, whereof we all are wit-
nesses. Being therefore by the right hand of God exalted,
and having received of the Father the promise of the
Holy Ghost, he hath poured forth this, which ye see
and hear. For David ascended not into the heavens;
but he saith himself, The Lord said unto my Lord, Sit
thou on my right hand, Till I make thine enemies the
footstool of thy feet. Let all the house of Israel therefore
know assuredly, that God hath made him both Lord
and Christ, this Jesus whom ye crucified.*

We will set aside for the moment verses 34 and 35, and consider verses 33 and 36 together. The former are a quotation from the 110th Psalm and are really a parenthesis, so we shall get the force of Peter's argument better if we ignore them for the time being. In verse 33 Peter states that the Lord Jesus was exalted "at the right hand of God" (mg.). What was the result? He "received of the Father the promise of the Holy Ghost." And what followed? The miracle of Pentecost! The result of His exaltation was—"this, which ye see and hear."

Upon what basis, then, was the Spirit first given to the Lord Jesus to be poured out upon His people? It was upon the fact of His exaltation to heaven. This passage makes it quite clear that the Holy Spirit was poured out because Jesus was exalted. The outpouring of the Spirit has no relation to your merits or mine, but only to the merits of the Lord Jesus. The question of what *we* are does not come into consideration at all here, but only what *He* is. He is glorified; therefore the Spirit is poured out.

Because the Lord Jesus died on the Cross, I have received forgiveness of sins; because the Lord Jesus rose from the dead, I have received new life; because the Lord Jesus has been exalted to the right hand of the Father, I have received the outpoured Spirit. All is because of Him; nothing is because of me. Remission of sins is not based on human merit, but on the Lord's crucifixion; regeneration is not based on human merit, but on the Lord's resurrection; and the enduement with the Holy Spirit is not based on human merit, but on the Lord's exaltation. The Holy Spirit has not been poured out on you or me to prove how great we are, but to prove the greatness of the Son of God.

Now look at verse 36. There is a word here which demands our careful attention: the word "therefore." How is this word generally used? Not to introduce a statement, but to follow a statement that has already been made. Its use always implies that something has been mentioned before. Now what has preceded this particular "therefore"? With which is it connected? It cannot reasonably be connected with either verse 34 or verse 35, but it quite obviously relates back to verse 33. Peter has just referred to the outpouring of the Spirit upon the disciples "which ye see and hear," and he says: "Let all the house of Israel *therefore* know assuredly, that God hath made him both Lord and Christ, this Jesus whom ye crucified." Peter says, in effect, to his audience: "This outpouring of the Spirit, which you have witnessed with your own eyes and ears, proves that Jesus of Nazareth whom ye crucified is now both Lord and Christ." The Holy Spirit was poured out on earth to prove what had taken place in heaven —the exaltation of Jesus of Nazareth to the right hand of God. The purpose of Pentecost is to prove the Lordship of Jesus Christ.

There was a young man named Joseph, who was dearly loved of his father. One day news reached the father of the death of his son, and for years Jacob lamented Joseph's loss. But Joseph was not in the grave; he was in a place of glory and power. After Jacob had been mourning the death of his son for years, it was suddenly reported to him that Joseph was alive and in a high position in Egypt. At first Jacob could not take it in. It was too good to be true. But ultimately he was persuaded that the story of Joseph's exaltation was really a fact. How did he come to believe in it? He went out, and saw the chariots that Joseph had sent from Egypt.

What do those chariots represent? They surely typify here the Holy Spirit, sent both to be the evidence that God's Son is in glory, and to convey us there. How do we know that Jesus of Nazareth, who was crucified by wicked men nearly two thousand years ago, did not just die a martyr's death but is at the Father's right hand in glory? How can we know for a surety that He is Lord of lords and King of kings? We can know it beyond dispute because He has poured out His Spirit upon us. Hallelujah! Jesus *is* Lord! Jesus *is* Christ! Jesus of *Nazareth is* both Lord and Christ!

If the gift of the Spirit depends thus upon the exaltation of the Lord Jesus alone, is it possible that *He* has been glorified and *you* have not received the Spirit? On what basis did you receive forgiveness of sins? Was it because you prayed so earnestly, or because you read your Bible from cover to cover, or because of your regular attendance at church? Was it because of your merits at all? No! A thousand times, No! On what ground then were your sins forgiven? "Apart from shedding of blood there is no remission" (Heb. 9:22). The sole ground of forgiveness is the shedding of blood; and since the precious Blood has been shed, your sins have been forgiven.

Now the principle on which we receive the enduement of the Holy Spirit is the very same as that on which we receive forgiveness of sins. The Lord has been crucified, therefore our sins have been forgiven; the Lord has been glorified, therefore the Spirit has been poured out upon us. Is it possible that the Son of God shed His Blood and that your sins, dear child of God, have not been forgiven? Never! Then is it possible that the Son of God has been glorified and you have not received the Spirit? Never!

Some of you may say: I agree with all this, but I have no experience of it. Am I to sit down smugly and say I have everything, when I know perfectly well I have nothing? No, we must never rest content with objective facts alone. We need subjective experience also; but that experience will only come as we rest upon divine facts. God's facts are the basis of our experience.

Go back again to the question of justification. How were you justified? Not by doing anything at all, but by accepting the fact that the Lord had done everything. And enduement with the Holy Spirit becomes yours in exactly the same way, not by your doing anything yourself, but by your putting your faith in what the Lord has already done.

If we lack the experience, we must ask God only for a revelation of this eternal fact, that the baptism of the Holy Spirit is the gift of the exalted Lord to His Church. Once we see that, effort will cease, and prayer will give place to praise. It was a revelation of what the Lord had done for the world that brought to an end our efforts to secure forgiveness of sins, and it is a revelation of what the Lord has done for His Church that will bring to an end our efforts to secure the baptism of the Holy Spirit. We work because we have not seen the work of Christ. But when once we have seen that, faith will spring up in our hearts, and as we believe, experience will follow.

Some time ago a young man, who had only been a Christian for five weeks and who had formerly been violently opposed to the Gospel, attended a series of meetings which I was addressing in Shanghai. At the close of one in which I was speaking on the above lines, he went home and began to pray earnestly, "Lord, I do want the power of the Holy Spirit. Seeing Thou hast now been glorified, wilt Thou not now pour out Thy Spirit upon me?" Then he corrected himself: "Oh no, Lord, that's all wrong!" and began to pray again: "Lord Jesus, we are in a life-partnership, Thou and I, and the Father has promised us two things—glory for Thee, and the Spirit for me. Thou, Lord, hast received the glory; therefore it is unthinkable that I have not received the Spirit. Lord, I praise Thee! Thou hast already received the glory, and I have already received the Spirit." From that day the power of the Spirit was consciously upon him. *(The Collected Works of Watchman Nee,* Vol. 33, pp. 84–88)

THE SPIRIT—THE REALITY OF CHRIST

Those who know Christ according to the flesh never actually know Him. One must have revelation before he can know Him. We cannot know Christ according to our outward senses of sight, sound, or touch. The knowledge of Christ is something that the Holy Spirit imparts to us. If a man does not have the Holy Spirit, he does not know the reality of Christ. In the eyes of God, if a man does not have the Holy

Spirit, he has not touched the reality of the Lord Jesus even if he has memorized the Lord's history and even if he has pressed upon Him, heard His voice, knelt before Him, and prayed to Him.

The Lord said, "The words which I have spoken to you are spirit and are life" (John 6:63). Hence, once a man touches the Holy Spirit, he will surely have life. It is impossible for a man to touch the Holy Spirit without receiving life. Anything that is of the Holy Spirit is of life. If a man touches reality, he receives life. But this is where the problem lies: many people receive their knowledge of the Lord from books, while others receive it from other men. Whether they receive it by reading or hearing from others, they may not be touching the Lord Himself. The Christ that one acquires through reading or hearing cannot be compared to the real Christ. The real Christ can only be known in the Holy Spirit; there is no other way to know Him.

Many Christians are discouraged at times. It seems as if their faith avails nothing. They say, "I have been listening to messages for many years. I know very much, but none of the things I know are useful and workable." This is because they have not touched reality. If a man tries to touch Christ with his fleshly hands, he can never expect any result. Power did not go out to those who pressed upon Him. It only went out to the woman who touched Him. Many pressed upon Him but did not touch Him. However, one touched Him. Whether or not our faith works depends on whether or not we have touched reality.

We must realize that the Christ in the flesh can be touched by fleshly hands, seen by fleshly eyes, and heard by fleshly ears. But the Christ in the Holy Spirit can only be touched when a man is in the spirit. To touch the Christ in the flesh is different from touching the Christ in the Spirit. When the Lord Jesus was on earth, there was already a difference between outward and inward knowledge. The same difference exists today with our knowledge of Him. The real issue is how we know Christ. If we know Christ in a real way through the Spirit and touch the spiritual reality of Christ, we will have an inward knowledge, even though we may not be able to articulate or explain it. Once there is inward knowledge, all doubts will be gone. We need to ask the Lord to give us true knowledge, true seeing, so that we will know the Lord, not according to ourselves or to the revelation of flesh and blood, but according to the revelation of the Father who is in the heavens. (*The Collected Works of Watchman Nee,* Vol. 36, pp. 236–238)

Now we must see how the Holy Spirit conveys the work of the Lord to us. The Lord's work includes all that He has done on the cross, in His resurrection, in His ascension, in His second coming, and in everything that He bestows upon us. We cannot go into detail concerning all these items. There is too much to say about them. To speak of them, we would have to mention the work of the Holy Spirit in the entire New Testament. Tonight we can only mention it in brief. The coming of the Holy Spirit is not merely for conveying the Lord's work to us. It is also for conveying the Lord Himself to us. The purpose of the fellowship of the Holy Spirit is to convey the Lord Jesus and His work to us. If a man has not received the work of the Lord, the Holy Spirit conveys this work to him. If a man has not received the Lord Jesus, the Holy Spirit conveys the Lord Himself to man. At the time we were saved, the work of the Holy Spirit was to convey the work of the Lord to us. Later His work is to convey the Lord Himself to us. The ministry of the Holy Spirit is to manifest the Lord Jesus. *(The Gospel of God,* Vol. 1, pp. 158–159)

THE SPIRIT—THE UNIQUE REALITY

God's children must realize that in God's eyes, every spiritual thing and matter has its reality. If we merely touch the outward appearance without touching the reality, what we touch has no spiritual value. What is the reality of a spiritual thing? The reality of a spiritual thing is spiritual; it is not physical. Although spiritual realities must be expressed in words, words alone are often not the reality. Although spiritual reality is expressed in our daily lives, legalistic formalities are not realities. Although spiritual reality is manifested through our behavior, human performance is not reality.

What is Spiritual Reality?

What then is spiritual reality? The Lord said that "God is Spirit, and those who worship Him must worship in spirit and truthfulness" (John 4:24). The word "truthfulness" can be translated as "reality." The Lord also said, "But when He, the Spirit of reality, comes, He will guide you into all the reality" (16:13). First John 5:6 says, "The Spirit is He who testifies, because the Spirit is the reality." This shows us that God is Spirit, and everything related to God has to be in spirit. The Spirit of truth is the Spirit of reality. Hence, spiritual reality must be in the Holy Spirit. Spiritual reality is something that transcends people and things. Only that which is in the Holy Spirit is spiritual reality. All spiritual things are sustained in the

Holy Spirit. Once a spiritual thing moves away from the Holy Spirit, it becomes letter and form, and it is dead. All spiritual things must be in the Holy Spirit before they can be real, living, and organic. The Holy Spirit leads us into all reality. Hence, any experience that we can acquire without the guidance of the Holy Spirit is surely not spiritual reality. Anything that we acquire through our ears, our mind, or our emotion alone is not spiritual reality. Only the things that the Holy Spirit guides us into are spiritual reality. We have to remember that the Holy Spirit is the Executor of all spiritual things. Whatever God is doing today is executed by the Holy Spirit. Only that which the Holy Spirit does is real, and only that is reality.

Everything that is in the Holy Spirit is reality. When man touches reality, he touches life. Life and reality are joined together. If a man wants to take care of the spiritual life, he has to take care of spiritual reality. If a man touches spiritual reality in the Holy Spirit, he will immediately respond when others touch spiritual reality; he will immediately say amen. When others who have touched spiritual reality touch him, they will also have an inward response and an amen. This is the meaning of Psalms 42:7, which says, "Deep calls unto deep." We can say that reality invokes others to touch reality. We will give a few concrete examples in the following pages to explain what spiritual reality is. *(The Collected Works of Watchman Nee,* Vol. 36, pp. 223–224)

The Spirit of Truth

Finally, I would say a little more about the work of the Holy Spirit. In earlier chapters, especially when discussing the ministry of Paul, we have spoken frequently of the need for a revelation of divine things. More than once have we said that it is essential to *see* the purpose of God, to *see* the Person and work of Christ, to *see* the Church, the Body of Christ. To this some reader may be goaded to reply, concerning one or other of these things: "I *don't* see that. What do you suggest that I do?"

For answer I could point once more to the Spirit of truth, recalling again that He is a Person, close at hand—nay, dwelling now within our hearts—ready to help each one of us in our need. It is the apostle John who tells us how, at a time of great mystification for the disciples, Jesus assured them of the Holy Spirit's coming, to bear witness of Himself, and to guide them into all the truth.

Whether it be for the initial revelation to our hearts of divine things, or amid the discipline that must follow ere those divine things become truly a part of us, we shall find it necessary to turn again and again to this gracious Helper of our infirmities. It is by His revelation alone that we behold spiritual realities; it is by His loving discipline that we enter into those realities. By the former, He opens the gateway to progress; by the latter, He leads us on in the pathway of progress. The former is the foundation, the latter the superstructure. Without revelation by the Spirit, we cannot commence the course, but without the discipline of the Spirit we cannot complete it. Both these aspects of the Spirit's work are equally essential, but for both we can assuredly count upon Him.

The Father has conceived a plan; the Son has carried it out; now it is the Spirit who communicates to us what the Son has accomplished for us. We readily acknowledge the completeness of the work of the Son, when He said, "It is finished," and sat down at the right hand of the Majesty on high. But if we do not doubt that the Son has perfected the work committed to Him by the Father, why then do we doubt that the Spirit will perfect the work committed to Him by the Son?

The work of the Son is as comprehensive as the work of the Father. It does not go one whit beyond it, but nor does it fall one whit short of it. As great as is the work of the Father, so great is the work of the Son; and as great as is the work of the Son, so great is the work of the Spirit. There is not one particle of the work completed by the Son for us that will not be completed by the Spirit in us. All the fullness of spiritual reality that is in Christ will be imparted to us by the Spirit of Christ. Of Himself, Jesus said, "I am the Reality," and of the Spirit, "He shall guide you into all Reality." The question of coming into all the fullness of spiritual reality rests, therefore, not with us but with the Spirit. It is not a question of our capacity, or of our ability, but of the absolute faithfulness of the Holy Spirit of God. Can He be depended on to do all the work committed to Him by the Son? We must learn to trust Him. We must learn to count upon His two-fold work, first of revealing to us the nature and the dimensions of divine reality, and secondly of bringing us into every whit of the reality He has revealed.

As we look around us, we cannot fail to observe a tragic lack in the experience of so many Christians. There is nothing about their lives to indicate fullness. They have not sufficient for their own needs, much less have they anything to spare for others. Why are they so poor? Is it not because they do not know the discipline of the Spirit? The Psalmist says, "In pressure thou hast enlarged me" (Psa. 4:1). The object of all pressure is enlargement. James says something similar in his Epistle: "Did not God choose them that are poor as to the

world to be rich in faith?" (James 2:5). The object of tempo-
ral poverty is eternal enrichment. God never intended that
pressure and poverty should issue in nothing. His purpose is
that all pressure should lead to enlargement, all poverty to
enrichment. God's goal for His people is neither continuous
straitness nor continuous poverty. For straitness and poverty
are never the end; they are only the means to God's end.
Straitness is the pathway to expansion, poverty the pathway
to wealth. *(The Collected Works of Watchman Nee,* Vol. 40, pp.
182–184)

THE SPIRIT—THE REALITY OF RESURRECTION

Transmitting the Resurrected Lord

What then is the Holy Spirit? In Acts 2:33 Peter preached the
gospel to the Jews. He told them that the Lord was exalted to
the right hand of God, had received the promise of the Holy
Spirit from the Father, and had poured out this Spirit on men.
Therefore, the power of the Holy Spirit is the power of resurrection. This means that the Lord installed the power of
resurrection and even resurrection itself into the Holy Spirit
when He sent this Spirit to us. As soon as a man touches the
Holy Spirit, he touches resurrection. Once a man is in the
Spirit, he touches the Lord of resurrection. The Holy Spirit
testifies to the resurrection of the Lord. While the Lord was on
the earth, some leaned on His bosom. Others kissed Him,
pressed upon Him, or received from His hands. He washed
the feet and touched the hands of many. It was possible to
touch the Lord then. However, this kind of touch cannot
compare with our touch today. Today we are not bound by

time and space. The resurrected Lord is now in the Holy Spirit. What we see today far exceeds what men saw then. The church has been able to go on continuously for two thousand years because men have inwardly, seen the Lord in a clear way. Outwardl,y we do not see as clearly as the men in the four Gospels, but inwardly, our knowledge of the Lord far exceeds that of those in the four Gospels. Once we are in the Spirit, we touch the resurrected Lord. The single, most important work of the Holy Spirit today is to transmit the resurrected Lord to men. The Holy Spirit is not transmitting the Christ of the Gospels to men, but the Christ in resurrection. When men saw the Lord on earth, they could only tell how tall He was, how wise He was, or how old He looked. Some could say that they saw Him when He was twelve or that they knew His brothers. However, we who are in the Holy Spirit today are not bound by time and space. We are touching the Christ who is not limited by time and space.

The Power of Resurrection Being in the Holy Spirit

The Lord has transcended all barriers. Today the Holy Spirit is here to testify of this transcendent Christ. If a man claims to know the Holy Spirit yet does not know the transcendency of the resurrected Christ, he does not know the Christ in the Holy Spirit. The power of resurrection is in the Holy Spirit. Ephesians 1:21 says that when the resurrected Christ was uplifted, He transcended all rule and authority and power and lordship and every name that is named not only in this age but also in that which is to come. God made the resurrected Christ to sit at His right hand and exalted Him to a place that is far beyond human understanding. He has transcended all the names that man can name, not only in this age but also in the age that is coming. Resurrection means the breaking down of all barriers. Only the self-existing and ever-existing One can transcend all, yet God decrees that even those who are not self-existing and ever-existing can transcend all as well. The work of the Holy Spirit today is to reveal this resurrection power to us. We have to see that the Holy Spirit is the Spirit of resurrection. The Spirit that transcends everything is the Holy Spirit. *(The Collected Works of Watchman Nee,* Vol. 59, pp. 84–86)

The Holy Spirit Is Resurrection

Acts 2 shows us clearly what resurrection is. It also shows us what the Holy Spirit is. Resurrection destroys the bondage of death for us. The resurrected Lord has transcended over everything. What then is the Holy Spirit? When the Lord resurrected, He was raised up by God's right hand to His side. Once He reached the right hand of the Father, He poured out the Holy Spirit. Therefore, the power of the Holy Spirit is the power of resurrection. The Lord put both resurrection as well as the power of resurrection in the Holy Spirit, and the Holy Spirit brings these down to earth. Therefore, we cannot separate resurrection from the Holy Spirit. Anyone who touches resurrection touches the Holy Spirit. Anyone who touches the Holy Spirit touches resurrection. On the day of Pentecost, that which was poured out from on high, which was seen and heard by men, was the Holy Spirit. What was the purpose of the outpouring of the Holy Spirit? It was to testify that the Lord has resurrected. Does the Holy Spirit testify in words only? No, everyone who touches the Holy Spirit knows that the Lord Jesus has resurrected.

When the Lord Jesus was on earth, some leaned on His bosom; others received things from His hand. Some touched the hem of His garment, and some had their feet washed by the Lord. The Lord raised up the body of one person and touched the eyes of another with His spittle mixed with clay. Now the Lord Jesus has resurrected; He is now in the Holy Spirit. The Lord we see could not be seen or touched by those who saw Him when He was on earth. The Lord we see today is much deeper than the Lord they saw. The Lord we touch is the resurrected Lord. Those who knew the Lord when He was on earth could say that His wisdom and stature grew. Those who encountered Him could say that they had met Him when He was twelve or when He was thirty years of age. They could say that they knew His brothers, His parents, and His history. But the Lord we have touched has transcended all "growth." This Lord has transcended over all boundaries. Even the last boundary, death, has been broken through.

How can the church extend itself for two thousand years? It continues to exist because at various times men have seen the resurrected Lord. During the past two thousand years of church history, various people here and there were clear within; they saw the Lord within them. Concerning the outward Christ, we admit that we cannot see as clearly as the men in the Gospels; we have not seen what they saw. We do not know what the Lord was like when He was in the flesh. Nevertheless, our knowledge of the Lord today is far clearer than the men in the Gospels. Within us, we are clearer than they were. We are touching the Lord from within.

Therefore, what is the Holy Spirit doing on earth today? The Holy Spirit is conveying to us the resurrected Christ. If anyone tells me that he knows the Holy Spirit but does not know resurrection, I will say that this is impossible. This Christ has transcended over everything; He has transcended over time, space, death, and all barriers. This Christ is now in the Holy Spirit! The Holy Spirit is the Spirit that raised Jesus from among the dead. The power of the Holy Spirit is the power of resurrection. Wherever the Holy Spirit works, there is the manifestation of the power of resurrection. Wherever the Holy Spirit is, there is resurrection. *(The Collected Works of Watchman Nee,* Vol. 19, pp. 593–595)

CHAPTER 9

CHRIST'S REDEMPTION AND GOD'S SALVATION

GOD'S REDEMPTION IN CHRIST

Our Redeemer Being God and Man

What then is the way to solve the problem of sin according to the Bible? There are only two righteous ways to solve the problem. One is to deal with the one who has sinned, and the other is to deal with the one who has been sinned against. There are only two parties in the world that are qualified to deal with this problem. There are only two persons in the world who have the right to deal with the problem of sin. One is the one who has sinned against another. The other is the one who has been sinned against. When a person sues another in court, no third party has the right to speak anything. In a court proceeding, only the one who has sinned against someone and the one who has been sinned against have the right to speak. Concerning the sinner's salvation, if the sinner does not take care of it himself, then God has to take care of it for him. The sinner is the sinning party, and God is the party being sinned against. Either party can deal with the problem of sin in a most righteous way. On the sinner's side, it is righteous for him to suffer judgment and punishment, perish, and go into perdition. But there is another way which is equally righteous. The party that has been sinned against can assume the punishment. This may be quite inconceivable to us, but it is a fact. It is the party being sinned against that bears the sins. It is not a third party that bears our sins. A third party has no authority or right to step in. If a third party comes in, it is unrighteousness. Only when the party that is being sinned against is willing to suffer the loss can the problem be solved. Since God has love and also has righteousness, He would not allow a sinner to bear his sins, for that would mean that God was righteous without love. The only alternative is for the party being sinned against to step in. Only by God bearing our sins will righteousness be maintained.

Do you know what forgiveness means? In the world, we have forgiveness. Between individuals, there is forgiveness. Between a government and its people, there is also forgiveness. Even between nations, there is forgiveness. With God and man, there is also forgiveness. Forgiveness is something universally recognized as a fact. No one can say that forgiveness is something unrighteous. It is something one does cheerfully to another. But the question is: Who has the right to forgive? If a brother has stolen ten dollars from me, and I forgive him, it means that I have taken up the consequence of his sin. I have taken up the loss of these ten dollars. As another example, let us say that you have hit me in the face. The blow was so severe that I bled. If I say that I forgive you, it means that you have committed the sin of hitting, and I have suffered the consequence of hitting. The sin was committed by you, but I suffered the consequence of it. This is forgiveness. To forgive means that one party sins, and another suffers the consequence of that sin. Forgiveness is the taking up of the responsibility of the sinning party by the party sinned against. A third party has no right to come in to forgive. He cannot come in to recompense. If a third party comes in to forgive and recompense, it is unrighteousness. If the Lord Jesus comes in as a third party to substitute for the sinner, it may be fine for the sinner, and God may also have no problem with it, but there is a problem with the Lord Jesus. He has no sin. Why did He have to suffer judgment? Only the sinning one can bear the consequence of sin; he has the right to bear his own responsibility and suffer judgment for his own sin. And there is only one who can take up his sins—the one whom he has sinned against. Only the one sinned against can take up the sin of the sinning one. This is righteousness. This is the principle of forgiveness. Both God's law and man's law recognize that this is righteous. Man has the right to suffer loss. Inasmuch as man has a free will, God also has a free will. A person with a free will does have the right to choose to suffer loss.

What then is Christ's redemption? The redemptive work of Christ is God Himself coming to bear man's sin against Him. This word is more lovely to the ear than all the music in the world. What is the redemptive work of Christ? It is God bearing that with which man has sinned against Him. In other words, if Jesus of Nazareth was not God, He would not be qualified to bear our sins righteously. Jesus of Nazareth was God. He is the very God whom we sinned against. Our God has come down to earth personally and borne our sins. Today, it is God rather than man who has borne our sins. This is why it was a righteous bearing. We cannot bear it ourselves. If we were to bear it, we would be finished. Thank God that He

Himself has come to the world to bear our sins. This is the work of the Lord Jesus on the cross.

Why then did God have to become a man? It is good enough for God to love the world. Why did He have to give His only begotten Son? One has to realize that man has sinned against God. If God requires man to bear his sin, how can he do it? The wages of sin is death. When sin motivates and acts within, it ends in death. Death is the rightful penalty of sin (Rom. 5:12). When man sins against God, he has to bear the consequence of sin, which is death. Hence, God is the other party. If He is to come and take up our responsibility and bear the consequence of our sin, He has to die. But 1 Timothy 6:16 tells us that God is immortal; He cannot die. Although God is willing to come into the world and bear our sins, and although He is willing to die and go into perdition, it is impossible for Him to do this. Death has simply no effect on God. There is no possibility for God to die. Hence, for God to bear the judgment of man's sin against Him, He has to take on the body of a man. This is why Hebrews 10:5 tells us that when Christ came into the world, He said, "A body You have prepared for Me." God has prepared a body for Christ so that Christ could offer Himself up as a burnt offering and sin offering. The Lord says, "In burnt offerings and sacrifices for sin You did not delight" (v. 6). Now He is offering up His own body to deal with man's sin. Hence, the Lord Jesus became a man and came into the world to be crucified on the cross.

The Lord Jesus is not a third party; He is the first party. Because He is God, He is qualified to be crucified on the cross. Because He is man, He can die on the cross on our behalf. We must distinguish between these two statements clearly. He is qualified to be crucified because He is God, and

He is able to be crucified because He is man. He is the opposite party; He has stepped over to man's side to suffer punishment. God has become a man. He has come among man, joined Himself to man, taken up man's burden, and borne all his sins. If redemption is to be righteous, Jesus of Nazareth must be God. If Jesus of Nazareth is not God, redemption is not righteous. Every time I look at the cross, I say within myself, "This is God." If He is not God, His death becomes unrighteous and it cannot save us, for He is but a third party. But thank and praise the Lord, He is the party opposite us. That is why I made the statement that only two parties are able to deal with our sins. One is we ourselves, in which case we have to die ourselves. The other party is the God whom we have sinned against, in which case He dies for us. Other than these two parties, no third party has the right or authority to deal with our sins.

Two Aspects of the Lord's Cross

Here is a question. The Lord died on the cross, but what is the significance of His death? Who sent Him to the cross? Everyone who reads the Gospels knows that the Jews sent Him to the Gentiles, and the Gentiles crucified Him on the cross. If I remember correctly, Pilate was a Spaniard. How can we say that the Lord Jesus died to bear our sins? He was clearly crucified by man. In Acts 2:23 Peter told the Jews that they had nailed Jesus to the cross through the hand of lawless men. Here it says that it was the Jews who nailed the Lord Jesus to the cross. But what did the Lord Jesus do on the cross? Before He went to the cross, He was praying in the garden of Gethsemane. Was His prayer, accompanied with sweat like drops of blood, caused by man's persecution and opposition? Was it because Judas was bringing men to arrest Him? Or was it because He had to go to the cross to redeem us from sin? Was it not because God made the sinless One to become sin for us and laid the sins of the whole world upon Him, so that He would bear our sins upon the tree? There He prayed, "Father, if You are willing, remove this cup from Me" (Luke 22:42).

If the cross was something out of man's hand, if it was just the tool for some evil men to kill Him, and if there was only the human aspect to the Lord Jesus, then I would not like to listen to this prayer of the Lord. I would not like to hear Jesus of Nazareth kneeling there praying to the Father to remove the cup from Him if possible. For the past two thousand years, many martyrs and disciples of the Lord had a much stronger voice than He did when they were about to die. Many martyrs, when locked inside cells and dungeons, prayed that the Father would glorify them, that they would rather die for the Son, and that they would rather testify to the Lord's Word with their blood. If it had not been God who had commenced to place the burden of sins on the Lord at Gethsemane, and if it had not been God who had laid the burden of bearing our sins on the Lord Jesus, we would have to say that the Lord Jesus did not even have as much courage as those who believed in Him. Hence, the problem is that the cross has the aspect of man and the aspect of God. Man crucified the Lord Jesus on the cross. But the Lord said that no man takes His life away; He gave it up by Himself (John 10:17–18). Man could crucify the Lord a thousand times or ten thousand times, but unless He Himself gave His life away, nothing could have been done to Him. Man considers that He was crucified by man. We consider Him to be crucified by God to redeem sins on our behalf.

We have to find out from the Bible what God did on the cross. First, let us read Isaiah 53:5–10:

"But He was pierced because of our transgressions;
He was crushed because of our iniquities;
The chastening for our peace was upon Him,
And by His stripes we have been healed.
We all like sheep have gone astray;
Each of us has turned to his own way,
And Jehovah has caused the iniquity of us all
To fall on Him.
He was oppressed, and it was He who was afflicted,
Yet He did not open His mouth;
Like a lamb that is led to the slaughter
And like a sheep that is dumb before its shearers,
So He did not open His mouth.
By oppression and by judgment He was taken away;
And as for His generation,
    who among them had the thought
That He was cut off out of the land of the living
For the transgression of my people
    to whom the stroke was due?
And they assigned His grave with the wicked,
But with a rich man in His death,
Although He had done no violence,
Nor was there any deceit in His mouth.
But Jehovah was pleased to crush Him,
    to afflict Him with grief.
If You make His soul a trespass offering,
He will see a seed, He will extend His days,
And the pleasure of Jehovah
    will prosper in His hand."

The apostles quote Isaiah 53 many times in the New Testament. The One spoken of in this passage of the Scriptures is the Lord Jesus. What did the prophet say when he wrote this portion of the Scripture? The last sentence in verse 4 says, "We ourselves esteemed Him stricken, Smitten of God and afflicted." At the beginning, the prophet thought that He was smitten and stricken by God, that He was punished for His own sins and smitten by God for His transgressions. But in verse 5, there is a turn. God showed him a revelation by means of the word *but*. We think that He was merely suffering from punishment and smiting. *But* He was not suffering from punishment and smiting.

> *"But He was pierced because of our transgressions;*
> *He was crushed because of our iniquities;*
> *The chastening for our peace was upon Him,*
> *And by His stripes we have been healed.*
> *We all like sheep have gone astray;*
> *Each of us has turned to his own way."*
>
> (vv. 5–6)

The next sentence is very precious, "And Jehovah has caused the iniquity of us all; To fall on Him" (v. 6). This is what the Lord has done. We can see that there is the aspect of man to the cross and there is the aspect of God. Although it was the hands of man that nailed the Lord Jesus up, manifesting man's hatred for God, it was also God who had laid all of our sins upon Him and crucified Him. The cross was God's doing; it was something that Jehovah accomplished.

What happened at the cross? "He was oppressed, and it was He who was afflicted,

Yet He did not open His mouth;
Like a lamb that is led to the slaughter
And like a sheep that is dumb before its shearers,
So He did not open His mouth.
By oppression and by judgment He was taken away;
And as for His generation,
  who among them had the thought
That He was cut off out of the land of the living
For the transgression of my people
  to whom the stroke was due?"

(vv. 7–8)

To be cut off out of the land of the living is to die. Those who stood by the cross at the time the Lord was crucified marveled and wondered why this man was being crucified. They did not know the reason why such a thing happened. The prophet said that "He did not open His mouth," and that He is brought "like a lamb that is led to the slaughter and like a sheep that is dumb before its shearers." Who knew that He was cut off out of the land of the living for the sin of the people? Who knew that it was God working on Him to accomplish the work of redemption? The cross was the way that the Lord accomplished redemption through His death. Verse 9 says,

"And they assigned His grave with the wicked,
 But with a rich man in His death,
 Although He had done no violence,
 Nor was there any deceit in His mouth."

Verse 10 is very precious:

> *"But Jehovah was pleased to crush Him,*
>   *to afflict Him with grief.*
> *If You make His soul a trespass offering."*

The cross is a work that God did. It was God Himself who bore our sins on the cross. He solved our problem of sin. Never give any credit to Judas for delivering the Lord Jesus to the Jews. Never think that without Judas the Lord would not have been able to be the Savior. Even if there had been a thousand or ten thousand Judases, it would still be useless. It was the Lord Jesus Himself who bore our sins.

When the Lord Jesus was praying in the garden of Gethsemane, He may have seemed like the weakest of all men, without any courage. He prayed for the Father to take the cup away from Him (Luke 22:42). But when He came out from the garden and met many evil men, He said, "I am," and "they drew back and fell to the ground" (John 18:6). Please remember that He did not fall while being confronted with man's evil. On the contrary, He caused them to fall. While He was at Gethsemane, considering the suffering involved in bearing man's sins, how the sinless One would be made sin, and how He was to take upon Himself the judgment of sin, He prayed for the cup to be removed from Him if possible. Had it not been for the question of redemption, the Lord Jesus would not have even matched a martyr. How brave were the many Christian martyrs when they marched to the lions' den. But the Lord Jesus pleaded to have the cup removed from Him if possible. Physically speaking, the Lord Jesus was vastly different from all the martyrs. But for redemption, for solving the problem of sin, for God to come to man and bear man's sin, even He had to ask for the removing of the cup if possible. The

Bible says that it was Jehovah that made Him an offering for sin. It was Jehovah who laid on Him the iniquity of us all. It was something Jehovah did. The cross was the work of God; it was not the work of man. The cross is God Himself coming to earth to bear man's sins. The cross is not the crucifixion of the Son of God by man.

Do you remember what the Bible says about the sixth to ninth hours? The sun's light failed (Luke 23:44–45). The Jews could mock Him, and the Gentiles could chastise and shame Him, but the sun was beyond the Jews' control. The Gentiles did not have the authority to manipulate the sun. Man could clamor and trumpet, but the earthquake was not something that Pilate could summon. Why was the sky darkened? These phenomena happened because God Himself had come to bear our sins. This was not something done by man. If it had been done by man, would God have added to His Son's pain when He was hanging on the cross? Would God not have sent twelve companies of angels to come and rescue Him? Such would indeed have happened had it not been for the redemption for sins. We thank and praise God that His Son came to redeem us from sins. This was why He said, "My God, My God, why have You forsaken Me?" (Matt. 27:46). No believer throughout the past two thousand years has ever said these terrible words when they died. For two thousand years, whether the believers died in peace or in woe, they were more bold than He was. Why was the Son of God rejected there by God? If it had merely been man's hand and man's crucifixion, that would have been the time He needed God's presence even more. When man plotted to persecute and kill Him, God should have manifested His presence more. That was the most crucial moment. God should have been with Him. Why did God leave Him instead? It was solely because the Son of

God had become sin and had borne the judgment. That was the reason He cried, "My God, My God, why have You forsaken Me?" God had forsaken Him. We who have believed in the work of redemption know that the work of the cross was for Him to be judged by sin. The cross of the Lord shows us how evil sin is and how much of a price God has paid for the work of redemption.

Besides Isaiah 53, another clear testimony of the Scripture can be found. In Romans 3:25, God set forth Christ "as a propitiation place." This also shows clearly that the work was done by God. Deuteronomy 21:23 tells us that he who is hanged on a tree is accursed of God. When the Lord was hanging on the cross, He was not accursed of man. Rather, He was accursed of God. That is why He can deliver us from the curse. First John 4:10 says that God loved us and sent His Son as a propitiation concerning our sins. It was God who sent His Son to be a propitiation. It was not man who crucified Him. Second Corinthians 5:21 also says, "Him who did not know sin He made sin on our behalf." This was something that God did. The cross is the work of God. It was God who sent the Lord Jesus to pass through the cross. Acts 2:23 mentions both the aspect of God and the aspect of man. "This man, delivered up by the determined counsel and foreknowledge of God, you, through the hand of lawless men, nailed to a cross and killed." The Lord Jesus was killed by the Jews through the hand of lawless men. However, such a death was according to the determined counsel of God. This shows us that everything was done by God. We have sin, and sin can only be taken care of by God Himself. For this reason, God came to the world to be a man. While He was a man, He was indeed righteous. But this righteousness was not imputed to us. It was the death of the Lord Jesus that delivered us from the curse of the law (Gal. 3:13). He did not deliver us from sin while He was living, but when He died. On the cross, it was God who crucified Him, rather than man. Man's hand is useless. It was God who took the opportunity to make manifest man's sin. *(The Gospel of God,* Vol. 1, pp. 109–112, 116–121)

GOD'S ETERNAL SALVATION

Eternal Salvation before God

The first kind of salvation is eternal salvation before God, which we obtained the moment we believed in the Lord. This salvation involves our being delivered out of the judgment of sins, the curse of the law, the threat of death, the punishment of hell, and the power of Satan. Our trespasses have been forgiven, and we have been cleansed of our sins. We are justified, sanctified, and reconciled to God. This salvation also includes regeneration, receiving the eternal life of the Lord, the quickening of our spirit, and the indwelling of the Holy Spirit within us. We receive this salvation entirely by the grace of God; it has nothing to do with our works. Ephesians 2:8 and 9 say, "For by grace you have been saved through faith, and this not of yourselves; it is the gift of God; not of works that no one should boast." Second Timothy 1:9 says, "Who has saved us and called us with a holy calling, not according to our works but according to His own purpose and grace, which was given to us in Christ Jesus before the times of the ages." Titus 3:5 says, "Not out of works in righteousness which we did but according to His mercy He saved us, through the washing of regeneration and the renewing of the Holy Spirit." Acts 15:11 says, "But we believe that through the grace of the Lord Jesus we are saved in the same way also as they are."

This eternal salvation was accomplished by our Lord Jesus. He is our Savior who came to die for us on the cross and bore our sins (1 Pet. 2:24), redeemed us out of the curse of the law (Gal. 3:13), and delivers us from the wrath which is coming (1 Thess. 1:10). By His death He destroyed the devil, who held the might of death (Heb. 2:14), and delivered us out of the authority of darkness (Col. 1:13) that we should not come into judgment, but pass out of death into life (John 5:24). By the resurrection of the Lord Jesus from the dead, we are born again, given eternal life, and become the children of God (1 Pet. 1:3; John 12:24). By the ascension of the Lord Jesus, we are brought near to God the Father so that we and the Father can have fellowship in the Holy of Holies (Heb. 9:12; 10:19–22), far above all the powers of darkness (Eph. 1:21). The Lord has accomplished all these matters. Our part is simply to believe and receive. "But as many as received Him, to them He gave the authority to become children of God, to those who believe into His name" (John 1:12). "For I am not ashamed of the gospel, for it is the power of God unto salvation to every one who believes, both to Jew first and to Greek" (Rom. 1:16). "Believe on the Lord Jesus, and you shall be saved, you and your household" (Acts 16:31).

This kind of salvation is eternal. Once a person is saved, he is saved forever. "And having been perfected, He became to all those who obey Him the source of eternal salvation" (Heb. 5:9). Since the salvation that the Lord has accomplished for us is eternal, our salvation is also eternal.

We can find at least twelve aspects in the Bible which

confirm the security of our salvation and the fact that we shall not perish once we are saved.

According to God's Will

We have been made children of God and have received sonship not according to our condition but according to the predetermined will of God (Eph. 1:5). God has saved us and called us with a holy calling, not according to our works but according to His own purpose (2 Tim. 1:9). Our condition may change, but God's will never changes (Heb. 6:17). In eternity past, God determined that He would save us and not lose any of us (John 6:39). How then could we be saved and later unsaved? Our salvation is eternally secure in God's unchangeable purpose.

According to God's Election

Our election by God is neither accidental nor temporary. God chose us in Christ before the foundation of the world (Eph.1:4). God chose us according to His purpose, not according to our works (Rom. 9:11). Furthermore, we did not chose the Lord, but He chose us (John 15:16). The Lord will never change. God's calling is irrevocable (Rom. 11:29). Therefore, our salvation is eternally secure and will never be changed.

According to God's Love

We are saved because God loved us, not because we loved God (1 John 4:10). Our love may easily change, but God's love is deeper than the love of a mother (Isa. 49:15); it is eternal (Jer. 31:3), to the uttermost (John 13:1), and unchanging. This everlasting love of God assures us that His salvation can never be a matter of concern and never be lost.

According to God's Grace

We are not saved by ourselves nor by our works but by the grace of God (Eph. 2:8–9). Our self and works may change, but the grace of God is constant and unchanging. Therefore, our salvation is forever secure. Furthermore, God has saved us according to His grace which was given to us in Christ Jesus before the times of the ages (2 Tim. 1:9). Our salvation is according to the riches of His grace (Eph. 1:7). The grace of God is sufficient and superabundant; it is able to bear all our burdens, meet all our needs, and save us to the uttermost.

According to God's Righteousness

God saved us not only because of His love and by His grace but also according to His righteousness. The Lord Jesus received the judgment of God's righteousness on the cross for us, thereby satisfying the requirement of God's righteousness. Consequently, God must save us if we believe. If God did not save us, He would fall into unrighteousness. The righteousness of God is revealed in His saving us (Rom. 1:16–17). We are justified by God, and God must save us because who can bring a charge against God's chosen ones? (8:33). Righteousness is the foundation of God's throne (Psa. 89:14) and is solid and unmovable. Our justification is based on the righteousness of God and, therefore, is eternally secure and unshakable.

According to God's Covenant

God has made a covenant to save us (Matt. 26:28; Heb. 8:8–13). Since this covenant cannot be altered (Psa. 89:34), neither can our salvation be changed.

According to God's Power

"My Father, who has given them to Me, is greater than all, and no one can snatch them out of My Father's hand" (John 10:29). Since God is almighty, so is His power. Therefore, no one can snatch us out of His almighty hand. Our salvation is secure according to God's power.

According to God's Life

The life of God is eternal. God has given us His eternal life so that we can become children of God. Thus, we have a life relationship with Him, an eternal relationship (John 3:16; 1 John 3:1). A life relationship can never be broken, and since we have the eternal life of God within us, we shall never perish (John 10:28).

According to God Himself

God never changes, and with Him there is no shadow cast by turning (James 1:17; Mal. 3:6). How can the salvation we received from such a God ever change?

According to Christ's Redemption

The Lord has become the source of eternal salvation unto us (Heb. 5:9). "For by one offering He has perfected forever those who are being sanctified" (10:14). What the Lord accomplished is eternal; therefore, our salvation is also eternal. Because of this accomplished fact, "Who is he who condemns? It is Christ Jesus who died and, rather, who was raised, who is also at the right hand of God, who also intercedes for us" (Rom. 8:34). No one can negate the Lord's redemption which He accomplished for us by His death and resurrection, and no one can condemn us. Therefore, our salvation is eternally secure.

According to Christ's Power

"And I give to them eternal life, and they shall by no means perish forever, and no one shall snatch them out of My hand" (John 10:28). The Lord and God are one. He is equal with God; therefore, His hand is as powerful as God's hand. No one can snatch us out of the Lord's hand. His mighty hand makes our salvation eternally secure.

According to Christ's Promise

"All that the Father gives Me will come to Me, and him who comes to Me I shall by no means cast out" (John 6:37). The Lord has promised that He will never cast out those who come to Him. Based on this promise, we have the assurance that our salvation is eternally secure.

Salvation before Men

"He who believes and is baptized shall be saved" (Mark 16:16). The salvation spoken of in this verse does not refer to eternal salvation, because the verse continues to say, "But he who does not believe shall be condemned." Since the first part says, "He who believes and is baptized shall be saved," we may wonder why the second part does not say, "He who does not believe and is not baptized shall be condemned." When the second part speaks of condemnation, it puts aside the matter of being baptized. This explains why "shall be saved" in the first part is not equal to "shall [not] be condemned" in the second part. Not being condemned is totally a matter of believing. Being saved requires us to believe and be baptized. Therefore, the salvation in Mark 16:16 does not refer to eternal salvation, which saves one from condemnation. What then does it refer to? It refers to the salvation before men. If a person only believes but is not baptized, he is not known in the eyes of men as a saved person, even though he may have the eternal life within him. He must rise up and be baptized, proclaiming to men that his sins have been forgiven and that he belongs to the Lord. Then men will know that he is saved. Baptism separates him from the worldly people. Therefore, the salvation of being baptized refers to the salvation before men.

Daily Salvation

"So then, my beloved, even as you have always obeyed, not as in my presence only but now much rather in my absence, work out your own salvation with fear and trembling" (Phil. 2:12). We cannot work out our salvation by ourselves. By God's grace we freely received our salvation. But this verse says, "Work out your own salvation." Although we have been saved, in our daily living we must still live out the salvation that we have received. As soon as we believed in the Lord, we received the life of God. God is dwelling within us through the Holy Spirit. "For it is God who operates in you both the willing and the working for His good pleasure" (v. 13). In our daily living we must live out the life of God. Day by day, moment by moment, we must live by obeying God who is operating within us. This cannot be accomplished quickly, but day after day we must live out our salvation with fear and trembling.

"Hence also He is able to save to the uttermost those who come forward to God through Him, since He lives always to intercede for them" (Heb. 7:25). This also speaks of the Lord's saving us in our daily living. The Lord is now interceding before God for us, keeping us, and saving us until the day He comes.

In the matter of daily salvation, we should also be aware that the Lord wants us to pray daily, petitioning God to deliver us from the evil one (Matt. 6:13). Day by day and moment by moment, Satan is tempting us, luring us, attacking us, and trapping us. Therefore, we need to pray that the Lord would deliver us from Satan day by day and moment by moment.

Salvation from Tribulation

There is another kind of salvation, in which God saves us out of tribulation. Paul said, "Who has delivered us out of so great a death, and will deliver us; in whom we have hoped that He will also yet deliver us" (2 Cor. 1:10). Deliverance does not refer to eternal salvation before God. The deliverance spoken of in this verse is a continuation of the preceding verses. In verses 8 and 9, Paul said that trouble came to him and his co-workers in Asia, so that they were excessively burdened, beyond their power, so that they despaired even of living. They even had the response of death in themselves. Yet God delivered them out from so great a trouble and so great a death. God had delivered them in the past, He was delivering them then, and they expected that He would deliver them in the future. God would deliver them from all the troubles in their circumstances.

"The angel of the Lord encamps around those who fear Him, and delivers them" (Psa. 34:7). God will send His angel to encamp round about those who fear Him to deliver them out of the troubles in their environment.

"For I know that for me this will turn out to salvation through your petition and the bountiful supply of the Spirit of Jesus Christ" (Phil. 1:19). "And I was delivered out of the lion's mouth. The Lord will deliver me from every evil work" (2 Tim. 4:17–18). This salvation also refers to salvation in troubled times. The Lord will deliver us from troubles and evil works.

Salvation of the Body

At the second coming of the Lord, our body will be redeemed, transformed, and conformed to His glorious body (Phil. 3:21). This, too, is called salvation in the Bible. It is the salvation of the body. "But we ourselves also, who have the firstfruits of the Spirit, even we ourselves groan in ourselves, eagerly awaiting sonship, the redemption of our body" (Rom. 8:23). Verse 24 says, "For we were saved in hope." "Saved" refers to "the redemption of our body" in verse 23. The redemption of our body will be achieved only at the time the Lord comes again. We must hope for this. At the time we believed in the Lord, we received eternal salvation; our spirit was made alive, but our body is still in the old creation groaning, laboring, restrained by corruption, and suffering illness and oldness. When the Lord comes, He will redeem and transform our body, the body that is restrained by the old creation, and He will bring it into the glorious freedom of the new creation.

"For now is our salvation nearer than when we believed" (Rom. 13:11). This also refers to the salvation of the body. We received the salvation of our spirit at the moment we believed. Our body will be saved in the future. Therefore, after we believe, the salvation of our body draws nearer and nearer.

The Salvation of the Soul

Since our whole being is composed of three parts—spirit, soul, and body (1 Thess. 5:23), our salvation involves the salvation of these three parts. The salvation of our spirit occurred at the time we believed in the Lord, when we were regenerated by the Holy Spirit. When God forgave all our sins, the Holy Spirit entered into us and enlivened our deadened spirit. The salvation of our body will occur at the coming of the Lord. By His power the Lord will change our vile body into a glorious body. In addition to these two parts, our soul also needs to be saved. The salvation of our soul relates to entering into the millennial kingdom and reigning with the Lord. The Lord will reward us, and our soul will enjoy with Him the joy of the kingdom.

"For whoever wants to save his soul-life shall lose it; but whoever loses his soul-life for My sake shall find it" (Matt. 16:25). "Save" in this verse does not refer to eternal salvation, which is received freely by believing. The salvation referred to here requires a price; one has to lose the soul and sacrifice the soul in order to gain the soul. This speaks of a person who, having been saved by the Lord, is willing to deny himself, take up his cross, and follow the Lord. He sacrifices his own soul for the Lord's sake, and by doing so, will enter into the millennial kingdom and participate in the joy of the Lord (25:21, 23). The soul is the part of our being where we perceive joy and sorrow. If we can endure the suffering and sacrifice temporary joy for the Lord's sake, when He comes we shall enter into the joy of the Lord. Man's soul is also his self.

If we deny the self today for the Lord's sake, the Lord will give us something that is truly our own in the future (Luke 16:11–12).

"But whoever will lose his soul-life for My sake and the gospel's shall save it" (Mark 8:35). The Lord's sake and the gospel's sake always go together and are inseparable. Whether it is for the Lord or for the gospel, if we sacrifice the soul and its pleasure in this age, our soul will gain special joy in the coming kingdom age; that is, we will reign with the Lord and enjoy the joy of the Lord in glory.

"Whoever seeks to preserve his soul-life will lose it, and whoever loses it will preserve it alive" (Luke 17:33). Believers who preserve their soul and the pleasure of their soul in this age will lose the joy during the kingdom age. Whosoever will lose his soul and its pleasure in this age, will save his soul and have the enjoyment in the coming kingdom.

"But he who has endured to the end, this one shall be saved" (Matt. 10:22). "In your endurance you will possess your souls" (Luke 21:19). If believers can endure to the end in persecution, they will gain the reward from the Lord. By then, their souls will not suffer but will participate in joy.

"But we are not of those who shrink back to ruin but of them who have faith to the gaining of the soul" (Heb. 10:39). The faith spoken of in this verse is the faith we receive after we are saved. It is not the initial faith but the faith by which we walk. It is not faith for life, but faith for our living. If we can walk the Lord's way by faith and live a victorious life after being saved, our soul will be saved in the future, and we will have a portion in the glory and joy of the kingdom.

"Receiving the end of your faith, the salvation of your souls" (1 Pet. 1:9). This "faith" is also the faith which we receive and live by after we are saved. This faith enables us to be kept by God and overcomes difficulties and trials. It will bring about the salvation that God has prepared and will be manifested when the Lord comes back. This is to be delivered from all sufferings and enjoy the joy of glory.

"Therefore putting away all filthiness and the abundance of malice, receive in meekness the implanted word, which is able to save your souls" (James 1:21). The salvation of the soul is not the same as the salvation of the spirit. For the salvation of the spirit, we do not need to do anything; just by believing and receiving, we obtain it. However, the salvation of the soul requires that we put away all filthiness and malice in our conduct and receive the implanted word in meekness.

"The Lord. . .will save me into His heavenly kingdom" (2 Tim. 4:18). "For doing these things you shall by no means ever stumble. For in this way the entrance into the eternal kingdom of our Lord and Savior Jesus Christ will be richly and bountifully supplied to you" (2 Pet. 1:10–11). The salvation of the soul is the salvation into the kingdom of the heavens— the eternal kingdom of our Lord and Savior Jesus Christ. *(The Collected Works of Watchman Nee,* Vol. 20, pp. 195–204)

SALVATION BEING OF GRACE NOT LAW

First, we have to see what is the nature of grace. What characteristics does grace have? We treasure the love of God, for without God's love as the source, there would not be the flow of salvation. The flow of salvation issues from the love of God. At the same time, without God's mercy there would be no possibility of salvation. Because God has shown mercy on us, He has given us His salvation. God's salvation is the concrete expression of God's love. Hence, we treasure love, and we also treasure mercy. But the most precious of all that reaches us is grace. Love is indeed good, but it does not give any concrete benefit to us. Mercy is also very good, but it also does not bring us any direct benefit; however with grace there is a direct benefit. Hence, grace is more precious. The New Testament is filled, not with the love of God, nor with the mercy of God, but with the grace of God. Grace is God's love coming forth to accomplish something for the fallen, lost, and perishing sinner. Now we not only have an abstract love and a sentimental mercy, but we have grace to meet our needs in a concrete way.

We may think that it is wonderful enough if God is merciful to us. A fleshly or fleshy person will think that mercy is good enough. The Old Testament is filled with words of mercy. There are not many words on grace. When man is in the flesh, he thinks that mercy is enough, that there is no need for grace. He thinks this way because he does not consider sin to be something serious. If man were without food or clothing or housing, mercy would not be adequate; there would also be the need of grace. But the problem with sin is not a lack of food, clothing, or housing. The problem with sin is unrest in man's conscience and judgment before God. For this, man thinks that if only God would be merciful to us and be a bit more lenient, everything would be fine. If God would overlook our sins, it would be good enough for us. In our hearts we hope that God would be merciful to us and let us go. Man's concept is to let go and to overlook. But God cannot mercifully overlook our sins. He cannot let us get by loosely. He must deal thoroughly with our sins.

Not only does God have to show mercy on us; He has to give us grace as well. What issues out from God's love is grace. God is not satisfied with mercy alone. We think that if there were mercy and that if God would let us go and not reckon with us, everything would be fine. But God did not say that since He has pity on us He would let us go. This is not the way God works. When God works, He must do so in harmony with Himself. Therefore, God's love cannot stop with mercy. His love must extend into grace. He must deal thoroughly with the problem of our sins. If the problem of sins were something that could be overlooked, God's mercy would be sufficient. But to Him, letting us go and overlooking our sins are not sufficient. Thus to have mercy alone is not sufficient. He must settle the matter of sins thoroughly. Here we see the grace of God. This is why the New Testament, though not void of mercy, is full of grace. In it we see how the Son of God, Jesus Christ, has come to the world to show forth grace and to become grace so that we might receive grace.

What is grace? Grace is nothing other than God's great work accomplished freely in His unconditional and boundless love for helpless, unworthy, and sinful man. God's grace is just God working for man. How does this contrast with the law? The law is God requiring man to work for Him, while grace is God working for man. What is the law? The law is God's demand for man to do something for Him. What is work? Work is man's effort to do something for God. What is grace? Grace is neither God requiring something nor God receiving man's work, but grace is God doing His own work. When God comes forth to do something for and on behalf of man, that is grace.

The emphasis in the New Testament is not on the principle of the law. In fact, the New Testament opposes the principle of the law because law and grace can never mix. Is it God who is working or is it man who is working? Is God giving something to man or is He asking for something from man? If God is asking for something from man, we are still in the age of the law. But if God is giving something to man, we are in the age of grace. You would not go to someone's home to give him money while you are there to collect money. Likewise, law and grace are opposite principles; they cannot be put together. If man is to receive grace, he must put the law aside. On the other hand, if he follows the law, he will fall from grace.

If man is to follow the law, he must have God accept his works. If there is the principle of the law and of works and if man is to give something to God, he must give God what He demands. The Bible indicates that man's works should be a response to God's law. God's law demands that I do something. When I do it, I am responding to God's law. This is what the Bible calls works. But when grace is here, the principle of law and of works is set aside. Here we see that it is God working for man instead of man working for God.

Grace, which is God working for helpless, poor, and troubled man, has three characteristics or natures. Everyone who wants to understand God's grace must remember these three characteristics or natures. If we forget these three characteristics, we as sinners will not be saved, and we as Christians will fail and fall. If we see the characteristics and nature of God's grace, we will receive more grace from God for timely help. Let us consider briefly these three characteristics from the Bible.

What are man's works? Generally speaking, there are three things to man's work: (1) his wrongdoings, (2) his achievements, and (3) his responsibilities. The works of man that are evil are his wrongdoings, those that are good are his achievements, and those that he is willing to bear are his responsibilities. Here we have three things: of the things that man does, those that are not done well become his wrong-doings, those that are done well become his achievements, and those that he promises to do for God are his responsibilities. In terms of time, wrongdoings and achievements are things of the past, and responsibilities are things of the future; they are things that a man is responsible for. If God's grace is God working for sinful, weak, ungodly, and helpless man, right away we see that God's grace and man's wrong-doing cannot be joined together. Neither can God's grace be joined with man's achievements and responsibilities. Where the question of wrongdoing comes into play, grace does not exist. Where the question of achievement comes into play, grace also does not exist. Likewise, where responsibility is, grace does not exist. If God's grace is indeed grace, wrong-doings, achievements, and responsibilities cannot be mixed in. Whenever wrongdoings, achievements, and responsibilities are mixed in, God's grace loses its characteristics. *(The Gospel of God,* Vol. 1, pp. 39–42)

SALVATION AND REWARD

We have seen that Revelation is a book on righteousness. If we want to understand the function of its righteous nature, we must differentiate between salvation and reward. The Bible as the Word of God has made a clear distinction between these two things; they are never mixed together. What God has separated, no man can put together by force. Let us now consider their distinctions a little:

Salvation is free; it is not obtained through man's work. It is God who has *graced* us. We are not saved through any *merit* of our own. We can look at a few verses from the Bible:

"Ho! Everyone who thirsts [the sinners],
Come to the waters [God's salvation],
And you who have no money [merits, righteous acts, etc.];
Come, buy and eat [every sinner can believe and be saved];
Yes, come, buy wine and milk [the joy of salvation]
Without money and without price [without righteous acts and without goodness in oneself]" (Isa. 55:1).
"The *gift* of God" (John 4:10).
"But the *gift* of God is eternal life" (Rom. 6:23).
"For by *grace* you have been saved through *faith,* and this not of yourselves; it is the gift of God; not of works that no one should boast" (Eph. 2:8–9).
"Not out of works in righteousness which *we did* but according to *His mercy* He saved us" (Titus 3:5).
"Let him who wills take the water of life *freely*" (Rev. 22:17).

We should pay attention to the above verses. These verses, and many others which we have not quoted, prove that our salvation is *free.* It does not come about through our work or our righteous acts. We are saved through the *grace* of God. All there is for us to do is to *believe* in God's gift of grace, that is, in God's free gift. We must be very clear about this. The work of salvation is *completely* accomplished *for* us by the Lord Jesus. He died on the cross to *accomplish* our salvation. If we want to be saved and have eternal life now, we *do not need* to have any more work or to accumulate any merit. All that is needed is for us to *believe* and to *receive.* None of our good deeds are acceptable before God. In the whole New Testament, there are over one hundred fifty times where it says that we receive salvation by believing or that we receive eternal life by believing. God never lies to us. He says, "Believe, believe, believe." When we believe, we are saved, have eternal life, and are justified. This is free. "God *gave* to us eternal life and this life is in His Son. He who has the Son has the *life;* he who does not have the Son of God does not have the life" (1 John 5:11–12). According to the Word of God, everyone who receives the Lord Jesus as Savior by faith has eternal life. Truly, "He who *believes* into the Son *has* eternal life" (John 3:36). The minute we believe, we have it!

But *reward* is different. It is different from *gift. Reward* is not given for free. It is obtained through *good works.* Reward is given according to the *saints'* work. We can look at the following verses:

"My *reward* is with Me to render to each one as his *work* is" (Rev. 22:12). This is a word to the church (see v. 16).

"Each will receive his own *reward* according to his *own labor*" (1 Cor. 3:8).

"Whatever you *do, work* from the soul as to the Lord and not to men, knowing that from the Lord you will receive the inheritance as recompense. . . . For he who *does* unrighteously will receive what he unrighteously did" (Col. 3:23–25).

"Now to the one who works, his wages are not accounted according to grace, but according to what is due" (Rom. 4:4).

We can quote many other verses, but these few are sufficient to prove to us that *reward does not come freely.* According to the teaching of the Bible, we can see that reward is awarded according to the *good works* of the believers. Whether it be as small as a cup of cold water (Matt. 10:42), or as hidden as a counsel of the heart (1 Cor. 4:5), or a humble service (Mark 10:43), or a suffering for the Lord (Luke 6:22), all these are opportunities for reward.

Hence, according to the Bible, what is set before man is two goals. While we were *sinners,* our goal was to *be saved.* After we are *saved* and have become *believers,* our goal is to receive the reward. Salvation is prepared for the sinners. Reward is prepared for the believers. A man should first receive salvation and then seek after the reward. The perishing ones need salvation. The saved ones need the reward. After reading 1 Corinthians 9:24–27 and Philippians 3:12–14, we see that some *believers* will not receive the *reward.* In those two passages, Paul was speaking of the question of reward rather than of salvation. Paul knew very well that he was saved. In his Epistles, he often expressed that he was a saved person, but in these two passages, he showed us what he was pursuing after he was saved. He was pursuing after the reward. At that time, he could not say for sure yet that he would receive the reward. He was still seeking after it. A sinner should seek for salvation, while a believer should seek for reward.

Even though a sinner may be corrupt to the uttermost, as long as he is willing to accept, that is, believe in the Lord Jesus as the Savior, he will immediately be saved. After he is saved, as one who has been regenerated by God, he should develop the new life, work for the Lord, and serve Him faithfully so that he can receive the reward. Man is saved by the merit of *Christ.* Man is rewarded through *his own* achievement. Man is saved by *faith.* Man is rewarded by *work.* God is willing to save a sinner who has no merit, but God is not willing to reward a believer who has no achievement. Before a man believes in the Lord, if he will confess that he is a sinner, and will come to Jesus, and will trust that His death on the cross is a substitution for him, he will be saved. He will be guaranteed eternal blessings. Once he is saved, according to the Bible, he is placed in an arena where he must run. If he wins, he will receive a reward. If he loses, he will not receive a reward. *However, he will not lose his eternal life, that is, his salvation, just because of his defeat.* Salvation is eternal. Here we have the most balanced teaching and the most appropriate truth. Unfortunately, many only know about salvation. They think that they will be adequately satisfied if they can be saved. They have no further capacity to strive for the reward. It is sad that many have confused salvation with reward. As a result they consider salvation to be extremely difficult and obtainable only through one's self-mortification. However, this is not the teaching of the Bible. The Bible says that salvation is very simple. The Lord Jesus has accomplished all the works for us. But to receive the reward is not that simple. It is an achievement we should attain through our trust in the Lord.

Here I can use an illustration. Suppose a certain rich man is setting up a free school. All those who come to join the school will not be charged any fee. The expenses are born by the rich man himself. Among all the students in the school, those with outstanding results will be rewarded. Salvation is like enrollment in this free school. Everyone who is willing to come to the Lord Jesus will be saved by the Lord. All the price for salvation has been paid by the Lord. It is very easy to become a student in a free school; there is no effort to it. As long as one *comes,* he will be accepted. Likewise it is very easy to be saved; one does not need to do anything. All he needs to do is *believe.* But it is not easy for a student to receive a reward. He has to put in the *effort.* Likewise it is not easy for a believer to receive the reward; he must have many *good works.*

The readers should never think that to be saved is good enough, and that there is no need to seek after any reward. We have to know that the Lord desires every genuine regenerated person to pursue after the reward. At the same time, it is spontaneous that a person would seek after the reward. This is not for one's self gain. To gain the reward is equivalent to gaining the Lord's heart, for those that the Lord rewards are the ones that are well-pleasing to Him. As sinners should seek for salvation, so believers should seek for reward. Just as salvation is crucial to a sinner, in the same way reward is crucial to a believer. The most important thing for a sinner is to be saved. The most important thing for a believer is to receive the reward. If a believer does not receive the reward, it does not merely mean that he has relinquished his rights. It means that he has not conducted a holy life, that he has not been faithful in his work, that he has achieved no performance in this world, and that he has not fully expressed the Lord Jesus Christ.

Recently, there have been two extreme teachings which have developed into two errors. Some think that to be saved is very difficult, that man has to do this and that before he can be saved. This annuls the merit of the Lord Jesus' substitution and redemption. This teaching puts all the responsibility on man and forgets the biblical teaching that salvation is by *grace* and justification is by *faith*. Some others think that everything is of grace. This is, of course, true, but they think that all those who believe in the Lord Jesus are not only saved but will also receive reward, glory, and kingship with the Lord Jesus in the future. They put all the responsibility on God and forget that the Bible also says that some will suffer loss, and that though they will be saved, they will be saved so as through fire (1 Cor. 3:15). We have the most balanced and sensible teaching. Before a person believes in the Lord, the Lord takes all the responsibility for him. After he believes in the Lord, he has to take up his own responsibilities. The work of salvation is fully accomplished by the Lord on our behalf. Once a man believes, he will receive. The matter of reward is fully accomplished by the believers themselves. It is not enough just to believe. A sinner cannot be saved by good works. A believer cannot be rewarded by his faith. Salvation is based on faith, while reward is only based on work. Without faith one cannot be saved. Without work one cannot be rewarded. If we read the New Testament carefully, we will see how clearly God separates the matters of salvation and reward. Salvation is for the sinners, while reward is for the believers. Both are God's commandments. A sinner should be saved, and a believer should obtain reward. Those who are reluctant to accept either of these commandments are bound to suffer great loss. We must never mix salvation with reward.

What is to be saved? We know that it is to receive eternal life and to be delivered from perdition. However, this does not determine our position in glory. The latter is determined by the reward. What is the reward? According to the Bible, we can see that the reward is to reign with the Lord Jesus in the millennial kingdom. Every believer has eternal life, but not every believer will be rewarded with the kingship with the Lord Jesus. The kingdom of the heavens mentioned in the book of Matthew refers to the *heavenly part* of the millennial kingdom [5:3, note 4]. There, believers will reign with the Lord Jesus. Every careful reader of the Bible should see the difference between eternal life and the kingdom of the heavens. The Lord permitting, we will discuss this more at a future date. To receive eternal life requires only faith, but to receive the kingdom of the heavens requires our striving.

To be saved is to receive eternal life. To be rewarded is to enter the kingdom of the heavens. Brothers, let us press forward towards the mark! May God cause us to be willing to relinquish everything for His sake so that we can obtain His reward. Salvation is for now. It is obtained instantly because the Scripture says that he who believes in the Son has eternal life (John 3:36). To have is to obtain now. But reward is something for the future; we will be rewarded in the future. The Scripture says that not *until the Lord comes* will there be praise (1 Cor. 4:5). We will all be recompensed (2 Cor. 5:10). "Will" means something for the future. Salvation is for now, but reward is for the future. The two cannot be mixed. There is a great difference in principle between salvation and reward. Salvation shows God's *grace* because God does not recompense man according to his sins; when he believes in the Lord, he is saved. Reward shows God's *righteousness* because God recompenses according to the believers' good work; if they serve the Lord faithfully, they will be rewarded. We have to remember that God is not either gracious or righteous; He is both gracious and righteous. To save the sinner is an act of His grace. To reward the believer is an act of His righteousness. We have said that Revelation shows God's righteousness. Hence, to understand the distinction between salvation and reward is the necessary condition in understanding the book of Revelation. If one fails to understand the difference between salvation and reward, he will not be able to explain God's righteous way of dealing with the believers in Revelation.

God spoke the words of the eternal life through John. In the Gospels, He spoke of the way to receive eternal life. In the Epistles, He spoke of the expression of the eternal life. In Revelation, He spoke of the judgment for those who have received eternal life, that is, the saved ones. Hence, Revelation seldom touches the question of the believers' salvation; it touches the question of their reward. This book is on righteousness. Reward is God's act in righteousness. Hence, this book is concerning reward. This is why when we study chapters two and three, there is no mention of the matter of salvation. They cover the Christian life, work, and victory. This realization will help not only to explain chapters two and three but the doctrines in all the following chapters also. *(The Collected Works of Watchman Nee,* Vol. 3, pp. 128–134)

REWARD AND GIFT

Now we want to see the third difference—the difference between reward and gift, in other words, the difference between the kingdom and eternal life. There are many Christians in the church today who cannot differentiate between the kingdom of the heavens and eternal life. They think that the kingdom of the heavens is eternal life and that eternal life is simply the kingdom of the heavens. They have mixed up the Word of God, taking the condition for the receiving of the kingdom as the condition for the preservation of eternal life. They take the losing of the kingdom as the losing of eternal life. However, the distinction between these two is very clear in the Bible. One may lose the kingdom of the heavens, but he will not lose eternal life. One can lose the reward, but he will not lose the gift.

What then is the reward, and what is the gift? We were saved because of the gift. God gave the gift to us freely by His grace; therefore, we were saved. The reward pertains to the relationship between us and the Holy Spirit after we were saved. When we were saved, we were related to Christ. This relationship allows us to obtain the gift that we are absolutely unworthy of receiving. Similarly, after we have been saved, we have a relationship with the Holy Spirit. This relationship allows us to obtain the reward which we could not otherwise obtain by ourselves. If one believes in the Lord Jesus as Savior, accepting the Lord Jesus as life, this one is saved before God. After he is saved, God immediately puts this one on a pathway, so that he will run in the race and will obtain the reward placed before him. A Christian is saved because of the Lord Jesus. After he is saved, he has to manifest the victory of Christ by the Holy Spirit day by day. If one will do this, then at the end of the race, he will obtain the heavenly glory and the heavenly reward from God.

Hence, salvation is the first step of this path, and the reward is the last step. Only the saved ones are qualified to gain the reward. The unsaved ones are not qualified for this. God has given us two things rather than one thing. God places the gift before the worldly people and places the reward before the Christians. When one believes in Christ, he receives the gift. When one follows Christ, he receives the reward. Gift is obtained through faith, and it is for the worldly people. Reward is obtained by being faithful and having good deeds, and it is for the Christians.

There is a big mistake in the churches today. Man thinks that salvation is the only thing and that there is nothing else besides being saved. He takes the kingdom of the heavens and eternal life as the same thing. He considers that since one is saved when he believes, he no longer has to be concerned with works. The Bible makes a distinction between God's part and man's part. One part is the salvation given by God, and the other part is the glory of the millennial kingdom. To be saved has absolutely nothing to do with one's works. Once anyone believes in the Lord Jesus, he is saved. But after his salvation, God immediately places the second thing before him, telling him that besides salvation, there is a reward, a coming glory, a crown, and a throne for him. God puts His throne, crown, glory, and reward before the believers. If one is faithful, he will obtain these. If he is unfaithful, he will lose them.

Therefore, we do not say that good works are useless. However, we do say that good works are useless as far as salvation is concerned. Man cannot be saved by his good works. Neither can he be prevented from salvation by his evil works. Good works are applicable to the matter of the reward, the matter of the crown, the matter of the glory, and the matter of the throne. Good works are useless regarding the matter of salvation. God cannot allow man to be saved by his work; neither will He allow man to be rewarded by his faith. God cannot allow man to perish because of his evil works. God can determine only man's salvation or perdition by whether or not he believes in His Son. Similarly, God cannot determine a man's receiving of His glory by whether or not one believes in His Son. Whether or not you have His Son in you determines the matter of eternal life or perdition. Whether or not you have good works before God determines the matter of receiving the reward and the glory. In other words, God will never save a person because he has merits, and He will never reward one who has no merit. If someone has merits, God will not therefore save such a one. On the other hand, God will never reward anyone who has no merit. Man has to come before God totally helpless and meritless in order for God to save him. But after salvation, we have to be faithful, and we have to endeavor to produce good works through His Son Jesus Christ in order to obtain the reward.

Please do not think that good works are useless. We are

saying that good works are useless towards salvation. Good works have nothing to do with salvation at all. Salvation depends on whether or not you would repent of your former position. It depends on whether you would have regret over your past to believe in His work on the cross and in His resurrection as the proof of your justification. This is the crux of all problems. The matter of work is related to reward. Work is useful, but only in the matter of reward.

Today's problem is that people will not differentiate between salvation and the kingdom. In the Bible, there is a clear distinction between salvation and the kingdom and between the gift and the reward. Because people would not differentiate these matters, the question of salvation is mishandled, and the question of reward is also mishandled. God has never placed the matter of reward before the unsaved ones. God only wants the unsaved ones to obtain salvation. However, after salvation, God places the reward before them so that they will endeavor, pursue, and run after the reward. Salvation is not the last step of the Christian experience. Rather, salvation is its first step. After we have been saved, we have to run and pursue after the reward before us. The problem is that we think that our salvation is our reward. The sinners think that to be saved is to obtain the reward, and therefore they rely on their works. The Christians think that the glory is simply grace, and therefore they become foolish in their living. Please apply work only to reward and grace to salvation.

Through salvation, God separates the saved ones from the unsaved ones; He separates the ones having eternal life from those being condemned. Similarly, God also separates His children into two groups by His reward. Just as salvation separates the worldly people, in the same way, reward also separates God's children. God separates His children into the obedient and disobedient ones. With the worldly people, it is a matter of having faith and not having faith. With the Christians, it is a matter of being faithful or not being faithful. With the worldly people, it is a question of being saved or not being saved. With the Christians, it is a matter of having or not having the reward. Today's problem with God's children is that they magnify salvation too much; all that they see is simply salvation. They think that only when their work is taken care of can they be saved. As a result, they have no more time to pursue after the reward. If one has not passed through the first gate, he cannot pass through the second. May God be merciful to us that we would realize that the matter of salvation is solved already. It cannot be shaken, for it has been accomplished by the Lord Jesus already. It is fully done. Today what we have to strive for is the reward before us. There will be a big differentiation in the kingdom. Some will have glory, and some will not have glory.

Now we need to see on what basis reward is given. God's Word says that the reward is given because of work. Just as the Bible says clearly that salvation is by faith, in the same way the Bible says clearly that reward is by work. The Bible reveals to us that salvation is by the faith of the sinners, and the reward is by the work of the Christians. Faith is related to salvation; this is more than clear. Work is related to reward; this is also more than clear. One should not mix up these two.

Romans 4:4 says, "Now to the one who works, his wages are not accounted according to grace, but according to what is due." To give a reward to one who works is not grace, but a debt. In other words, how can one obtain a reward? Reward comes by works and not by grace.

Revelation 2:23 says, "And her children I will kill with

death; and all the churches will know that I am He who searches the inward parts and the hearts; and I will give to each one of you according to your works." This verse says that the Lord will make all the churches know that He is the One who searches the inward parts and the hearts, and will give to each one according to his works. In other words, He will reward each one according to his works. How does He reward or recompense? It is according to our work. Of course, this work is not our own work. We only wash our clothes to be white in the blood. When the Holy Spirit lives out Christ in us, we have the works of a Christian. Some will live out Christ, and some will not live out Christ. All the capital comes from Christ. All the power also originates from Christ. But some let the Lord work within them and some do not. Therefore, this verse clearly shows us the matter of recompense. The matter of reward depends on whether or not a Christian is worthy. Today, God will not save a person who is worthy, and in the future, God will not reward a Christian who is not worthy.

First Corinthians 3:14 says, "If anyone's work which he has built upon the foundation remains, he will receive a reward." Here it says that if his work remains, he will be rewarded. It does not say that if his faith remains he will be rewarded. The matter of reward depends on one's work. The Bible distinguishes clearly between salvation and reward. It never mixes up salvation and reward, and it never mixes up faith and work. Without faith, man cannot be saved. Without good works, man cannot be rewarded. One's works must withstand before the judgment seat and survive under the scrutiny of the burning eyes before there is the possibility of receiving a reward.

Luke 6:35 says, "But love your enemies, and do good and lend, expecting nothing in return, and your reward will be great." Reward is entirely due to one's work. To lend money to another without hoping to be repaid is your work, and to love your enemy is your work. You have to do these to obtain the reward. Nowhere does the Bible mention that one has to love his enemies and do good before he can receive eternal life. Neither is there any verse that says one has to lend to others before he can be saved, or that he has to lend to others before he can avoid perdition. But there is such a verse that says if you lend to others and do good to others, your reward in heaven will be great. Reward is of work and not of faith. Faith can save you, but faith cannot help you obtain the reward.

Second Timothy 4:14 says, "Alexander the coppersmith did many evil things to me; the Lord will recompense him according to his works." Here an example is cited. A Christian was trying to hurt Paul; he had sinned against Paul. The person mentioned here was a Christian. He was not a worldly person. In the future, Christians will be rewarded before God according to their works. *(The Gospel of God,* Vol. 2, pp. 394–395)

Chapter 10

The Believers

Man Composed of Three Parts

The Spirit, the Soul, and the Body

Most men today consider man as being made up of two parts: the soul and the body. The soul is the invisible part, the psychological part within man, and the body is the visible part, the outward form of man. This is man's fallen concept. Although there is some ground to it, it is not accurate. Outside of God's revelation, no ideas in this world are reliable. It is, of course, true that the body is the outward shell of man. But the Bible never mixes the soul with the spirit or considers the two as the same thing. In addition to being different terms, the soul and the spirit are actually two different substances; they are not the same. The Word of God has not divided man into two parts, the soul and the body. Rather, it has divided man into three parts: the spirit, the soul, and the body. First Thessalonians 5:23 says, "The God of peace Himself sanctify you wholly, and may your spirit and soul and body be preserved complete." This verse clearly divides a

THE RICHES OF WATCHMAN NEE

person into three parts: the spirit, the soul, and the body. Here the apostle mentioned the believers' being sanctified "wholly." This means that the whole being of the believers is to be sanctified. What did he mean when he said that a person is to be sanctified wholly? He meant that a person's spirit, soul, and body are to be preserved complete. This is very clear; a *complete* person has a spirit, a soul, and a body. This verse also tells us clearly that there is a distinction between the spirit and the soul. Otherwise, it would not have said "your spirit *and* soul." Instead, it would have said "your spirit-soul." Since God has spoken this, we can see that there is a distinction between man's spirit and his soul, and from this we can conclude that man is composed of three parts: spirit, soul, and body.

The Creation of Man

Genesis 2:7 says, "And the Lord God formed man of the dust of the ground, and breathed into his nostrils the breath of life; and man became a living soul." In the beginning, God created the figure of a man with the dust of the earth and then breathed into his nostrils "the breath of life." When the breath of life came in contact with man's body, the soul was produced. The soul is the consummation of man's body and his spirit. This is why the Bible calls man "a living soul." This "breath of life" is man's spirit, the source of man's life. The Lord Jesus tells us that "it is the Spirit who gives life" (John 6:63). This breath of life comes from the Creator. Yet we should not confuse this spirit, which is the "breath of life," with the Holy Spirit of God. There is a difference between the Holy Spirit and the human spirit. Romans 8:16 shows us that the spirit of man is different from the Holy Spirit; the two are not the same. "The Spirit Himself witnesses *with* our spirit that we are children of God." The word "life" in the expression "the breath of life" is *chay;* it is *plural* in number. This tells us that God's breathing produces two lives, a spiritual one and a soulish one. This means that when God's breath of life entered the human body, it became the spirit. At the same time, when this spirit came in contact with the body, it produced the soul. This is the source of the two lives, the spiritual life and the soulish life, within us. But we should make a distinction here: this spirit is not the life of God Himself; it is merely "the breath of the Almighty [which] hath given me life" (Job 33:4). It is not the entrance of the uncreated life of God into man. The spirit that was received in the beginning is not the life of God that we received at the time of our regeneration. The life which we received at the time of our regeneration is the life of God Himself; it is the life represented by the tree of life. This spirit of man is eternal, but it does not have the "eternal life."

"And the Lord God formed man of the dust of the ground." This refers to man's body. "And breathed into his nostrils the breath of life." This refers to the fact that man's spirit comes from God. This man then became "a living soul." This speaks of man's soul. When the spirit caused the body to come alive, man became a living soul, a living person with his own consciousness. A complete person is a tripartite being, a person with a spirit, a soul, and a body. According to this verse, man was created with two independent materials—spirit and body. When the spirit entered the body, the soul was produced. The soul is the result of the union of the spirit and the body. The body was dead, but when it met the spirit of life, a third entity was produced, the soul. Without the spirit, the body is dead. When the spirit came, the body became alive. When the spirit is in the body, something organic is produced. This something that is organic is called the soul.

Here it says that the man became "a living soul." This signifies not only that the soul is produced from the union between the spirit and the body, but that after the soul is produced from this union of the spirit and the body, both the spirit and the body are *incorporated* into the soul. In other words, the soul and the body are fully joined to the spirit, and the spirit and the body are incorporated into the soul. Before Adam fell, his spirit and his flesh were of course not in conflict with each other daily as it is with us today. The three elements of his being were *fully in harmony* one with another. These three were mingled together. The soul served as the linking chain, the seat of man's personality, making it possible for man to exist independently. The soul is the consummation of the spirit and the body, the totality of the elements within man. After man's spirit and body were fully integrated, man became a living soul. This soul is the very result of the union of the two things; it is man's own personality. We may consider an incomplete illustration: If we put a drop of ink into a cup of water, the ink and the water mingle together and become ink-water. You can say that it is ink; it is indeed ink. You can also say that it is water, for it is still water. The ink and the water are integrated together and have become a third thing—ink-water. (Of course, the soul produced from the union of the spirit and the body is an independent and insoluble element, just as the spirit and the body are.) In the same way, the spirit and the body were two independent elements, but after they combined, the combination became a living soul.

God characterizes man by his *soul* because in His creation man's characteristics lie in his soul. This is similar to the angels being characterized by their spirit. Man is not only a body, and he is not only a body with the breath of life, but he has become a living soul. This is why later on in the Bible we see God calling man a "soul"; He did not call man a man, but He called him a soul. The reason for this is that a man is judged by his soul. The soul represents the man and expresses the characteristics of his personality. The soul is the organ of man's free will, and both the spirit and the body are incorporated into it. It has a free will. If it chooses to obey God, it can make the spirit the master of everything, according to God's design. But it can also suppress the spirit and take as its master the part that it likes. The three things—the spirit, the soul, and the body—are like a lighted electric bulb. Within a bulb, there is the electricity, the filament, and the light. The body is like the filament, the spirit is like the electricity, and the soul is like the light. Electricity is the source of light, and light is the consequence of electricity. The filament is a physical material for conducting electricity and for emitting the light. When the spirit and the body combine together, they produce the soul. The soul bears the characteristics of the combination of the spirit and the body; it is the product of the union of the two things. The spirit is the motivating force behind the soul, while the body is the means to express the soul. This is like electricity being the source of light, while the filament is the means through which light shines.

However, we should clearly remember that in this life the soul is man's consummate expression, while in the next life and in resurrection, the spirit will be man's consummate expression. This is why the Bible says, "It is sown a soulish body, it is raised a spiritual body" (1 Cor. 15:44). Since we are now joined to the resurrected Lord, through Him the spirit can control our whole being. We can control our being because we are not joined to the first man Adam, who was a living soul, but to the last Adam, who is the life-giving Spirit.

The Temple and Man

The apostle said in 1 Corinthians 3:16, "Do you not know that you are the temple of God, and that the Spirit of God dwells in you?" After reading this verse, we can see that the apostle was inspired to consider man a temple. Just as God dwelt in the temple in time past, in the same way the Holy Spirit dwells in the believers. The Bible compares man to the temple. In doing so it depicts the three elements of man most conspicuously.

We know that the temple is divided into three parts. The first part is the outer court, which everyone can see and into which everyone can go. All outward worship is offered to God here. Further in, there is the Holy Place. Here, only the priests can enter. In the Holy Place the priests offer the blood, the oil, the incense, and the bread to God. Although they are very close, they are not the closest, because they are still outside the veil and cannot enter into God's presence. God dwells in the Holy of Holies from which He radiates His infinite glory. The Holy of Holies is *otherwise* dark. No one can come before Him. Although the high priest is allowed once a year to enter the Holy of Holies, this only demonstrates all the more that before the rending of the veil there was no one within the veil.

Man is a temple of God. Within man there are also three parts. The body is like the outer court; it is outside, and its life is seen by all. It is here that man should obey all God's commandments. It is also here that God's Son died for man. Further in, there is man's soul, which is the inward life in man; it includes man's feelings, will, and mind. This is the Holy Place to a regenerated one. His love, thoughts, and desires are all here. In this place there is much light, everything is clear and obvious, and the priests come in and out to serve God. However, further in, there is the Holy of Holies behind the veil, which is unreachable by human light and is a place invisible to the human eyes. This is "the secret place of the Most High" (Psa. 91:1). It is the habitation of God, a place that no man can reach unless God removes the veil. This is the hu-man spirit. Man not only has a body and a soul but a spirit as well. This spirit is deeper than man's consciousness; it is the place unreachable by man's feelings. It is in this place that man fellowships with God.

In the Holy of Holies there is no light, for this is God's habitation. In the Holy Place there is light because there is the lampstand with seven branches. In the outer court everything is exposed under the sun. This is a picture of a regenerated person. His spirit is like the Holy of Holies, where God dwells. This place is entered by faith and is totally dark. This is a place which the believer cannot see, feel, or understand. The soul is like the Holy Place, where there is much power of understanding, many thoughts, much knowledge, and many rules and where one comprehends both the things in the psychological world and the things in the physical world. In this place there is the shining of the lampstand. The body is like the outer court; it is seen by all. All its activities and living are visible to everyone.

The order that God gives to us can never be wrong. It is: "spirit and soul and body" (1 Thess. 5:23). It is not "soul and spirit and body," nor is it "body and soul and spirit." Rather, it is "spirit and soul and body." The spirit is the noblest; hence, it is mentioned first. The body is the lowest; hence, it is mentioned last. The soul lies in between; hence, it is placed in between the soul and the body. After we have clearly seen God's order, we will see the wisdom God has in comparing man to the temple. We see how the Holy of Holies, the Holy Place, and the outer court correspond with the order and the degree of importance of the spirit, the soul, and the body.

The work of the temple revolves around the revelation in the Holy of Holies. All the actions in the outer court and the Holy Place are determined by the presence of God in the Holy of Holies. The holiest place within the temple and the place which all other places are subject to and depend on is the Holy of Holies. In the Holy of Holies there does not seem to be much work; it is very dark. All the activities are in the Holy Place. All the works in the outer court are controlled by the priests in the Holy Place. Indeed, the Holy of Holies is a quiet and still place. Yet all the activities of the Holy Place are directed by the inspiration of the Holy of Holies.

The spiritual significance of this is not difficult to understand. The soul is the organ of our personality. It includes the mind, the will, the emotion, etc. The soul appears to be the master of the activities of the whole being. Even the body is under its direction. Yet before man fell, although there were many activities and works with the soul, they were all under the control of the spirit. God's order is: (1) the spirit, (2) the soul, and (3) the body. *(The Spiritual Man,* Vol. 1, pp. 3, 5–8, 11–13)

REGENERATED WITH THE LIFE OF GOD

Before man is regenerated, his spirit is far away from God and is dead. The meaning of death is to be separated from life. The ultimate name of life is God. Since death means to be separated from life, and God is life, then to be dead is to be separated from God. Man's spirit apart from God is deadened, having no fellowship with Him. The soul controls the whole man so that he lives either in his ideas or in excitement. The lusts and desires of the body bring the soul into subjection.

Man's spirit became deadened; therefore, there is the need for the spirit to be resurrected. The rebirth which the Lord Jesus spoke about to Nicodemus is the rebirth of the spirit. To be born again is not a matter related to our body, as Nicodemus thought, nor is it a matter related to our soul, because not only is the "body of sin" to be made of none effect (Rom. 6:6), but also "they who are of Christ Jesus have crucified the flesh with its passions and its lusts" (this is the soul) (Gal. 5:24). We ought to especially emphasize that regeneration is the impartation of God's life into man's spirit. Because Christ has made redemption for our soul and destroyed the principle of the flesh, we who are one with Him can have a share in His resurrected, deathless life. Our being one with Christ's death and our initial step of obtaining His resurrection life are in our spirit. To be born again is completely a matter in the spirit; it has no relationship with the soul or the body.

"The spirit of man is the lamp of the Lord" (Prov. 20:27). At the time of regeneration the Holy Spirit comes into us. He enters into man's spirit like the lighting of a lamp. This is the "new spirit" spoken of in Ezekiel 36:26. Because the old spirit was dead, the Holy Spirit puts the uncreated life of God inside it, causing it to have life and to live.

Before regeneration, man's soul ruled over his spirit. His "self" dominated his soul. His lust governed his body. The soul became the life of the spirit, the "self" became the life of the soul, and the lust became the life of the body. After man's regeneration, the Holy Spirit rules his spirit, causing his spirit to govern his soul, then through the soul to rule over his body. Now the Holy Spirit becomes the life of the spirit, and the spirit becomes the life of the entire being.

At the time of regeneration, the Holy Spirit revives the human spirit and renews it. In the Bible, regeneration refers to the step in which a man comes out of death and enters into life. This regeneration, like the physical birth, occurs only once, and once is sufficient. It is at this time of rebirth that man receives God's own life, is born of God, and becomes God's child. "Being renewed" in the Bible refers to the Holy Spirit's work of increasingly filling and permeating our being with His life and thus completely overcoming our life in the flesh. It is a lengthy, continuous, and progressive work. In such a regenerated one, the original order of the spirit and the soul is restored.

There is another point we ought to pay attention to. That is, regeneration not only restores us to the condition of Adam before his fall, but it also affords us something additional. Adam had a "spirit," but that spirit was only created by God and did not contain the uncreated life of God Himself, as signified by the tree of life. There was no life-relationship between Adam and God. As the angels were called sons of God, Adam was also called a son of God (Luke 3:38), because he was created directly by God. We who believe in the Lord Jesus are "begotten" of God (John 1:12–13) and thus have a life relationship with God. The life of a father is the life inherited by the sons. Since we are born of God, we automatically have the life of God (2 Pet. 1:4). If Adam had been willing to receive the life which God offered him by means of the tree of life, Adam would have had the eternal life, the uncreated life of God. His spirit came from God and exists forever, but how this life would become everlasting depended on how he regarded God's command and how he made his choice. What we Christians obtain at regeneration is God's life, a life which was possible for Adam to obtain, but he did not obtain it. Regeneration serves not only to restore man's spirit and soul from the original state of confusion and darkness, but furthermore, puts man in possession of the supernatural life of God.

Man's deadened, fallen spirit is made alive by receiving God's life imparted through the power of the Holy Spirit. This is regeneration. The basis upon which the Holy Spirit regenerates man is the cross (please read John 3:14–15). The eternal life in John 3:16 is the life of God which is put into man's spirit by the Holy Spirit. Because this life is God's life, which can never die, all who have been regenerated have this life and are said to "have eternal life." If God's life were to die, man's eternal life would immediately perish!

After regeneration, man's relationship with God is that of birth. Regardless of what happens, once a man has been born of God, God cannot deny that He has begotten him. Therefore, man, once born of God, despite how long eternity may be, has a relationship and position which cannot be canceled. Man obtains this through regeneration by believing in the Lord Jesus as Savior and not through his progress, spirituality, or holiness gained after believing in the Lord. What God gives to the regenerated ones is eternal life. Therefore, this position and life can never be annulled.

When man is regenerated, he obtains God's life. This is *the starting point of a Christian life. This is the minimum for every believer.* Whoever has not believed in the death of the Lord Jesus and received a supernatural life which he originally did not have, regardless of how zealously he may be progressing in the areas of religion, morality, and learning, is still a dead man in God's sight. *All who do not have God's own life are dead.*

With regeneration as the starting point, the spiritual life now has the possibility to grow. This rebirth is the first step in the spiritual life. At such a time the spiritual life is complete but not mature. The capabilities of this life are complete and able to reach the highest plane. However, because this life is newly born, it is not grown-up or mature. It is like a fruit which is green; the life is complete, but it is still unripe. The completeness is in its life capabilities, not yet in all of its organic parts. Man's regeneration is the same. After regeneration there is still an immensely great capacity in God's life that will allow him to advance unceasingly. From here on, the Holy Spirit can lead him forward until the body and soul are totally overcome.

How can one know whether or not he has been regenerated? John 1 has already told us that a man is born anew because of his believing in the name of the Son of God and his receiving Him. The name of God's Son is "Jesus." *Jesus* means "He. . .will save His people from their sins" (Matt. 1:21). Therefore, to believe in the name of the Son of God is to believe in Him as the Savior from sins, to believe that He died on the cross for my sins that He might save me from the punishment and power of sin, and thus to receive Him as my Savior. Therefore, if any man wants to know whether or not he has been regenerated, he only need ask himself whether he has come to the cross as a helpless sinner to *receive* the Lord Jesus as his Savior. If he has done so, he has been regenerated. All who believe in the Lord Jesus are regenerated. *(The Spiritual Man,* Vol. 1, pp. 47, 52–54, 68)

MEMBERS OF THE BODY OF CHRIST

The Difference between Being a Member and Being a Christian

The New Testament shows us that there is a difference between being a member and being a Christian. Being a Christian is something individualistic, whereas being a member is something corporate. Being a Christian is something one does for himself, whereas being a member is something for the Body. In the Bible there are many terms with opposite meanings, such as purity and uncleanness, holiness and commonness, victory and defeat, the Spirit and the flesh, Christ and Satan, the kingdom and the world, and glory and shame. All these are opposites. In the same way, the Body is in opposition to the individual. Just as the Father is versus the world, the Spirit is versus the flesh, and the Lord is versus the devil, so also is the Body versus the individual. Once a man sees the Body of Christ, he is free from individualism. He will no longer live for himself but for the Body. Once I am delivered from individualism, I am spontaneously in the Body.

The Body of Christ is not a doctrine; it is a realm. It is not a teaching, but a life. Many Christians seek to teach the truth of the Body, but few know the life of the Body. The Body of Christ is an experience in a totally different realm. A man can know the book of Romans without being justified. Similarly, a man can know the book of Ephesians without seeing the Body of Christ. We do not need knowledge; rather, we need revelation to know the reality of the Body of Christ and to enter the realm of the Body. Only a revelation from God will usher us into the realm of the Body, and only then will the Body of Christ become our experience.

In Acts 2 it seems as if Peter was preaching the gospel alone and that three thousand people were saved through him. But we must remember that the other eleven apostles were standing beside him. The Body of Christ was preaching the gospel; it was not the preaching of an individual. If we have the view of the Body, we will see that individualism will not bring us anywhere.

If we realize that a Christian is nothing more than a member, we will no longer be proud. Everything depends on our seeing. Those who see that they are members will surely treasure the Body and honor the other members. They will not see just their own virtues; they will readily see others as being better than themselves.

Every member has a function, and all the functions are for the Body. The function of one member is the function of the whole Body. When one member does something, the whole Body does it. When the mouth speaks, the whole body is speaking. When the hands work, the whole body is working. When the legs walk, the whole body is walking. We cannot divide the members from the body. Therefore, the movement of the members of the Body must be focused around the Body. Everything that the members do should be for the Body. Ephesians 4 says that the Body is growing into a full-grown man. It does not say that individuals are growing into full-grown men. In chapter three the ability to know the love of Christ and to apprehend the Lord's breadth, length, height, and depth is with all the saints. No one can know or apprehend by himself. An individual does not have the time or the capacity to experience the love of Christ in that kind of way.

First Corinthians 12:14 through 31 speaks of two erroneous concepts that members may have: (1) "Because I am not. . .I am not of the body" (v. 15). This is to despise oneself and covet the work of others. (2) "I have no need of you" (v. 21). This is to be proud of oneself, thinking that one man can be all-inclusive, and despising others. Both concepts are harmful to the Body. We should not imitate other members or be covetous of other members. In this way we will not become discouraged and give up when we find that we cannot be like others. At the same time, we should not despise other members, thinking that we are better and more useful.

The Consciousness of the Body

In the church life, we should learn to have the consciousness of the Body. When we are at odds with the brothers and sisters, it means that we are surely at odds with God. Some Christians are like butterflies; they act independently. Others are like bees; they live and move together. The butterfly flies from flower to flower, going its own sweet way; but the bee works for the hive. The butterfly lives and works individually, but the bee has a body-consciousness. We should all be like bees, having the consciousness of the Body so that we can live together with other members in the Body of Christ. Wherever there is Body-revelation, there is Body-consciousness, and wherever there is Body-consciousness, individual thought and action are automatically ruled out. Seeing Christ results in deliverance from sin; seeing the Body results in deliverance from individualism. Seeing the Body and deliverance from individualism are not two things but one. As soon as we see the Body, our life and work as individuals cease. It is not a matter of changing our attitude or conduct; revelation does the work. We cannot enter the realm of the Body by anything other than seeing. A real inward seeing settles the whole problem. *(The Mystery of Christ,* pp. 16–19)

SANCTIFIED WITH THE DIVINE NATURE

God's desire is for sons who shall be joint-heirs with Christ in glory. That is His goal; but how can He bring that about? Turn now to Hebrews 2:10 and 11: "It became him, for whom are all things, and through whom are all things, in bringing many sons unto glory, to make the author of their salvation perfect through sufferings. For both he that sanctifieth and they that are sanctified are all of one: for which cause he is not ashamed to call them brethren."

There are two parties mentioned here, namely, "many sons" and "the author of their salvation," or, in different terms, "he that sanctifieth" and "they that are sanctified." But these two parties are said to be "all of one." The Lord Jesus as Man derived His life from God, and (in another sense, but just as truly) we derive our new life from God. He was "begotten. . .of the Holy Ghost" (Matt. 1:20 mg.), and we were "born of. . .the Spirit," "born. . .of God" (John 3:5; 1:13). So, God says, we are all of One. "Of" in the Greek means "out of." The first begotten Son and the many sons are all (though in different senses) "out of" the one Source of life. Do you realize that we have the same life today that God has? The life which He possesses in heaven is the life which He has imparted to us here on the earth. That is the precious "gift of God" (Rom. 6:23). It is for this reason that we can live a life of holiness, for it is not our own life that has been changed, but the life of God that has been imparted to us. *(The Collected Works of Watchman Nee,* Vol. 33, pp. 81–82)

CHAPTER 11

THE CHURCH

THE UNIVERSAL CHURCH AND THE LOCAL CHURCHES

The Word of God teaches us that the Church is one. Why then did the apostles found separate churches in each of the places they visited? If the *Church* is the Body of Christ, it cannot but be one. Then how does it come about that we speak of *churches?*

The word "church" means "the called-out ones." The term is used twice in the Gospels, once in Matthew 16:18 and once in Matthew 18:17, and we meet in quite frequently in the Acts and the Epistles. In the Gospels the word is used on both occasions by our Lord, but it is employed in a somewhat different sense each time.

"You are Peter, and upon this rock I will build My church, and the gates of Hades shall not prevail against it" (Matt. 16:18). What church is this? Peter confessed that Jesus was the Christ, the Son of the living God, and our Lord declared that He would build His Church upon this confession—the confession that as to His Person He is the Son of God, and as to His work He is the Christ of God. This Church comprises all the saved, without reference to time or space, that is, all who in the purpose of God are redeemed by virtue of the shed blood of the Lord Jesus, and are born again by the operation of His Spirit. This is the Church universal, the Church of God, the Body of Christ.

"And if he refuses to hear them, tell it to the church" (Matt. 18:17). The word "church" is used here in quite a different sense from the sense in Matthew 16:18. The sphere of the church referred to here is clearly not as wide as the sphere of the Church mentioned in the previous passage. The Church there is a Church that knows nothing of time or place, but the church here is obviously limited both to time and place, for it is one that can hear you speak. The Church mentioned in chapter sixteen includes all the children of God in every locality, while the church mentioned in chapter eighteen includes only the children of God living in one locality; and it is because it is limited to one place that it is possible for you to tell your difficulties to the believers of whom it is composed. Obviously, the church here is local, not universal, for no one could speak at one time to all the children of God throughout the universe. It is only possible to speak at one time to the believers living in one place.

We have clearly two different aspects of the Church before us—the Church and the churches, the universal Church and the local churches. The Church is invisible; the churches are visible. The Church has no organization; the churches are organized. The Church is spiritual; the churches are spiritual and yet physical. The Church is purely an organism; the churches are an organism, yet at the same time they are organized, which is seen by the fact that elders and deacons hold office there.

All Church difficulties arise in connection with the local

churches, not with the universal Church. The latter is invisible and spiritual, therefore beyond the reach of man, while the former is visible and organized, therefore still liable to be touched by human hands. The heavenly Church is so far removed from the world that it is possible to remain unaffected by it, but the earthly churches are so close to us, that if problems arise there we feel them acutely. The invisible Church does not test our obedience to God, but the visible churches test us severely by facing us with issues on the intensely practical plane of our earthly life.

The Basis of the Churches

In the Word of God we find "the church of God" spoken of in the singular (1 Cor. 10:32), but we find the same Word referring to the "churches of God" in the plural (1 Thess. 2:14). How has this unity become a plurality? How has the Church which is essentially one become many? The Church of God has been divided into the churches of God on the one ground of difference of locality. [The word "divided" is used here in its purest sense.] Locality is the only scriptural basis for the division of the Church into churches.

The seven churches in Asia, referred to in the book of Revelation, comprised the church in Ephesus, the church in Smyrna, the church in Pergamos, the church in Thyatira, the church in Sardis, the church in Philadelphia, and the church in Laodicea. They were seven churches, not one. Each was distinct from the others on the ground of the difference of locality. It was only because the believers did not reside in one place that they did not belong to one church. There were seven different churches simply because the believers lived in seven different places. Ephesus, Smyrna, Pergamos, Thyatira, Sardis, Philadelphia, and Laodicea are clearly all the names of places. Not only were the seven churches in Asia founded on the basis of locality, but all the churches mentioned in Scripture were founded on the same basis. Throughout the Word of God we can find no name attached to a church save the name of a place, for example, the church in Jerusalem, the church in Lystra, the church in Derbe, the church in Colosse, the church in Troas, the church in Thessalonica, the church in Antioch. This fact cannot be overemphasized, that *in Scripture no other name but the name of a locality is ever connected with a church, and division of the Church into churches is solely on the ground of difference of locality.*

Spiritually, the Church of God is one; therefore, it cannot be divided—but physically its members are scattered throughout the earth; therefore, they cannot possibly live in one place. Yet it is essential that there be a physical gathering together of believers. It is not enough that they be present "in the spirit"; they must also be present "in the flesh." Now a church is composed of all "the called-out ones assembled" in one place for worship, prayer, fellowship, and ministry. This assembling together is absolutely essential to the life of a church. Without it, there may be believers scattered throughout the area, but there is really no church. *The Church* exists because of the existence of its members, and it does not require that they meet in a physical way; but it is essential to the very existence of *a church* that its members gather together in a physical way. It is in this latter sense that the word "church" is used in 1 Corinthians 14. The phrase "in the church" (vv. 19, 23, 28) means "in the church meetings." A church is a church assembled. These believers are not separated from other believers in any respect but that of their dwelling places. As long as they continue in the flesh, they will be limited by space, and this physical limitation, which in the very nature of things makes it impossible for God's people to meet in one place, is the only basis sanctioned by God for the forming of separate churches. Christians belong to different churches for the sole reason that they live in different places. That division is merely external. In reality the Church as the Body of Christ cannot be divided; therefore, even when the Word of God refers to the different assemblies of His people, the places named vary, but it is still "the church" in every one of these places, such as "the church in Ephesus," "the church in Smyrna," "the church in Pergamos."

In the New Testament there is one method, and one alone, of dividing the Church into churches, and that God-ordained method is division on the basis of locality. All other methods are man-made, not God-given. May the Spirit of God engrave this truth deeply on our hearts, that the only reason for the division of God's children into different churches is because of the different places in which they live.

What is a New Testament church? It is not a building, a gospel hall, a preaching center, a mission, a work, an organization, a system, a denomination, or a sect. People may apply the term "church" to any of the above; nevertheless, they are not churches. A New Testament church is the meeting together for worship, prayer, fellowship, and mutual edification, of all the people of God in a given locality, on the ground that they are Christians in the same locality. The Church is the Body of Christ; a church is a miniature Body of Christ. All the believers in a locality form the church in that locality, and in a small way, they ought to show forth what the Church should show forth. They are the Body of Christ in that locality, so they have to learn how to come under the headship of the Lord, and how to manifest oneness among all the

members, guarding carefully against schism and division.
(The Normal Christian Church Life, pp. 51–55)

THE KINGDOM OF GOD

*God Desires That the Church Be
the Kingdom of God*

The Lord came to the earth to establish God's kingdom.
There are two sides to the gospel. On the one hand, there
is the individual aspect. On the other hand, there is the corporate aspect. Individually, the gospel gives eternal life to
those who believe. Corporately, the gospel calls people to repentance unto the kingdom of God. God's eyes are upon the
kingdom. In the Lord's prayer in Matthew 6:9–13, the kingdom is spoken of at the beginning and the end. Verse 10 says,
"Your kingdom come; Your will be done, as in heaven, so also
on earth." The kingdom of God is the sphere where His will
is accomplished in an unhindered way. Verse 13 says, "For
Yours is the kingdom and the power and the glory forever.
Amen." The kingdom, the power, and glory are related. Revelation 12:10 says, "Now has come the salvation and the
power and the kingdom of our God and the authority of His
Christ." The kingdom is the sphere of authority. In Luke
17:21 the Lord said, "For behold, the kingdom of God is in
the midst of you." (He did not say that it is in you.) This word
indicates that the Lord Jesus is the kingdom of God. For the
Lord Jesus to be in the midst of you is for the kingdom of God
to be in the midst of you, because the authority of God is fully
executed in Him. The kingdom of God is upon the Lord.
It is also upon the church. Because the Lord's life has been

released to the church, His kingdom must also be propagated and established through the church. From the time of Noah, God established a kingdom. But that was just a kingdom of man; it was not the kingdom of God. The kingdom of God began with the Lord Jesus, but how small was its sphere! Today the one grain of wheat has produced many grains. Today the sphere of the kingdom of God is not limited to the Lord alone. It is also in the many believers.

God's purpose is not only for us to become the church, but also for the church to become the kingdom of God. She is to be the sphere of God's kingdom, the place where God executes His authority. Hence, God's desire is not only to gain ground in a few, but to have the whole church free from rebellion. There must be an absolute submission and an absolute position for God so that His authority can be perfectly carried out. In this way authority is established among God's creatures. Not only does God want man to submit to His direct authority, He wants man to submit to all of His appointed, deputy authorities as well. God does not ask for a little submission; He demands a perfect submission.

*The Gospel Being Not Only for Man to Believe
but Also for Man to Submit*

The Bible speaks not only of faith. It also speaks of obedience. We are not only sinners; we are sons of disobedience. In Romans 10:16 we have the obedience to the gospel. In principle believing in the gospel is obeying the gospel. Second Thessalonians 1:8 says, "Rendering vengeance to those who do not know God and to those who do not obey the gospel of our Lord Jesus Christ." Those who do not obey are those who rebel. Romans 2:8 speaks of those who are disobedient to the truth. This is also rebellion, and God will render wrath and anger to those who rebel against the truth. First Peter 1:22 says, "Since you have purified your souls by your obedience to the truth. . ." By this we see that salvation comes through obedience. To believe is to obey. A disciple in faith should really be a disciple in obedience. Not only must there be the faith; there must also be the submission to the Lord's authority. When Paul was enlightened, he said, "What shall I do, Lord?" (Acts 22:10). He not only believed in the Lord; he became obedient to the Lord. Paul's conversion not only made him realize grace, but also made him submit to authority. When he was moved by the Holy Spirit to see the authority of the gospel, he acknowledged Jesus as Lord.

God has called us not only to receive life through faith, but also to maintain His authority through obedience. God's plan for us in the church is for us to submit to His authority and to all the authorities He has established. This covers our home, our government, our school, the church, and so forth. He does not want to specifically mark out whom we should submit to. As long as we have met God's authority in the Lord, we should learn to submit to authority.

Many can submit and be obedient if they are under certain ones, but to others they cannot submit. This is due to a failure in seeing authority. It is useless to submit to man. What is needed is to see authority. All kinds of systems are for us to learn submission. After a man has touched authority, a slight disobedience will cause him to have an inward sense of rebellion. Those who do not know authority do not realize how rebellious they are. Before Paul was enlightened, he did not know that he was kicking against the goads (26:14). After a man is enlightened, he will first see authority. Then he will see many authorities. When Paul met a little brother, Ananias, he did not see just a man. He did not ask who Ananias was or whether or not he was educated. He recognized Ananias as a sent authority, a deputy authority. Therefore, Paul submitted to him (9:17–18). How easy it is to submit when one has met authority!

*God Desires to Make the Nations
the Kingdom of God through the Church*

If the church does not take God's authority, He has no way to establish His kingdom. First, God gained the kingdom in the Lord Jesus. Then He established His kingdom in the church. In the end His kingdom will be established on the whole earth. One day there will be a declaration, "The kingdom of the world has become the kingdom of our Lord and of His Christ" (Rev. 11:15). Between the time in which the kingdom was in the Lord Jesus individually and the kingdom of the world becomes the kingdom of our Lord and of His Christ, there is the church. Only when the kingdom was established in the Lord Jesus could it be established in the church. Only when the kingdom is established in the church can the kingdom of the world become the kingdom of God. Without the Lord Jesus, there is no church. Without the church, there is no expansion of the kingdom of God.

When the Lord was on earth, He was obedient even in the smallest thing. For example, He was not negligent in the matter of paying the temple tax. Even when there was no money, a coin was found in the mouth of a fish to pay it (Matt. 17:24–27). He also said, "Render then the things that are Caesar's to Caesar and the things that are God's to God"

(22:21). Although Caesar was rebellious, he was set up by God, and as such, one must obey him. When our obedience is perfect, the Lord will rebuke the disobedient ones. When we become submissive, the kingdom can be expanded to the whole earth. Many have strong feelings concerning sin, but they have no feeling concerning rebellion. Man must not only have the consciousness of sin; he must also have the consciousness of authority. Without the consciousness of sin, one cannot be a disciple of Christ. Without the consciousness of authority, one cannot be a disciple of submission.

The Church Must Submit to God's Authority

We have to know how to submit in the church. There is not a single authority in the church that we can ignore. God wants to see the kingdom issuing forth from the church. He wants all authority to be executed through the church. When the church is so submissive, the earth will submit to the authority of God. If the church will not give the kingdom of God a free way, the kingdom of God will have no way among the nations. For this reason, the church is the highway to the kingdom. If this is not the case, the church will become a hindrance to the kingdom.

Today, if the church cannot submit to God because of a little difficulty, how can the kingdom of God be manifested? When men reason with one another and argue with one another, how can God's kingdom come? We have delayed God. We must rid ourselves of all disobedience so that God will have a free way. When the church submits, the nations will submit. For this reason, the church bears a great and heavy responsibility. When God's life, God's will, and God's commands are executed in the church, the kingdom will come. *(Authority and Submission,* pp. 149–153)

THE HOUSE, THE DWELLING PLACE, AND THE TEMPLE OF GOD

Fifth, the church is not only a Body. When the individual Christians come together before God, they become a temple. Every Christian is like a stone, and the church is the spiritual house that God is building. The Lord Jesus is the foundation of this spiritual temple. He is a great stone. Every Christian is a small stone built upon the Lord Jesus to become the temple of God and the habitation of God. This is what is spoken of in 1 Peter 2:5. If there were a possibility for Christians to perish, the temple of God would become more unsightly than our run-down meeting hall; one minute the stones would be taken out, and another minute they would be put back in again, and the walls would be full of holes. If that were the case, why would God not make up His mind before He saved men? God intends that we be built up into a spiritual house. If it is a spiritual house, then not one stone can be lost. If any stone can be lost, the spiritual house would be in trouble and would not be up to standard.

The Old Testament record in 1 Kings 6:7 tells us how the temple of Solomon was built. Chapter five is an account of Solomon sending men to the mountains to cut the stones. The stones were cut in the mountains. By chapter six, they were moved to mount Moriah for the building. Hence, when the temple was being built, there was no sound from iron tools. There was no need for further cutting.

The skilled workmen had calculated accurately and prepared everything on the mountain before the materials were moved to the building. There was no more need of improvement; everything was done properly. If, while building the earthly temple, Solomon's skilled men could cut the stones so well that they were exact in every way and had no need for improvement, could God change us, the living stones, once every two or three days when He builds the spiritual temple? Could God have such oversight? Would God not know how to calculate? Is God worse than man? In the Old Testament, God used men to build. In the New Testament, He builds by Himself. Is God's own work inferior to man's? If the believers are stones for the building of the spiritual house, can they be lost? Therefore, if we are in God's temple, we can never be lost. *(The Gospel of God,* Vol. 2, pp. 303–304)

THE BODY OF CHRIST

In this message we will speak on the Body of Christ. In the New Testament, Paul was the only apostle who used the expression *the Body of Christ* to denote the church. In other places in the New Testament, the church is called the temple of God, the household of God, etc. But Paul specifically said that the church is the Body of Christ. The subject here is not us becoming the sons of God or becoming Christians. We are talking about how the church becomes the Body of Christ. We can say that the church is Christ in a different form. Christ was the only begotten Son of God. Now He has become the Firstborn. Christ plus all the sons—the church —is the one Body. There are no individual persons in the church; there is only Christ in the church. Anything that issues from Christ is the church. The church comes fully out of Christ and is one with Christ. There is no need for a Christian to do anything or change anything in order to be in Christ. As long as a man is regenerated, he is in Christ and becomes a part of the Body of Christ.

The Body of Christ Being the Expression of Christ

What is the Body of Christ? The Body of Christ is the continuation of Christ's life on earth. When He came to the earth and lived on earth, He expressed Himself through a body. Today He still requires a body to express Himself. Just as a man needs a body to express all that he is, Christ needs a body to express Himself. The function of the Body is to be the full expression of Christ. We cannot manifest our personality through any one member of our body— the ears, mouth, eyes, hands, or feet—alone. Similarly, Christ cannot manifest His personality through any one member of His Body. It takes His whole Body to manifest Him. We must see that everything of Christ is expressed through His Body. This is not all. The Body of Christ is the extension and continuation of Christ on earth. He spent more than thirty years on earth to reveal Himself. He did this as the individual Christ. Today He is revealing Himself through the church. This is the corporate Christ. Formerly, Christ was expressed individually; now He is expressed corporately.

*The Body of Christ Being
the Corporate Vessel to Fulfill God's Plan*

God is after a corporate vessel, not individual vessels. He is not choosing a few zealous, consecrated ones to work for Him individually. Individual vessels cannot fulfill God's goal and plan. God has chosen the church, and He is after the church. Only the church as the corporate Christ can fulfill God's goal and plan.

Consider our human body. No member of our body can act independently. It is impossible for a body to depend on one hand or one leg. However, if the body loses a member, it will not be complete. The Body of Christ is composed of all the believers. Every believer is a member in the Body of Christ, and every believer is indispensable.

The Body of Christ is a reality. The church life is also a reality. The Word of God does not say the church is *like* the Body of Christ; it says the church *is* the Body of Christ. Nothing external can become part of our physical bodies. We may clothe our bodies, but the clothes do not become part of our bodies. Nothing that is of us can ever become part of the Body of Christ, because "Christ is all and in all" in the Body (Col. 3:11). Anything in us that is not a part of Christ frustrates our inward knowledge of the Body of Christ. Sin hinders us from seeing Christ, and the natural life hinders us from seeing the Body. We all must see our position in the Body of Christ. If we truly see our position in the Body, it will be as though we were saved a second time.

The Adamic life is individualistic and independent. Even though everyone in Adam shares the same life, there is no fellowship among them. We all commit sin, yet we each take our own way. Everyone in Adam lives as separate individuals.

In Christ everything that is individualistic is ruled out. If we want to know the Body life, we need deliverance not only from our sinful life and our natural life, but also from our individualistic life. All individual elements must go because nothing that is individualistic can reach God's goal. *(The Mystery of Christ,* pp. 11, 15–16)

THE BRIDE OF CHRIST

In the Lord's eyes, the church has two positions: as to her life, the church is the Body of Christ, but regarding her future, she is the bride of Christ. As to the union of Christ with the church, the church is His Body; regarding the intimate relationship of Christ with the church, the church is His bride.

Whenever God's Word speaks of the oneness between Christ and the church, we see Christ as the Head and the church as His Body. Whenever the Word shows the distinction between Christ and the church, we see the church as the bride to Christ. Adam and Eve were spoken of as two becoming "one flesh," but they were still two persons; God still counted them as two. Adam was Adam, and Eve was Eve. They were united to be one. This is the relationship between the church and Christ. From one they became two, and from two they became one. When God first created man, He made male and female. Eve came out from Adam; thus, she and Adam were one. Even so, the church comes out from Christ; therefore, the church and Christ are also one. However, since Adam and Eve both existed at the same time, there was a distinction between them. Likewise, since the church and Christ coexist, there is also a distinction between them. Regarding oneness, they are one, but as to the matter of distinction, they differ from each other.

These two positions have to do with a difference in time. Today the church is the Body of Christ, but in the future the church will be the bride of Christ. Today the church is the Body of Christ for the purpose of manifesting the life of Christ. One day, when the church is mature in life, God will bring the church to Christ; in that day she will become the bride of Christ. Some people think that the church is the bride of Christ today, but this is wrong. There is no such thing. Since the Lord Jesus is not yet the Bridegroom, how could the church already be His bride? God will not bring the church to Christ as His bride until the work of the church as the Body of Christ has been accomplished.

If we look at the type in Genesis 2, we can also see the relationship between the Body and the bride. Eve was made out of Adam's rib, so she was the body of Adam. Since a portion of Adam's body was used to make Eve, her position was the body of Adam. But after Eve was made, God brought her to Adam, and she became the bride of Adam. This is the relationship between the Body and the bride. When reference is made to Eve coming out of Adam, it means that she is the body of Adam; but when Eve was brought to Adam and became his help meet; she became Adam's bride. That which was out of Adam was the body of Adam, and that which was brought to Adam was his bride.

Only that which came out of Adam could become the help meet of Adam. Whatever was not out of Adam could never be his help meet. Thus, when all the birds of the air were brought to him, Adam did not take any of them as his help meet, for they were not out of him. When all the cattle were brought to him, Adam did not take any of them, because they also were not out of him. It was the same with all the beasts. Their origin was not right. Since they were not out of Adam, they could not be his help meet. Who then could be the help meet of Adam? Eve could! Eve was brought to Adam just as the birds of the air, the cattle of the field, and the beasts were brought. However, there was a basic difference between Eve and them; they were not out of Adam. Since Eve was the only one who came out from Adam, she alone was qualified to be his bride. Coming out from him, she was brought back to him. Whatever comes out from him is his body; whatever is brought back to him is his bride.

Only that which comes out of Christ can return to Christ. That which does not come out from Christ can never return to Him. Only that which comes from heaven can return to heaven. If we have not come down from heaven, we will not be able to return to heaven. Home is the place of our origin. When we say that we are going home, we mean that we are returning to the place from which we have come. Only that which is from heaven can return to heaven. Only that which was from Adam could return to Adam. Adam could receive only that which was out of himself. This was a type—showing that Christ will receive only that which is out of Himself. Only those who come out from Christ can return to Him. Only those who receive life from Him can be received by Him.

There are many people who feel that they should offer all that they are and all that they have for the Lord's use. But God cannot accept anything which is offered from a human source. God cannot take or use anything which comes out from man himself. Among all Christians, especially among those who are quite zealous, a serious mistake is often made. They think that everything will be fine as long as they offer themselves, their abilities, their talents, and all they have to the Lord. But we

277

must remember that Christ will accept only that which comes out of Himself; He will not accept anything which comes out of man.

You may say, "Among the apostles, was there not a Paul? Was he not well educated? Was he not a man of great intelligence?" But we must remember the words that Paul spoke about himself. "For I did not determine to know anything among you except Jesus Christ, and this One crucified. And I was with you in weakness and in fear and in much trembling; and my speech and my proclamation were not in persuasive words of wisdom but in demonstration of the Spirit and of power" (1 Cor. 2:2–4). We thank God that intelligent and eloquent men can come into the church, but their natural, original intelligence and their natural, original eloquence are of no spiritual use in the church. In the church only one thing is recognized—that which comes out of Christ. Only that which is out of Christ can return to Christ. The material for the building of such a bride is Christ Himself.

The matter we need to attend to is this: only that which is out of Christ can be of any value and spiritual use in the church. God never uses the old creation to construct the new creation. Neither does God use that which is of man to construct that which is of God. He can never, never use fleshly things to produce something spiritual. The Lord Jesus said, "That which is born of the Spirit is spirit" (John 3:6b). Would it be possible for that which is born of the flesh to become spirit? No! "That which is born of the flesh is flesh." All problems issue from the matter of source. If we want to know whether the result will be spiritual, we need only ask whether the source is spiritual. The Lord Jesus said, "That which is born of the Spirit is spirit." We cannot use anything of the flesh to produce something of the spirit. A message which issues from thoughts only produces thoughts. Work done by stirring up the emotion only produces emotional stimulation. Only work from the spirit produces the spirit. The question is not whether the goal or the purpose is right, but what the process is. Man considers that as long as the goal is right, everything else is right. But God not only asks if the goal is right, He also asks how we do it. Someone may say, "I am for the Lord, and the work I am doing is for the church—the work of saving souls, spiritual work, the work of extending the heavenly kingdom. I have given all my ability and intelligence to it. Isn't this good?" In spite of this, man's natural ability and intelligence—that which has not been dealt with by the cross—are of no spiritual use. The Lord said, "That which is born of the flesh is flesh" (v. 6a).

Thus, it is not only necessary to have a spiritual purpose, but the process must also be of the spirit. The method must be of the spirit, and the man himself must be one who is of the spirit. Only that which is from the Holy Spirit can be spiritual. Only that which was out of Adam could return to Adam. First it must be Adam's body, and then it could be Adam's bride. First we must be the Body of Christ, and then we can be brought back to be the Bride of Christ. We hope that we may touch some spiritual reality in this matter. We need to see what God is really after. He requires that everything be out of Christ, that everyone be born of the Spirit. *(The Glorious Church,* pp. 44–48)

In Genesis 2:18–23 there are two types: Adam, who typifies Christ, and Eve, who typifies the church (Eph. 5:31–32).

Ephesians 5:25–29 speaks of the believers' relationship with Christ; Genesis 2:18–23 speaks of the believers' relationship with God.

In Genesis 2 we can see a big difference between the thoughts of God and the thoughts of man. God said, "It is not good that the man should be alone; I will make him an help meet for him." *Man did not say this.*

The thought stressed in the Bible is *what God has said.* When we desire sinners to be saved, we usually think only in terms of the benefit to the sinners themselves. We think if they do not repent, they will perish and suffer, and if they believe in the Lord Jesus, they will receive eternal life. But in Genesis 2:18–23, *God's thought is on Christ, not on man.* When sinners are saved, they are given by God to Christ—"the men whom You gave Me out of the world" (John 17:6). God has not only given Christ to men, but has also given men to Christ. God has presented a special gift to Christ, which is the sinners. God's intention in doing this *is to satisfy Christ's heart.*

The one great purpose for the believers to live on earth is to live *for Christ.* Adam was not created for Eve, but Eve was created for Adam. In the same way, believers are made for Christ. For this reason, we should satisfy Christ.

There are two stories of marriages in the Bible. They show, on the one hand, the direct relationship between Christ and the church, and on the other hand, the indirect relationship of God giving the church to Christ. The two stories are Abraham seeking Rebekah for Isaac, and Jacob marrying Rachel through suffering under Laban. Isaac did not know Rebekah; his father, Abraham, arranged the marriage. As to Rachel, however, Jacob himself suffered for the marriage. If Rebekah was not good, Isaac could have complained to his father, since Rebekah was selected by his father. Of course, we know that the one whom Abraham chose for his son was a true satisfaction to his son. God has chosen the church for Christ, and God must make the church a satisfaction to Christ. Rachel was dispositionally not that pure, and she was jealous. But Jacob did not murmur because he loved Rachel and was willing to suffer much for Rachel's sake. Christ is to the church as Jacob was in his marriage to Rachel, while God is to the church as Abraham was to Rebekah in the marriage of his son. The church is given to Christ through the hand of God. Our attention now is on the aspect of the church as Rebekah, who was given to Christ by His Father.

In God's view, Christ seems to be incomplete without us, as though it was not good for Christ to live alone, and as though He would still be lacking if He did not have the sinners. God's purpose in saving us is not just for us but also for Christ. God wants Christ to be satisfied, pleased, and completed. Therefore, He gives us to Christ. Let us see that we are called not just for our own blessings, but also to satisfy Christ's heart. Our responsibility is not to fail God. To whatever extent we satisfy Christ is the same extent God has not failed Christ.

There are two passages in the Bible which speak of "satisfaction." One says that in the coming days, Christ will see "the travail of His soul. . .and will be satisfied" (Isa. 53:11). The other says that "when [the believers] awake [in resurrection], [they] will be satisfied with Your [Christ's] likeness" (Psa. 17:15b). May we be able to satisfy Him. *(The Collected Works of Watchman Nee,* Vol. 8, pp. 141–142)

THE INCREASE OF CHRIST

My friends, please remember that death and resurrection have the same boundary line. Before the Lord's death, God had only one Son. After the Lord's resurrection, God has many children. The Lord became the first grain. God's only begotten Son has become the firstborn Son. Originally, there was only one grain. Now there are hundreds of grains. What is the difference between the hundreds of grains and the first grain? When a mustard seed is sown, mustard comes out. When a grain of wheat is sown, wheat comes out. When the Lord Jesus is planted, what comes out must be the Lord Jesus.

There was an elderly black woman in Africa who was a very spiritual sister. She did not have any education and was not eloquent at all. Yet many people went to her for the truth. One British pastor once went to her and asked, "What are Christians?" She answered, "They are fragments of Christ." This is indeed well said. I am afraid that many doctors of divinity cannot answer the question the way she did. Every Christian has a little bit of Christ in him. The hundreds of grains are produced from the first grain. When the hundreds of grains are put together, you have the original grain. When Christ and all the Christians are added together, we have the Christ.

I have often been amazed by 1 Corinthians 12:12. I do not know whether others are equally amazed when they read this. This verse tells us that just as a body has many members and is still one body, so also is Christ. Brother Paul, have you made a mistake? Why did you not use the word *church?* You should have said, "So also is Christ and the church." But was Paul wrong? No! He did not speak of the church, because the church is Christ. He did not have to say Christ and the church, because the church is Christ!

In reading the Bible, we should make a distinction between two different aspects of Christ. In Greek, when the name *Christ* is used without a definite article, it refers to Christ Himself. When it is used with a definite article, it refers to the church of Christ. Most versions do not make this distinction clearly. Only Darby's translation brings out this distinction. There is a difference between *Christ* and *the Christ*. The former refers to the individual Christ, while the latter refers to the church. The Christ refers not only to one individual, but to the corporate man composed of all those who are in Christ. This corporate man becomes the Christ. The individual Christ refers to Jesus; He was not corporate. He is the Head, and all Christians combined together form His Body. The individual Christ becomes the Head of the corporate Christ, and the whole is called *the Christ.*

Through His death Christ becomes us. Within every saved person there is now a little bit of Christ. Everyone has a little bit of Him. This is why we break the bread. Originally, there was one bread, but God charges us to break it and each take a piece of it. There is only one bread before us, and when we put together all the pieces that each one has taken, we have the same one bread. Within each one of us there is a little bit of that bread. Within each one of us there is a little bit of Christ. This is God's goal. Our Lord was God's only begotten Son. After death and resurrection, He begot many sons, and He Himself became the firstborn Son.

In the physical world, how does one grain produce many grains? It was most suitable for the Lord to use this illustration. In the natural realm, one grain can be turned into many grains. In the same way, one Christ can be multiplied to become the corporate Christ. This is a fact. How does one grain become so many grains? We do not know, but we do know that this multiplication is a fact. Christ is the seed of God. God has sown Christ into the earth, and many Christians have been produced. Through His death and resurrection, Christ released His life into us. After resurrection, He said to His disciples, "I ascend to My Father and your Father, and My God and your God" (John 20:17). Originally, God was His Father. After the Lord's resurrection, God became our Father also, and Christ, who had been the only begotten Son, became the firstborn Son among many sons. *(The Collected Works of Watchman Nee,* Vol. 43, pp. 658–660)

THE NEW MAN

The Mystery Hidden in the Ages

In Ephesians 3:4–6 Paul speaks of his understanding of the mystery of Christ. This mystery was not made known to the sons of men in other generations. The men of old did not know of the mystery that God spoke through Paul, which involves the Jews and Gentiles becoming one new man in Christ Jesus. This is the corporate Christ, which is the church. Verse 6 of chapter three is a precious verse. The words "fellow members" refer to the new man in Ephesians 2:15. The new man stands in contrast to the old man. There are many individual men in this world, but there is only one old man. In the same way, there are many Christians, but there is only one new man—the church.

One New Man

In order to understand what the new man is, we must first understand what the old man is. The old man is the God-created man who fell through sin. Every person in Adam is not only a sinner before God, but also an old man. When such a sinner, the old man, hears the gospel and believes in Christ and is saved, he becomes a new man. Not only has he become a new man individually; he is joined to all other Christians to become one corporate new man as well. Ephesians 1 speaks of the church as the Body of Christ; chapter two speaks of the church as the new man; chapter three speaks of the mystery of Christ; chapter four speaks of the way to build up the Body of Christ; chapter five speaks of the responsibility of the church; and chapter six speaks of the warfare of the church. The peak of God's work is the church, which is the new man. God saves us so that we will become a new man in Christ.

A great lack among Christians today is that everyone wants to be an individual Christian. Everyone wants to be good and zealous; everyone wants to sit and listen to good sermons. In short, everyone wants to be a Christian in an individual way. But God does not just want us to be good on an individual basis. He is after a corporate vessel that will destroy Satan and accomplish His plan. God does not want to see Christians scattered like a pan of sand. He wants Christians to be joined together to become a corporate new man.

What Is the New Man?

Ephesians 2 speaks of Christ creating one new man out of two groups of people, but it does not tell us what the new man is like. According to Colossians 3:10–12, the new man is renewed unto full knowledge according to the image of Him who created him. In the new man there is no Greek or Jew, circumcision or uncircumcision, barbarian or Scythian, slave or free man, but Christ is all and in all. The new man is not a matter of having or not having distinctions; it is a matter of either being the new man or being nothing. The new man is not in the realm of being a Greek or a Jew. The new man is simply Christ. The nature of the new man is Christ. In the new man, Christ is all and in all. We can even venture to say that Christ is the church and the church is Christ, because everything in the new man—the church—is simply Christ. The constitution of the new man is nothing less than Christ Himself. *(The Mystery of Christ,* pp. 7–8)

CHAPTER 12

THE NEW JERUSALEM

THE TABERNACLE OF GOD

Revelation 21:3 says, "And I heard a loud voice out of the throne, saying, Behold, the tabernacle of God is with men, and He will tabernacle with them, and they will be His peoples, and God Himself will be with them and be their God." This verse reveals what it will be like in the new heaven and new earth. The new heaven and new earth are in the eternal blessing, and positive blessing is spoken of here. This verse is followed by statements that say there will be no more of this and no more of that. These are the negative aspects, not the positive aspects. What is the positive and eternal blessing? It is that God will be with us. The presence of God is the blessing. All that the Scriptures have ever said about the blessing in eternity is summed up in these words, "God Himself will be with them." The severest suffering is to be without God's presence. But all of the enjoyment in eternity will be God's presence. The blessing of that day, is nothing other than God being with us. Solomon once said, "Behold, the heaven and heaven of heavens cannot contain thee; how much less this house that I have builded?" (1 Kings 8:27). The heaven and the heaven of heavens cannot contain Him, but we may say that the New Jerusalem can contain Him. God dwells in the New Jerusalem, and God's throne is established there.

The New Jerusalem is the woman whom we have been considering. In Genesis we saw a garden and a woman. This woman sinned, and God drove her out of the garden. Now in the new heaven and new earth, the woman and the holy city are one; they are no longer two separate entities. Since the New Jerusalem is the woman, the New Jerusalem is the wife of the Lamb; therefore, the woman and the holy city are one. Not only so, but God's throne is established in the New Jerusalem, or we may say that God Himself dwells within this woman. The Almighty One is dwelling in her. Therefore, it does not matter how great the force or temptation that can come from without. Evil powers can no longer enter, nor can man fall again, because God dwells within her. The blessing of the new heaven and new earth is the presence of God. All who have tasted something of God's presence in their experience know that it is indeed a blessing. No other blessing is greater or more precious than this.

Verse 16 says, "And the city lies square, and its length is as great as the breadth. And he measured the city with the reed to a length of twelve thousand stadia; the length and the breadth and the height of it are equal." There is another place in the Bible where the measurements of length, breadth, and height are equal, that is the Holy of Holies in the temple. "And the oracle in the forepart was twenty cubits in length, and twenty cubits in breadth, and twenty cubits in the height thereof" (1 Kings 6:20). The length, the breadth, and the height are all the same. In the Bible, only the Holy of Holies in the temple and the city of the New Jerusalem have equal measurements of length, breadth, and height. In other words, in the new heaven and new earth, the New Jerusalem becomes the Holy of Holies to God. When David gave Solomon the pattern for the temple, he said, "All this. . .the Lord made me understand in writing by his hand upon me, even all the works of this pattern" (1 Chron. 28:19). Everything in the temple was built according to divine revelation. In the new heaven and new earth, the New Jerusalem is the very temple of God. Everything that constitutes the city is something in God. There is nothing that is outside of Him.

Verse 22 says, "And I saw no temple in it, for the Lord God the Almighty and the Lamb are its temple." These words are especially precious. We know that in the Jerusalem of the Old Testament there was the temple. Whenever man wanted to have fellowship with God at that time, he had to go to the temple. The temple was the place set aside for God, and it was to that place that man had to go for fellowship with God. In the New Jerusalem, however, there will be no temple, because God and the Lamb are the temple of the city. This means that the fellowship between God and man in that day will be intimate and direct; it will be face to face. Man will no longer need to go to a specified place in order to have fellowship with God.

In the Old Testament there was a veil in the temple. No one could pass through this veil and enter into God's presence except the High Priest, and then only once a year. Today in the church the veil has been split. Now we all can enter into God's presence to worship Him in spirit and in truthfulness. But in that day God and the Lamb will be the temple of the city. We will not have to go to God; He will be right where we are. Today we go to God, but in that day we will live in His presence. God and the Lamb are the temple of the city. Therefore, if we do not learn to live in the Holy of Holies today, we are the most foolish people. Today the veil has been split, and we can enter into the Holy of Holies with boldness. We must not stay outside.

Verse 23 says, "And the city has no need of the sun or of the moon that they should shine in it, for the glory of God illumined it, and its lamp is the Lamb." This passage is connected with the previous verse about the temple. God and the Lamb are the temple of the city, and the glory of God lights the city. Therefore, there is no need for the sun or the moon to shine. We know that in the temple of the Old Testament the outer court was lighted by the sun and the moon, and the Holy Place by the light of the lamp. But in the Holy of Holies there was no window; the light of the sun and the moon could not shine in. Neither was there a lamp as in the Holy Place. The glory of God provided the light. Even so, the New Jerusalem is not lighted by the sun or the moon, but by the glory of God. This reveals that the whole city will be the Holy of Holies. The church in the future will become the very Holy of Holies. *(The Glorious Church,* pp. 117–118, 131, 142–143)

THE BRIDE OF CHRIST

We have already seen that the woman in Genesis 2 is the same woman seen in Ephesians 5 and in Revelation 12. Now let us look at another woman, recorded in Revelation 21 and 22.

Although there is a long distance between them, the last two chapters of Revelation correspond with the first three chapters of Genesis. God created the heaven and the earth in Genesis, and the new heaven and the new earth are in the last two chapters of Revelation. In both Genesis and Revelation there is the tree of life. In Genesis there is a river flowing out from Eden, and in Revelation there is a river of living water flowing from the throne of God and of the Lamb. In Genesis there is gold, pearl (bdellium), and a kind of precious stone (onyx), and in Revelation there is gold, pearl, and all kinds of precious stones. In Genesis 2 Eve was Adam's wife. In Revelation 21 the Lamb also has a wife. The Lamb's wife is the New Jerusalem, and God's eternal purpose is fulfilled in this woman. In Genesis 3 man's fall was followed by death, sickness, suffering, and the curse. But, when the New Jerusalem descends from heaven in Revelation 21, there is no more death, sorrow, crying, or pain because the former things have all passed away. If we read the Scriptures carefully, we will see that Genesis 1 through 3 does indeed correspond with Revelation 21 and 22. They face each other at the two ends of the expanse of time.

Now we have seen four women: Eve in Genesis 2, the wife (the church) in Ephesians 5, the woman in the vision of Revelation 12, and the wife of the Lamb in Revelation 21. These four women are actually one woman, but her history can be divided into four stages. When she was conceived in the plan of God, she was called Eve. When she is redeemed and manifesting Christ on earth, she is called the church. When she is persecuted by the great dragon, she is the woman in the vision. When she is completely glorified in eternity, she is the wife of the Lamb. These four women reveal God's work from eternity to eternity. The woman in Genesis 2 is the woman purposed in God's heart in eternity past, and the woman in Revelation 21 is the woman who fulfills God's purpose in eternity future. Of the two women in between, one is the church, prepared for Christ by God, and the other is the woman who will bring forth the man-child at the end time. In other words, these four women show us the four stages of the history of one woman: one stage is in eternity past, two stages are between the eternities, and another stage is in eternity future. Even though these four women appear to be different when we speak of them separately, they are the same when we put them together. The wife of the Lamb is the woman of Ephesians 5. Since the Lord Jesus is the Lamb, it is impossible for the woman in Ephesians 5 to be anyone other than the wife of the Lamb. The woman in Ephesians 5 is also likened to Eve, and Eve is also likened to the wife of the Lamb in Revelation 21. When there are overcomers, whose work represents that of the whole church, the woman in Revelation 12 will introduce the woman in Revelation 21. As a result, God in eternity future will indeed obtain a woman, a ruling woman who has dealt thoroughly with Satan. God will truly obtain a wife for the Lamb, and His purpose will be fulfilled. Let us see how the woman of Revelation 12 becomes the woman of Revelation 21.

The angel said to John, "I will show you the bride, the wife of the Lamb" (21:9). The angel said that he would show him the wife of the Lamb, but John saw "the holy city, Jerusalem, coming down out of heaven from God" (v. 10). The wife of the Lamb whom John saw was the holy city, Jerusalem. Therefore, the description of the city is also the description of the wife of the Lamb. The city is a figure, describing the characteristics and spiritual condition of the corporate Body whom God chose before creation.

This city comes down out of heaven from God. This means that God not only is concerned about the destination of this corporate man, but also about the place from which this corporate man comes. It is not just a matter of the future, but a matter of the source. The wife of the Lamb comes down out of heaven. The New Jerusalem is from heaven, not from earth. God is not showing us a man with a history of sin, who was later saved. (This is not to say that we do not have a history of sin and that we do not need to repent and be saved by grace.) Rather, this passage shows us only that portion which is out from God. It shows us the glorious church of Ephesians 5 which is to be presented to Christ.

In the Old Testament, one woman represents in a special way the church which is to be offered to Christ. She is Rebekah. Abraham said to his old servant, "Thou shalt not take a wife unto my son of the daughters of the Canaanites, among whom I dwell: but thou shalt go unto my country, and to my kindred, and take a wife unto my son Isaac" (Gen. 24:3–4). Rebekah was not an inhabitant of the land west of the Euphrates, nor an inhabitant of the land west of the Jordan, but she was of the kindred of Isaac.

God desires to have a corporate man of the kindred of Christ. Since Christ is from heaven, the church, too, must come from heaven. Thus Hebrews 2:11 says, "For both He who sanctifies and those who are being sanctified are all of One, for which cause He is not ashamed to call them brothers." What are brothers? Brothers are those who have been born of the same mother and father. How we thank God that, on one hand, we were purchased with the precious blood of the Lord, and on the other hand, we were truly born of God. There are two aspects to the history of every Christian: one is that we were outwardly purchased of God, and the other is that we were inwardly born of God. From the standpoint of our history with sin, we were outwardly purchased;

but from the standpoint of our history apart from sin, we were born of God, for whoever is born of God cannot sin. This portion has no beginning of sin nor history of sin. The fact that the New Jerusalem comes down from God implies that the church has never been on this earth. It appears that the church is coming down to earth for the first time. This is not to say that we did not come to God as sinners, but that there is a portion in us which is from God and is entirely of God. How we must thank the Lord that the New Jerusalem descends out of heaven from God!

This city is completely different from the city recorded in chapter seventeen. That city is called the great city, and this city is called the holy city. The characteristic of Babylon is its greatness, and the characteristic of the New Jerusalem is its holiness. Among Christians there are some who are taken up with greatness, but there are some who pay attention to holiness. Those who concentrate on greatness are in the principle of Babylon, while those who pay attention to holiness are in the principle of the New Jerusalem.

What is the meaning of holiness? Since God alone is holy, anything which issues from Him must also be holy. Saying that "both He who sanctifies and those who are being sanctified are all of One" means that Christ is holy because He is of the One and that we also are holy because we also are of the One. Only those who are of the One are holy. Only that which issues from God is of value; that which comes out from God, and only that, is the New Jerusalem. Everything that is of man must be left aside. The matter of the rapture is based upon this. Why will some be left out? It is because they have so many things which are not of Christ, and anything that is not of Christ cannot be brought to heaven. Nothing which is not of heaven can return to heaven. Everything that is of earth must be left on earth; while everything that is of heaven can return to heaven. *(The Glorious Church,* pp. 99–100, 123–125)

THE ULTIMATE CONSUMMATION OF THE CHURCH, THE BODY

Revelation 21:2 continues, "And I saw the holy city, New Jerusalem, coming down out of heaven from God, prepared as a bride adorned for her husband." In chapter nineteen there is a declaration that the marriage of the Lamb has come and His wife has made herself ready. But in this chapter, the New Jerusalem is prepared as a bride adorned for her husband. This is the actuality. There are many declarations in Revelation, but the most important declaration is Revelation 11:15. According to the order of occurrence, the rapture of the man-child and the casting down of the dragon from heaven take place after this declaration. Then how can the words, "The kingdom of the world has become the kingdom of our Lord and of His Christ," be spoken at this time? It is possible because this declaration was made at the beginning of things, not at the point of their accomplishment. This means that a turning point has come. When there is a definite turn towards God's eternal purpose, God can make such a declaration in heaven. In chapter nineteen God makes another declaration, saying that the marriage of the Lamb has come and that His wife has made herself ready. This declaration is also made at the starting point of events which are about to occur. Because before Him the overcomers represent the bride and because this group of people is ready in His sight, God is able to declare that the marriage of the Lamb has come and His wife has made herself ready. However, the "has come" is fully realized in the new heaven and the new earth. In Revelation 21:2, John actually saw the New Jerusalem coming down from God out of heaven. At that time the bride was truly ready in every sense. This is not merely the readiness declared in chapter nineteen, but the readiness in actual fact.

Now we must turn back to read Ephesians 5:26 and 27. "That He might sanctify her, cleansing her by the washing of the water in the word, that He might present the church to Himself glorious, not having spot or wrinkle or any such things, but that she would be holy and without blemish." "That He might present the church to Himself" is fulfilled in Revelation 21. Now, before God, the bride is ready to be presented to the Lord. "Prepared as a bride" is no longer difficult to comprehend. By the end of the kingdom age, the whole church will be brought to this place. What we fail to see today will be fully seen in that day. Today we may say that God's standard for the church is high and ask how the church will ever attain to such a condition. We may not know how God will do it, but we do know that the church will attain to that position at the time of the new heaven and new earth. Some may think that the church will reach the stage of Ephesians 5 before the age of the kingdom. However, the Lord did not say this. The church will not arrive at that place until Revelation 21. At the time of the new heaven and new earth, there will not be just a group of saints who are perfected, but all the saints, the whole Body, from all the nations throughout all the ages. They will all be together before God and glorified in His presence. *(The Glorious Church,* pp. 115–117)

John the apostle reaffirms that God's end is certain, and that His ways now are consistent with that end. Just as, in the heavenly City at the last, the principles of the Body find their fullest development and expression, so is the reverse also true. Whenever the life of the eternities has a free course in us today, we shall find every feature of the heavenly City, every true character of the Lord Jesus, manifesting itself through His Body here on the earth. And who that has once caught a glimpse of God's heavenly Man can ever be satisfied with anything less than this? *(The Collected Works of Watchman Nee,* Vol. 40, p. 169)

THE INHABITANTS

Revelation 21:12–14 says, "It had a great and high wall and had twelve gates, and at the gates twelve angels, and names inscribed, which are the names of the twelve tribes of the sons of Israel: on the east three gates, and on the north three gates, and on the south three gates, and on the west three gates. And the wall of the city had twelve foundations, and on them the twelve names of the twelve apostles of the Lamb." How many are included in this corporate man? We are told that the names of the twelve tribes of Israel are written upon the gates, and the names of the twelve apostles are written upon the foundations. This shows us that the city includes the saints from both the Old and the New Testament.

This can be proved by reading the following passages of Scripture. Luke 13:28–29 says, "There will be weeping and gnashing of teeth there when you see Abraham and Isaac and Jacob and all the prophets in the kingdom of God, but you being cast outside. And they will come from the east and the west, and from the north and the south, and will recline at table in the kingdom of God." Here we see that the kingdom of God includes Abraham, Isaac, and Jacob, who represent the Old Testament saints. Those who come from the east, west, north, and south represent the New Testament saints. These two groups of people are participants in the kingdom of God; therefore, they will all enter into the New Jerusalem together.

Hebrews 11:8–10 says, "By faith Abraham. . .dwelt as a foreigner in the land of promise as in a foreign land, making his home in tents with Isaac and Jacob, the fellow heirs of the same promise; for he eagerly waited for the city which has the foundations, whose Architect and Builder is God." The city referred to in this passage is the New Jerusalem. Only this city is a city with foundations, whose Architect and Builder is God. Verse 13 says, "All these died in faith." "All these" are Abel, Enoch, Noah, Abraham, Isaac, Jacob, and many others. Verse 16 continues, "But as it is, they long after a better country, that is, a heavenly one. Therefore God is not ashamed of them, to be called their God, for He has prepared a city for them." "They" in verse 16 are the "these" in verse 13. This shows us that the Old Testament saints have a portion in the New Jerusalem. From Abel at the beginning and for all the saints in the Old Testament, God has appointed a city, the New Jerusalem. They all have their share in it. Verses 39–40 say, "And these all, having obtained a good testimony through their faith, did not obtain the promise, because God has provided something better for us, so that apart from us they would not be made perfect." God has kept all the Old Testament saints waiting; they have not yet obtained that city. He has bid them to wait so that both we and they might go

THE RICHES OF WATCHMAN NEE

there together. From this we see that both the saints of the Old Testament and the saints of the New Testament will be in the New Jerusalem.

Ephesians 2:11–14 says, "Therefore remember that once you, the Gentiles in the flesh, those who are called uncircumcision, . . .that you were at that time apart from Christ, alienated from the commonwealth of Israel, and strangers to the covenants of the promise, having no hope and without God in the world. But now in Christ Jesus you who were once far off have become near in the blood of Christ. For He Himself is our peace, He who has made both one and has broken down the middle wall of partition." From verse 11 to 13, the pronoun "you" is used, but in verse 14, it changes to "our." When "you" is used, it refers to the saints in Ephesus, but when "our" is used, it refers both to the Jewish saints and the Ephesian saints as well as all the saints of both the Old and New Testaments. Christ is our peace and He has made both one, breaking down the middle wall of partition. Verse 15 says, "Abolishing in His flesh the law of the commandments in ordinances, that He might create the two in Himself into one new man, so making peace." The "two" in this verse corresponds with the "both" in verse 14. This also refers to Old Testament saints as well as New Testament saints. It does not refer to the relationship between man and God. Could God and man be created together to become a new man? No. This passage refers to both the saints of the Gentiles and the saints of the Jews, the Old Testament saints as well as the New Testament saints.

Verse 16 says, "And might reconcile both in one Body to God through the cross, having slain the enmity by it." To reconcile "both in one Body" to God means that the Old Testament saints as well as the New Testament saints are reconciled to God. Verses 17–19 say, "And coming, He announced peace as the gospel to you who were far off, and peace to those who were near, for through Him we both have access in one Spirit unto the Father. So then you are no longer strangers and sojourners, but you are fellow citizens with the saints and members of the household of God." The saints in Ephesus were no longer strangers but fellow citizens with the saints and members of the household of God. Verses 20–22 say, "Being built upon the foundation of the apostles and prophets, Christ Jesus Himself being the cornerstone; in whom all the building, being fitted together, is growing into a holy temple in the Lord; in whom you also are being built together into a dwelling place of God in spirit." Thus, the habitation of God includes all the saints of the Old and New Testament. Abraham, Isaac, and Jacob are there, and we also are there. In conclusion, at the time of the new heaven and new earth, all those who have the life of God will be included in the New Jerusalem. *(The Glorious Church,* pp. 126–128)

CONSTITUTED WITH:

Of what materials is this city built? Revelation 21:18 says, "And the building work of its wall was jasper." We have noted jasper already. We have seen that the brightness of the city is as jasper. The meaning of this is that when we behold the glory of the city we are looking at God's real image. By knowing God's real image, man can know the God who is sitting upon the throne. God is not far away from man, nor is He an unknowable God.

The function of the city wall, as we have seen, is to separate that which is within the city from that which is without.

The fact that this wall is made of jasper means that the separation is based upon what is seen in God's true light. The basis of separation is the seeing of what God requires, the seeing of what God is after. If man is not clear about God's requirement, he will have no separation. *(The Glorious Church,* pp. 132–133)

The Divine Nature of God

Let us read further in Revelation 21:18: "And the city was pure gold, like clear glass." In other words, all that is in the city is of God. Gold signifies that which is of God, that which is placed in God's new creation. Peter said that we are partakers of the divine nature. Within everyone who belongs to God, there is a portion which is of God. Before we were saved, everything in us was of the flesh, everything was natural; there was nothing whatever of a spiritual nature. But when we received the Lord, God imparted His life to us. This is the gold which He has given us. Within us there is a portion of gold; there is something which is truly of God. It is regrettable, however, that although we have this gold in us, it is mixed with many other things; it is an alloy. We have God's nature, but at the same time, we also have many things in us which are completely different from God. For this reason, the greater portion of God's work with His children is to reduce them, not to add to them.

Many times men would like to obtain more of God, to be filled with the Holy Spirit, and to know Christ better. All of these things have their place. We dearly need to obtain more of God, to be filled with the Spirit, and to know more of Christ. But there is another work—it is not of increasing but of reducing. God's basic work is to reduce us. From the day we were saved, God has been doing this work, and the instrument for this work of subtraction is the cross. The work of the cross is to cancel out. It is not to bring things into us but to take things away from us. Within us there is so much that is refuse. There are so many things that are not of God, which do not bring glory to Him. God wants to remove all of these things through the cross so that we may become pure gold. What God has put into us is pure gold, but because there is so much dross in us, so many things which are not of God, we have become an alloy. Therefore, God must expend much effort to make us see those things in us which are of self and those things which cannot bring glory to Him. We believe that if God speaks to us, we will discover that what needs to be removed is much more than what needs to be added. Christians who are especially strong in the soul must remember that God's work in them through the Holy Spirit is to remove things from them and to reduce them.

The outstanding feature of the New Jerusalem is that of gold, pure gold. There is nothing there which contains a mixture; everything is entirely of God. The one lesson which God wants us to learn today is to see that everything coming from us is but dross. Apart from the gold in us, everything which comes from us is refuse. When added to the gold, our goodness is dross; when added to the gold, our zeal is also dross. Everything from us is dross. In other words, anything which is not of God is dross. No one can stand before God and say that he has something to contribute to Him. God demands pure gold. In the New Jerusalem everything is pure gold, without any dross. The day will come when we see that everything that is not of God is on the cross. Everything that is in the New Jerusalem is of God. God must attain His purpose.

When God says that it will be pure gold, it will be pure gold. There is nothing which can be mixed with God's work. *(The Glorious Church,* pp. 133–134)

The Transforming Spirit

Revelation 21:19 and 20 say, "The foundations of the wall of the city were adorned with every precious stone: the first foundation was jasper; the second, sapphire; the third, chalcedony; the fourth, emerald; the fifth, sardonyx; the sixth, sardius; the seventh, chrysolite; the eighth, beryl; the ninth, topaz; the tenth, chrysoprase; the eleventh, jacinth; the twelfth, amethyst." What do precious stones imply? There is a basic difference between precious stones and gold. Gold is a chemical element, while a precious stone is not a chemical element, but a compound. Gold is an element because God created it as gold; it was made directly by God. But a precious stone has been formed from various kinds of elements, which have been composed together through chemical combination through countless years of heat and pressure in the earth. In other words, the precious stones do not signify something given directly by God, but something which the Holy Spirit has produced in man by much effort and many years of burning. The work of the Holy Spirit on earth is to continually put us into trials so that we may have all kinds of experiences and become precious stones before Him. The precious stones, therefore, are the product of our being disciplined by Him.

Let us illustrate. Isaac's birth represents gold, but Jacob's experience represents precious stone. Isaac was born a son through the promise of God. He never suffered, nor was he ever seriously at fault. Jacob's case, however, was quite different.

He suffered very much and passed through many trials. God's hand was upon him all the time. Day after day and year after year, God wrought something into Jacob which caused him to become a precious stone.

That life which God has imparted to us is the gold, while the life which God is constituting in us is the precious stone. Day after day, in all kinds of circumstances, He is making us in the image of Christ. This is the precious stone. God does not stop by just giving us a portion of Christ's life; He wants to have the life of Christ wrought into us. On one hand, we must realize that, except for the Lord's life in us, we are not any different than we were prior to our salvation. But on the other hand, after following the Lord for five or ten years and being disciplined and dealt with by Him, a portion of the life of Christ has been constituted in us by the Holy Spirit. There is something within us which has been formed by the Lord, and this is the precious stone.

You should not be surprised when God continually puts you into the fire to burn. It seems that the things which other people encounter are all good, but the things which you are up against are not prosperous or easy. You are even misunderstood and attacked by others; more things have happened to you than to anyone else. But you must realize that it is not without a cause. God is continually burning you; the Holy Spirit is working to constitute more of the life of Christ in you so that you may be transformed into His image.

In Revelation we find not just one kind of precious stone, but all kinds of precious stones. Some are jasper, some sapphire, some chalcedony, some emerald, some sardonyx, some sardius, and other kinds. All of these precious stones are the product of burning. They were not formed by God in a moment of time but obtained after being wrought upon through long years of God's working. Precious stone was not given to us at creation, nor is it something we obtained when we became a new creation. Precious stone is formed in us through God's burning day after day. It is a substance which is constantly put into the fire. When the fire burns in a certain way, a certain kind of mineral is melted into that substance, and it becomes a certain kind of precious stone. When the fire burns in another way, it causes another kind of mineral to be dissolved into that substance, causing it to become another kind of precious stone. Different ways of melting certain minerals together form various kinds of precious stones.

The precious stones represent the work of the Holy Spirit. When we were saved we obtained God's nature, but from that time, day after day, the Holy Spirit has been working the nature of God into us so that we may bear the fruit of the Spirit. There is not just one fruit of the Spirit. There are love, joy, peace, longsuffering, kindness, goodness, faithfulness, meekness, and many others. The Holy Spirit must continually work in us to cause us to bear all these different kinds of fruit. When we were saved, God imparted His life into us. But the fruit of the Spirit is not something imparted to us by God. We bear these fruits when the Holy Spirit works within us to a certain extent. Even so, precious stone is something formed in us through the Holy Spirit by means of many different circumstances.

Not only has God shared His nature with us, but day by day He is making us a certain kind of people who can bring glory to His name. When you were saved, you obtained God's nature, and when I was saved, I obtained His nature. In this regard, all Christians are the same; they all have obtained God's nature. But in the ensuing days, God may have put you into certain circumstances in order to give you certain kinds of experience. He may have let you go through certain trials, certain difficulties, and certain sufferings so that you will become a Christian like chrysolite, chalcedony, sardius, or some other precious stone. God is working in every Christian so that each one may become a certain kind of precious stone. We all have gold in common before God, but after we become precious stones before Him, we will each be a certain form.

What the Holy Spirit forms in us by means of the environment will abide forever. When a Christian receives more dealings in a certain way, he will learn more lessons in that way. This will produce an outstanding character in him, a character which will not come to an end after several years, but which will abide for eternity. What he has obtained will forever be a precious stone in the New Jerusalem.

In many of God's children who have walked with Him for ten or twenty years, there is something which God has wrought through the Holy Spirit. It is not just that God has imparted something to them, but they themselves have become that something; it is their very constituent. They have been disciplined by the Holy Spirit for many years. By passing through many trials and experiences, the Holy Spirit has formed a certain kind of life in them. Those who are acquainted with them acknowledge that something has indeed been accomplished in them. They not only possess the life that is given to them by God, but they also have a transformed life which the Holy Spirit has wrought within them. Not only do they live an exchanged life but also a transformed life. This is the precious stone. Precious stone is that which has been formed in us by the burning work of the Holy Spirit. The New Jerusalem will be filled with these precious stones.

At this point we must realize how useless it is to put our emphasis merely on doctrine. We must never think that we will benefit if we only know a little more theology or scriptural teaching. These are not of much use. Only that which is burned into us by the Holy Spirit is of value. If something has not been burned into an article, a little rubbing will remove it. What spiritual value is there in something which can be wiped away from us with a little rubbing? This does not mean that we should not read our Bible, but it does mean that what we read is of value only when the Holy Spirit burns it into us. All precious stones have come out of fire. To have precious stones, we need the fire. Without fire, there will never be any precious stone.

For this reason we should never refuse the trials that come upon us through our environment. We should never refuse the discipline of the Holy Spirit, nor complain when God's hand encircles and encloses us in every way. How bound and pressed we feel many times! How we would like to break through all the bondage and limitation and be released for a while. But we must remember that we are in God's forming hand. He is forming us so that one day we will come out as precious stones. God has not only given us His life, but He is also working in us to the extent that we may possess a special quality. This is what the Holy Spirit is forming in us through all the circumstances which God allows, and this is called precious stone. What use is it then to merely have knowledge or doctrine? Only that which the Spirit burns into us is of any value. Only when a Christian has received something through burning will he be able to preach messages from what he really knows rather than from books. Only that which has been burned into us by the Holy Spirit is precious stone. Otherwise, it is wood, grass, and stubble.

Sometimes when we sit in the presence of an elderly person, we feel that he is one who is really walking with the

Lord. There is a life in him which very much characterizes him; it has become his special nature. We can only bow down before him. There may be others who have a greater ministry than he and others who have undertaken a greater work, but he has an abundant life; something has been formed within him by the Holy Spirit. He has a special quality, something which has come out from the fire; he is a precious stone. In the presence of such a one we can only bow and say, "How we wish that we also may have something that is so inspiring, so touching." It is not words which inspire and touch people, but something which has gone through the fire.

In the New Jerusalem there are precious stones. Without precious stones, the New Jerusalem will never come into existence. God needs precious stones. He needs a group of people who will manifest the quality of precious stones. Oh, may God deliver us from being shallow! Only what the Holy Spirit has wrought into our life is of any value or use. *(The Glorious Church,* pp. 134–139)

The Redeeming Christ

Revelation 21:21 continues, "And the twelve gates were twelve pearls; each one of the gates was, respectively, of one pearl." The New Jerusalem consists not only of pure gold and precious stones, but also of pearls. Pearls are not formed by burning; they are the result of a gradual formation within a sea creature after it has been wounded. Therefore, the meaning of pearl is life which issues from death. Pearl signifies the life released by the Lord Jesus in the non-redemptive aspect of His death.

Matthew 13 also speaks about a pearl. To whom does this

pearl refer? It is a reference to the church, which the Lord has formed out of His death. He was willing to sell all that He had in order to purchase this pearl. Pearl signifies something positive, not something passive or negative. It is the church, the new man, that God desires to create. Within such a One there is no problem of sin, nor of redemption. He was willing to sell all to obtain this pearl. This shows us how precious is the life which is wholly out of Christ. How precious it is to God, and how precious it is to Christ!

In the New Jerusalem, pearls function as the gates of the city. This means that everything of God starts from here. In other words, in order for man to obtain life before God, the life must not be something of man, but of the death of Christ, of the non-redemptive aspect of Christ's death.

First Corinthians 3:12 says that spiritual building should have materials of gold, silver, and precious stones, not wood, grass, or stubble. In 1 Corinthians 3 there are gold, silver, and precious stones; but in Genesis 2, in the garden of Eden, there were gold, precious stones, and pearl—there was no silver. In Revelation 21, in the New Jerusalem, there are, once again, gold, precious stones, and pearl; there is no silver. What is the significance of this? Gold, precious stones, and pearl— these three items—are found both in the garden of Eden and in the New Jerusalem. This means that gold, precious stones, and pearl are from eternity to eternity.

In eternity God did not plan to have silver, because silver represents redemption. God knew that men would sin and need redemption, but this was not something of His eternal plan. In God's work there is redemption, but in His eternal purpose there is no redemption. Therefore, the New Jerusalem, in this respect, is the same as the garden of Eden —there is no silver. This means that in eternity future, we will be brought to the place where there is no trace of sin. Today, however, we cannot disregard or lightly esteem the silver. If anyone thinks he has no need of silver today, he must ask God for mercy. We cannot go on without silver. If we have no silver, we have no redemption, and we can do nothing. But redemption has no part in God's purpose. In the New Jerusalem we will not be able to find any silver. This shows us that God will wipe away all history of sin, because redemption is not included in that city. In the New Jerusalem man will no longer need redemption, because they will sin no more. God will bring us to such a firm ground that there will be no possibility for us to fall again. There is a life within us which has nothing to do with sin and which requires no redemption. That life in us is from Christ and it is Christ Himself. As Christ Himself needs no redemption, we who have a portion of His life will no longer need redemption. Thus, in eternity there is no need of silver.

Thank God that we have His redemption today. Thank God that although we have sinned, the blood of Jesus Christ His Son cleanses us from every sin. However, God has shared the life of His Son with us, a life which forever needs no redemption. One day we will live completely by this life and the history of sin will pass away. Redeeming silver will no longer be of any use.

We must see that the fall is not in the purpose of God, redemption is not in the purpose of God, and neither is the kingdom something in the purpose of God. The fall is not in God's purpose; it is something which happened on the way. Redemption is not in God's purpose; it is the solution to the fall. And the kingdom is also not in God's purpose; it is also the solution to the fall. Because of the fall there is redemption, and because of the fall there is the kingdom. All these

310

things are but remedies; they are not in the purpose of God. Even so, we would never make light of redemption and the kingdom. If there was no redemption, there would be no way to solve the problem of the fall. If there was no kingdom, could the matter of the fall be solved? Nevertheless, we must bear in mind that God did not create man that he might sin. God created man for His own glory. This line is straight; this heavenly line is straight. *(The Glorious Church,* pp. 139–141)

The River of Water of Life and the Tree of Life

We have yet to see what God will show us at the end. Revelation 22:1–2 says, "And he showed me a river of water of life, bright as crystal, proceeding out of the throne of God and of the Lamb in the middle of its street. And on this side and on that side of the river was the tree of life, producing twelve fruits, yielding its fruit each month; and the leaves of the tree are for the healing of the nations." Here we are reminded of verse 2:7, which says, "To him who overcomes, to him I will give to eat of the tree of life, which is in the Paradise of God." The tree of life is planted in the Paradise of God. Since the tree of life is in the city, this tells us that the New Jerusalem is the Paradise of God.

Recalling the book of Genesis, God created man as a type of Christ and the woman as a type of the church he desired to obtain in Genesis 2. God then put them, husband and wife, in the garden of Eden. Thus we have the man, the woman, and the garden. Then in Genesis 3 the serpent came in and they fell; as a result, God drove them out of the garden. In Revelation 21, whom do we see in the New Jerusalem? There is the Lamb, the One whom Adam typified in

Genesis 2; He is wholly for God. There is also the wife of the Lamb, who was typified by Eve in Genesis 2; she is wholly for Christ. The New Jerusalem is the wife of the Lamb and is also the Paradise of God. In Genesis 2 there were three entities—Adam, Eve, and the garden. But in Revelation 21 and 22 there are only two—the Lamb and the city. The city is the bride and also the Paradise; the woman and the Paradise have become one. The woman in Genesis could be driven away, while the woman at the end of Revelation can no longer be driven out.

Some people may worry and ask, "What will happen in eternity? What if the devil should come in again—then what would we do?" We can answer that it is impossible for this to happen again, because in eternity God Himself will dwell in the holy city. Praise God! He set up a garden in Genesis, a garden which had no wall and which was not guarded well. Therefore, the serpent and sin could enter. But God finally obtains a city for the sake of protection. It is impossible for this city to be ever involved in a fall. The woman and Paradise have been so joined that nothing can ever separate them again. Henceforth, this woman cannot be driven out by any means.

Verse 22:1 speaks of a river of water of life being in the middle of the street of the city. In Genesis there were four rivers, two of which have always oppressed the children of God. Babylon was built upon the river Pison, and Nineveh upon the river Hiddekel. God's children have always been persecuted by these two rivers. But in the New Jerusalem there is only one river—the river of water of life. This river gives life and joy to man. Psalm 46:4 says: "There is a river whose streams gladden the city of God, the holy place of the tabernacles of the Most High." This river especially gives gladness to God. The water of this river proceeds "out of the throne of God and of the Lamb." The throne is singular because God and the Lamb are sitting on one throne. This means that the reign of Christ is the reign of God.

Verse 2 says, "And on this side and on that side of the river was the tree of life, producing twelve fruits, yielding its fruit each month." Once again the number twelve is used. What does it mean that the tree bears twelve kinds of fruits and yields its fruit every month? This is a way of saying that everything is satisfied, and that this satisfaction is for eternity. Every month there is life. In eternity we will continue to know Christ and continue to receive the life of the Lord without any interruption—there will not be a month when there is no fruit. This means that there will be no regression. Today we see something which is very sad—that which the Scripture shows as the evaluation of man. Men from twenty years of age to sixty years of age were given a certain valuation, but the value was lowered for those over sixty years of age (Lev. 27:3, 7). This is going backward, but in eternity there will be no going backward. There will be new life and new fruit every month.

Even so, before the New Jerusalem comes into being, we need to seek a new experience of life every month. The particular experience we had twenty years ago is no longer fresh, nor can it be of any help to us today. Neither can the experience of five years ago be fresh or of any profit to us now. We cannot live by the fruit of the tree of life from former months. Each month we must continue to have fresh fruit. Before God we must receive life continuously; we must receive Christ. Not only do we need fruit each month, we need a different kind of fruit each month. We cannot be satisfied before God only having a little portion, a certain part. We must learn to know the Lord in many aspects; we must bear all manner of fruits.

Verse 2 continues, "And the leaves of the tree are for the healing of the nations." Fruit represents life; leaves, the clothing of the tree, represent our external behavior. The Lord Jesus cursed the fig tree because it only had leaves; there was no fruit. It only had the outward behavior without the inward life. In the new heaven and new earth, the people of the nations will have no sin, no death, no pain, no curse, nor any demons. This group of people, the nations, will continue living in the earth with the holy city in their midst. Being healed by the leaves of the Lord Jesus means that the deeds of the Lord Jesus will be their example. We will obtain the fruits of the tree of life, and they will obtain the leaves. By following the behavior of the Lord Jesus, they will be able to live on in well-being; and this way the nations will dwell together in peace and blessing.

In these verses the street, the river of water of life, and the tree of life are all linked together. In the New Jerusalem, wherever you find the street, you will find the river of water of life, and wherever you find the river of water of life, you will find the tree of life. In other words, wherever there is activity, there will be the river of life and the tree of life. This means that as we learn to follow the Lord, all our conduct should include the river of water of life and the tree of life. Then everything will be well. The street is a place for people to move about. In order to move about we need to have all of our activities based upon the tree of life, not upon the tree of the knowledge of good and evil. When the life within us generates the activity, the result will be the outflow of the river of the water of life in the Spirit. The outflowing of life is our street, our way. If the life of the Lord Jesus is not moving in us, we simply cannot walk. If there is not the life of the Lord and if there is not the outflow of the river of water of life in the Spirit, we cannot move. If, according to our own wisdom, we judge whether a certain way to act is good or bad, we are planting the tree of the knowledge of good and evil, not the tree of life. But if we act according to the moving of the life within, the result will be that the water of life will flow out to others. All of these things are linked to-gether. All of God's work is based upon the tree of life and results in the river of water of life. *(The Glorious Church,* pp. 145–148)

THE ULTIMATE AND ETERNAL EXPRESSION OF GOD

Revelation 21:11 describes this city as "having the glory of God. Her light was like a most precious stone, like a jasper stone, as clear as crystal." Jasper has been already mentioned in Revelation 4. John saw One sitting upon the throne whose appearance was like a jasper and sardius. The One whom John saw sitting upon the throne was the same as jasper. In other words, the meaning of jasper is God seen, God made visible. When man stands before the throne, God will be known to him as jasper. This is how we will recognize Him when we go there, but not while we are here. What we realize today is quite obscure in many areas, but in that city the glory of God has the brightness of jasper. This means that when the New Jerusalem descends to earth we will be able to see God Himself. We shall never again misunderstand Him, nor will we ever need to ask the reason for anything. The light of the New Jerusalem is as clear as crystal, without a trace of mixture. In that day, everything will be transparent and clearly shown to us. In that day we will see God, and we will know God.

When John recorded the description of the city, all the numbers he used were *twelve* or products of twelve— twelve gates, twelve foundations, twelve apostles, twelve tribes, etc. The measurement of the city wall is one hundred and forty-four cubits, the product of twelve times twelve. Twelve is the number used in eternity. It is the most precious number in the Bible. In the first part of Revelation, there are many sevens—seven churches, seven seals, seven trumpets, seven bowls, seven angels, etc. But in the latter part, there are many twelves, such as those already mentioned. Seven means perfection, and twelve also means perfection, but they are not altogether the same. Seven is composed of three plus four, while twelve is composed of three multiplied by four. Since God is the Triune God, the number three represents God, while four is the number which represents creation, such as the four winds, the four seasons, and the four living creatures. When three is added to four, it means that God is added to man. How complete and perfect it is to have the Creator plus the creature! But anything which is added can also be subtracted and thereby lost again; so this completion is not a lasting one. But in the New Jerusalem, the union of God and man is no longer seven, but twelve. It is no longer three plus four, but three multiplied by four. Multiplication is a perfect union, something which can never be separated. When the Creator mingles with the creature it is twelve, and twelve is the number of perfect union. In the new heaven and new earth, God and man will become one, and God and man can no longer be separated.

God wanted man to have dominion over the earth and to destroy Satan. Now man is reigning, and Satan has been cast into the lake of fire. God's purpose for the man He created has been attained. On the one hand, God wanted man to be like Himself, and on the other hand, God's appointed work for man was that he should rule. Now we have seen a bride—golden, glorious, and beautiful—with all kinds of treasure within her. She lacks nothing and is without spot, wrinkle, or any such things. Furthermore, she is holy and without blemish. She is truly clothed with glory. The glorious church spoken of in Ephesians 5 has been fulfilled in this way. What kind of work will those in the church do? They will reign forever and ever.

We may say that God's plan can be frustrated, but His plan can never be stopped. Since creation God's work has suffered much frustration. In fact, it seemed as if His work was being destroyed and that His plan would never succeed. But in Revelation God has reached His goal. There is a group of people full of pure gold, which is something of God. They are full of pearl, which is the work of Christ. And they are filled with precious stones, the work of the Holy Spirit. They will reign forever and ever.

Now that we have seen God's purpose and how He is working, what should we do? Should we hold a revival? Should we open a seminary? Or should we go back to our housework as usual? What are we doing here? God is doing a great thing. When we compare our work with His, how short we feel! May God be gracious to us, that having seen such a vision we will pay the full price. Once a man sees a vision he will be changed. May God give us a vision of what He is doing and what He is after. May He show us the kind of people He desires to obtain and how precious is that which He has set His heart upon. If we see these things, we will cry out and say, "Oh, how small I am! How much attention I have paid to myself!" And we will say, "If God does not work in me, I will never be able to do His work. Only when God Himself moves in me with His mighty power can I go on well." This great vision must overthrow us. It must cause us to see that our condition today can never satisfy God's heart. Our hope is that God would give us this vision. Once we have seen it, we will give our whole being to it; every part of us will be changed. Today we are standing between these two alternatives—being an overcomer or being a failure. How can any of us afford to be slack in prayer? If we neglect to pray, we will never be God's overcomer.

May the Lord Jesus, who has risen from the dead, that great Shepherd of the sheep, sustain us and lead us by His own mighty power that we may henceforth and forever belong to Him, forever consecrate to Him, forever serve Him, and forever go His way. May the Lord be gracious to us now and to eternity. Amen. *(The Glorious Church,* pp. 125–126, 132, 150–151)

THE
ESSENTIAL CHRISTIAN
LIBRARY

Books That Stand the Test of Time. . .
Priced as if Time Were Standing Still

Essential reading for every Christian, these hardbound, time-tested classics will form a priceless collection of Christian writing that will bring inspiration and encourage devotion to God for years to come. Beautifully bound, affordably priced at $9.97 each!

Best of Andrew Murray on Prayer, The
Christian's Secret of A Happy Life, The by Hannah Whitall Smith
Faith's Great Heroes, Volume One
Great Sermons, Volume One
God Calling edited by A. J. Russell
Hiding Place, The by Corrie ten Boom
Hinds' Feet On High Places by Hannah Hurnard
In His Steps by Charles M. Sheldon
Morning & Evening by Charles H. Spurgeon
My Utmost for His Highest by Oswald Chambers
Pilgrim's Progress, The by John Bunyan
Prison to Praise by Merlin Carothers
Riches of Bunyan, The
Search for Holy Living, The

Available wherever books are sold.
Or order from:

Barbour Publishing, Inc.
P.O. Box 719
Uhrichsville, OH 44683
http://www.barbourbooks.com

If you order by mail, add $2.00 to your order for shipping.
Prices subject to change without notice.

ISBN 1-57748-585-8

9 781577 485858

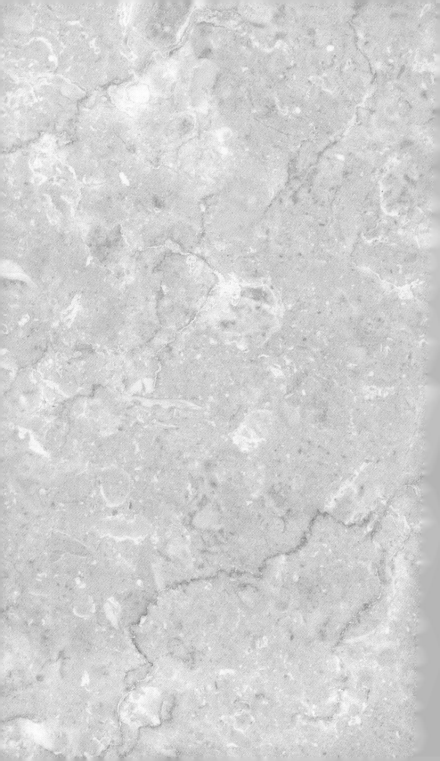